7

LIFE IN A WELSH COUNTRYSIDE

A Social Study of
Llanfihangel yng Ngwynfa

ALWYN D. REES

UNIVERSITY OF WALES PRESS
CARDIFF
1996

© Alwyn D. Rees, 1975
© Foreword, Harold Carter, 1996

First published in hardback in 1950
Second edition 1951
Reprinted 1961, 1968, 1971, 1975
New edition in paperback with new Foreword, 1996

British Library Cataloguing-in-Publication Data.
A catalogue record for this book is available from
the British Library.

ISBN 0-7083-1271-3

**Published with the financial support of the Arts Council
of Wales**

Cover design by Chris Neale, Gwaelod-y-garth
Printed in Wales by Dinefwr Press, Llandybïe

I'M RHIENI

PREFACE

This book is based upon a survey of Welsh life as it exists today in the Parish of Llanfihangel yng Ngwynfa in northern Montgomeryshire, which I made while serving as a University Extra-Mural Tutor in that County. Llanfihangel was selected as a field of study partly for reasons of convenience and partly because it is a relatively secluded and entirely Welsh-speaking area which could be expected to have retained many features of the traditional way of life. I believe that in spite of its proximity to the English Border, the social organisation of the area remains fairly representative of the Welsh uplands generally, but in many other respects the culture has probably been further modified by English influence than is the case in the rural areas of the neighbouring counties of Merioneth and Cardigan.

The suggestion that I should undertake such a study emerged in 1938 during discussions with Principal Ifor L. Evans of the University College of Wales, Aberystwyth, and Professor Daryll Forde, who was at that time Professor of Geography and Anthropology at Aberystwyth. A series of such studies of selected communities in various parts of the Principality were planned, but the outbreak of war delayed the progress of the work. It has, however, been resumed during the last few years when studies of localities in a number of Welsh Counties have been made by post-graduate research students of the College. My own investigations extended over a period of eight years. The basic field-work was carried out during the summers of 1939 and 1940 when questionnaires were completed for every household in the parish and other data collected by means of interviews and observation ; the statistics in the text refer to 1940 except where otherwise specified. I was able to maintain contact with the life of the parish by frequent visits during 1940-1943 and gradually completed my investigations, including a survey of house and farmstead types, during periods of residence in 1944, 1945 and 1946.

I am deeply grateful to Principal Evans, to Professor Forde, and to his successor Professor E. G. Bowen for constant encouragement and inspiration. I have also to thank them for taking the trouble of reading various drafts of the book and advising me on a great many points. Professor Forde's wide experience of field studies in other parts of the world was invaluable in planning the scope and method of my work, and in helping me to cultivate some degree of objectivity in dealing with a culture to which I myself belong. I cannot adequately acknowledge what I owe to Professor Bowen's insight into Welsh culture, and I also thank him for the opportunities he has given me to develop social studies in his Department. Professor H. J. Fleure has read the proofs of the book and I am grateful to him for his valuable suggestions and comments.

Acknowledgement is due to my wife for assistance in analysing the data, and to my brother, Mr. Brinley Rees who has read the proofs and with whom I have discussed most of the contents of the book from time to time. I have also been helped in many ways by Mr. E. D. O'Brien, Mr. Lewis Hywel Davies, Dr. Emrys Jones, Mr. Glanville Jones and Mr. Richard Phillips, to all of whom I extend my most sincere thanks. I am indebted to Mr. C. A. Fisher and Mr. Brynmor Thomas for many of the photographs, to Mr. R. L. Gapper and students of the Arts and Crafts Department of the College for the drawings reproduced on Plates viii, ix and xi, to the Editor of the *Montgomeryshire Collections* for permission to print Figure 34 and to Sir Ifan ab Owen Edwards for permission to reproduce Plate xa from *Cymru*.

I owe a great debt of gratitude to Mr. Thomas Davies, now of Cwm Du, Breconshire, who was schoolmaster at Llanfihangel when this survey was made, and to the Reverend W. Evans Jones of Pen-y-bont Fawr, who was formerly rector of Llanfihangel. Both helped substantially in the collection of data and their support facilitated my acceptance by the community which they served. I must also thank the Reverend B. Llewelyn Evans for helping with the questionnaires in his section of the parish. Above all I should like to place on record my gratitude to the people of Llanfihangel yng Ngwynfa who received me into their homes with the customary hospitality of the Welsh countryside and made my work among them a pleasure. My helpers were so many that I must resist the temptation to mention names. In thanking them collectively, I can only hope that they will not find my picture of their daily life lacking in appreciation and sympathy.

Finally, it has been my good fortune to have in Dr. Elwyn Davies, Secretary of the University of Wales Press Board, a publisher whose academic interests are akin to my own.

ALWYN D. REES.

CONTENTS

Chapter   *Page*

PREFACE   v

LIST OF PLATES   viii

LIST OF FIGURES IN TEXT   ix

I. INTRODUCTION   11

II. THE ECONOMY   18

III. HOUSE AND HEARTH   32

IV. FARMSTEADS   47

V. THE FAMILY   60

VI. KINDRED   73

VII. YOUTH   82

VIII. NEIGHBOURS   91

IX. NEIGHBOURHOODS AND HAMLETS   101

X. RELIGION   109

XI. RECREATION AND ENTERTAINMENT   131

XII. STATUS AND PRESTIGE   142

XIII. POLITICS   154

XIV. EPILOGUE   162

NOTES   171

INDEX   186

PLATES

Facing page

I a.	The hamlet of Llanfihangel viewed from the South	16
b.	A part of the hamlet of Llanfihangel	16
II a.	The neighbourhood of Braich-y-waun	17
b.	A view in the Township of Dolwar	17
III a.	Dolanog	32
b.	Pen-y-graig	32
IV a.	Cyfiau	33
b.	Y Fachwen Ganol	33
V a.	Dolwar Hall	48
b.	Pen-y-parc	48
VI a.	Brynffynnon	49
b.	Maes-y-gelynnen	49
VII a.	Braich-y-waun	64
b.	Ceunant	64
VIII.	A farmhouse living-room	65
IX.	A dresser and a screen	128
X a.	The Parish Church	129
b.	Pen-llys Independent Chapel	129
XI.	Interior of a Nonconformist Chapel	144
XII a.	Llwydiarth Hall today	145
b.	Plas Dolanog and the Vyrnwy Valley	145

FIGURES IN TEXT

		Page
1.	The location of the parish of Llanfihangel yng Ngwynfa	x
2.	The physical features of the parish	12
3.	Llanfihangel and Dolanog hamlets	13
4.	Population changes, 1801—1939	15
5.	Agricultural holdings, 1940	19
6.	Agricultural holdings, 1840	19
7.	Classification of holdings, 1840 and 1940	21
8.	Cultivation and principal stock in selected years	22
9.	Seasonal distribution of marriages (1885—1940)	26
10.	The farmhouse of Pen-y-graig : ground plan	33
11.	The farmhouse of Y Fachwen Ganol : ground plan	34
12.	The farmhouse of Dolwar Hall : ground plan	35
13.	The farmhouse of Pen-y-parc : ground plan	36
14.	Types of cottages	37
15.	The farmhouse of Y Farchwel : ground plan	41
16.	The cottage of Y Fronheulog : ground plan	42
17.	Sketch-plan of a farmstead : Pen-y-graig	48
18.	Sketch-plan of a farmstead : Cyfiau	49
19.	Sketch-plan of the homestead of a smallholding : Brithdir Coch	50
20.	Sketch-plan of the homestead of a smallholding : Maes-y-gelynnen	50
21.	Sketch-plan of a farmstead : Y Farchwel	51
22.	Sketch-plan of a farmstead : Ceunant	52
23.	Sketch-plan of a farmstead : Braich-y-waun	53
24.	Sketch-plan of a farmstead : Halfen	54
25.	Family farming	60
26.	Age at marriage	67
27.	Degrees of kinship	73
28.	Kinship	76
29.	Co-operation between neighbouring farms	94
30.	The townships of Llanfihangel	102
31.	Neighbourhoods and places of worship	102
32.	Denominational areas	116
33.	Distribution by counties of children and siblings of occupiers and of their wives, living outside the parish in 1940	149
34.	Llwydiarth Hall in 1684	151
35.	Examples of cruck building	177

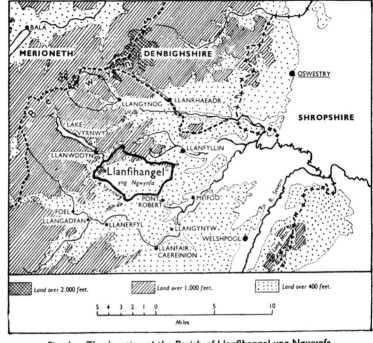

Fig. 1.   The location of the Parish of Llanfihangel yng Ngwynfa.

FOREWORD

LIFE IN A WELSH COUNTRYSIDE: A RETROSPECT

Harold Carter

THE VOLUME *Life in a Welsh Countryside* was first published in 1950. But its publications had been delayed, and an original plan for it to be but one of a number of studies had been disrupted, by the Second World War. The basic field work had been carried out in 1939–40. Against that background, the detailed provenance of the book is of considerable significance for it reveals the environment in which the study was conceived and in which the content of the book was framed.

It is generally accepted that the earliest studies of rural communities in the British islands were those undertaken in western Ireland by Arensberg (1939) and Arensberg and Kimball (1940). The authors were American anthropologists who sought to evaluate the significance of custom in the contemporary life of two small townlands in County Clare. It was an Irish-speaking area dominated by small farms and thus had something in common with rural Wales. The innovative character of their work is made clear by Frankenberg who wrote: 'This was a pioneer study. For the *first* time, in the British Isles, anthropologists looked at a community, and tried to describe and analyse its life as others had done in the South Seas and in Africa' (Frankenberg, 1966, 43). The theme of the work was 'how in a community of economic identity of interest such as exists among the small farmers, economic and social life, politics and kinship are inseparably linked together' (Frankenberg, 1966, 43).

That Alwyn Rees was familiar with this early work is quite certain, indeed there is a reference to Arensberg (p.80, note 12) where Irish evidence is put forward in regard to the particular issue of the age of marriage and the birth rate. But Alwyn Rees's work was conceived entirely independently and its inspiration must be sought in other sources.

When H. J. Fleure was appointed in 1917 to a new chair in a new department at the University College of Wales at Aberystwyth, in accordance with Fleure's wishes the names of chair and department were to be 'Geography and Anthropology'. That name was to be retained until 1968 when the department name was changed to 'Geography' alone and that of the chair to 'Human Geography'. To a large extent the chair had been created for Fleure and it epitomized his broad and catholic interests which were predominantly in the fields of anthropology and archaeology. During his tenure of the Gregynog chair (it had been endowed by the Misses Davies of Gregynog) Fleure inspired a group of greatly gifted Welsh students to concentrate their work on rural western Britain. Among them were Estyn Evans, later to become professor of geography at Queen's University, Belfast, and to initiate a whole generation of students into Irish 'folk' life, and Iorwerth Peate who was to create the Welsh National Folk Museum at St Fagans. The department under Fleure thus developed a new phase of enquiry into Welsh rural society.

In 1930 Fleure accepted an invitation to a new chair of geography at Manchester University. The College at Aberystwyth appointed in his place a young scholar, C. Daryll Forde, who at that time was working at the University of California. Forde had no Welsh connections whatsoever. He had graduated in geography from the University of London, but his postgraduate work had been in the field of archaeology; his doctoral thesis was on 'The Prehistoric Geography of Brittany'. Forde had taught geography at University College, London, for five years between 1923 and 1928, but in the latter year had travelled to the University of California on a Commonwealth Fellowship. There he spent the two years 1928–30 engaged in research on the Hopi pueblos of the lower Colorado. Although a complete contrast to Fleure in both age and personality, Forde's academic interests were similar and a research direction in anthropology and archaeology was certainly common to both. Forde continued to develop these interests whilst at Aberystwyth. Indeed, the degree to which they had become dominant precipitated a crisis when Forde moved back to London at the end of the war. E. G. Bowen, who was appointed to the chair which still retained its old name, was given a specific remit by the College Council to lay emphasis on geography rather than on anthropology (Bowen, Carter and Taylor, 1968, xxvii). Forde's main contribution to the teaching of geography was the publication of *Habitat, Economy and Society,* subtitled 'A Geographical Introduction to Ethnography' (1934). It was a book which sought to interlink the nature of the habitats, or the physical environments, and the economies and societies of so-called 'primitive peoples', on the assumption that, since such societies were less complex then, relationships were more easily identified.

Among the staff of the Department of Geography and Anthropology under both Fleure and Forde was another distinguished former student, E. G. Bowen. As has been noted, Bowen was later to succeed Forde in the Gregynog chair, and, indeed, to appoint Alwyn Rees to his staff for a brief but crucial period between 1946 and 1949. It is perhaps worth noting that when he was in the department Alwyn's main teaching courses were 'Ancient Civilizations' and 'Social Anthropology', thus continuing directly in the Fleure-Forde tradition. E. G. Bowen's interests too, were in the same fields, very much on the fringes of conventional geography, as his main focus of research on the Celtic Church suggests. But in contrast to the cosmopolitan Forde, he was a Welsh-speaking Welshman with a profound concern with the human geography of Wales.

These then were the men who made up the academic environment in which Alwyn conceived and executed his study of life in a Welsh countryside. He acknowledged his debt to them in the preface to his book. There were two others who must be noted. The first was the College principal of the time, Ifor L. Evans. He, too, was a committed Welshman and thoroughly convinced that the College should be closely concerned with its own rural environment, not only in its economic aspect where he actively supported the Department of Agriculture, but also with its social character. The second was Elwyn Davies who had also been a geography student of Fleure's at Aberystwyth. Elwyn Davies had undertaken his doctoral research with Fleure on rural Wales and had been appointed by Fleure to a post in the Geography Department at Manchester. But he returned to Wales, eventually to become secretary to the Council of the University of Wales and secretary of the University of Wales Press Board. He always retained his interest in research on Welsh rural life and through the Press Board provided a ready medium for publication. Again, the

fact that Elwyn Davies appeared as joint editor with Alwyn Rees of the subsequent work, *Welsh Rural Communities* (1960), is evidence of the close link
between the two.

There was, therefore, a set of stimulating individuals and traditions surrounding Alwyn Rees and they brought support and encouragement to his
work. On the one hand there was Forde urging that studies of Welsh societies
should be undertaken to parallel those which had long been in process in
Africa, Oceania and America. On the other hand at Aberystwyth there was a
developing tradition that geography should turn its attention more to its own
environment, to life in the Welsh countryside, and that modern communities
demanded formal and proper study.

All these influences worked on a man committed to his country and its
culture and convinced of the 'value' of its social character in a world which
was already changing as urbanization and materialism made a concerted
impact. If the research was properly an academic undertaking, it also had its
origin in an entirely engaged position. The conflict between the necessarily
engaged position of the investigator who is internal to the group under study
and the objectivity of the external researcher is one which inevitably arises in
social research. But there is no doubt what Alwyn's position was, and from it
the book draws much of its insight and strength. Even so, it is necessary to
examine three points which are inherent in the nature of the study, and relative
to the time when it was undertaken.

The first is that there was hardly any social anthropological theory in the
book at all, a point which will come up again and again in any review. It is an
entirely empirical study where even the bases of the empiricism are not
examined. It is certainly interpretative where the characteristics observed are
related to the nature of early Welsh society and the extent to which older traditions are still discernible in Llanfihangel yng Ngwynfa in the late 1930s.
But even if there is no explicit theoretical basis, implicit is a wide range of
speculation as to the nature of community. In his teaching of social anthropology Alwyn used as a text Ralph Linton's *Study of Man* (1936) and its
influence on his work is apparent. But he reached back to what Bell and
Newby (1971) call the most eminent of sociology's founding fathers – de
Tocqueville, Comte, Tönnies, Le Play, Marx and Durkheim. Of these Tönnies
was undoubtedly the foremost for Alwyn, and especially his book *Gemeinschaft
und Gesellschaft* which had been published originally in 1887. 'For Tönnies
there are three central aspects of *gemeinschaft*: blood, place (land) and mind
with their sociological consequences of kinship, neighbourhood and friendship' (Bell and Newby, 1971, 25). *Life in a Welsh Countryside* is woven about
those three main aspects. *Gemeinschaft* is usually translated as 'community'
and signifies the traditional, integrated way of life of long-standing social
groups in specific areas. In contrast *gesellschaft*, often translated as 'society',
refers to the large-scale impersonal and contractual ties which become characteristic of populations massed together in industrial settlements. Alongside
Tönnies was set the work of Durkheim and especially his *The Division of
Labour in Society* which was published in 1893. Central to Durkheim's theme
was the transition from mechanical to organic solidarity, that is from a
situation where status was ascribed to one where it was achieved; from one
where the valuation of an individual is based on who he or she is, on antecedents, to one based purely on achievement, by what has been won. The price

paid for movement out of a community where the individual from birth had a clear role, and a clear recognition of it, was alienation and eventually anomie, the situation which was to become known popularly as 'lost in the lonely crowd'. These ideas were to become widespread in the period about the Second World War. They were to form the basis of Louis Wirth's seminal paper 'Urbanism as a way of life' (1938) and lead into the whole realm of urban ecological studies (Shevky and Bell, 1955). They were to be elaborated by a number of authors into the notion of a rural-urban continuum, most effectively presented by Frankenberg in *Communities in Britain* (1966). There, some twenty-five themes were set out – described as 'not exhaustive' – which demonstrated the opposed rural-urban contrasts in social character. Thus the first is a contrast of community with association, essentially of *gemeinschaft* with *gesellschaft*, mechanical with organic solidarity. Frankenberg notes under the heading 'rural' that 'rural societies have a community nature, people are related in diverse ways and interact frequently. They have, or feel they have, interests in common'. In contrast, under the heading urban or 'less rural' is association: 'Urbanized societies have an associative nature. Although there may be a greater number of possible relationships, they do not overlap. There is comparative infrequency of interaction' (Frankenberg, 1966, 286). The consequence is that relationships are transitory and superficial.

There is little point here in developing what became a very extensive literature. The main purpose of introducing it is to stress that Alwyn Rees was thoroughly immersed in it and it was in the context of that literature that *Life in a Welsh Countryside* was written. It was only in the last paragraph, however, that an explicit statement was made: 'The failure of the urban world to give its inhabitants status and significance in a functioning society, and their consequent disintegration into formless masses of rootless nonentities, should make us humble in planning a new life for the countryside. The completeness of the traditional rural society – involving cohesion of family, kindred and neighbours – and its capacity to give the individual a sense of belonging, are phenomena which might well be pondered by all who seek a better social order' (p.170).

The second feature of the book is one of method. It is clearly of the era before quantitative methods in the social sciences. The preface does note a question-naire completed 'for every household in the parish' during the summers of 1939 and 1940. But, unlike most later studies, no copy is included. More-over, there is little formal analysis of the questionnaires, although they are used from time to time to uphold points which are being made, such as the nature of land holdings or the character of inter-farm linkages. Even in the section on the economy, data are used only to a minimal degree. Alwyn Rees was never greatly convinced of the value of formal data derived from survey. His method was participant observation. But, more than that, he was con-vinced that to understand a community and appreciate the way in which it functioned one had to live in it, be part of it and fully empathize with it. Other-wise work was superficial in the proper meaning of that word, of the surface only. It has already been noted that such a method has its critics. But as Gareth Lewis has noted, 'those studies undertaken by Welsh-speaking re-searchers, "from within", are preoccupied with religion and the values it represents, whilst those by non-Welsh-speakers, "from without", give greater attention to secular activities like, for example, the football club, carnival and local government' (Lewis, 1979, 176). Lewis also notes (p.180) that there have been criticisms that these studies by Welsh speakers from within over-emphasized the isolation of the social systems they were investigating, failed to examine the implied unchanging, static condition and underestimated class differences, all this because they were inward-looking by virtue of their methodology. These shortcomings will be reviewed later but, however justi-fied these criticisms were, it is apparent that what Alwyn Rees presented was a unique and original insight into the way of life in the area he studied.

The third feature of the book is perhaps the most surprising. The study is crucially about a Welsh community and, although there are references to the Welsh language, they are limited to a brief comment in the Introduction on the proportions speaking Welsh and a note on its significance in Noncon-formity in the chapter on religion. The fact that there was no census in 1941, because of the war, meant that formal data were only available for 1931 and were outdated. Perhaps the totally Welsh nature of the parish meant that there was no need for development of the topic. In the first post-war census of 1951 the Welsh-speaking proportion was still 92.4 per cent, and it was only to decline significantly after 1971, falling to 78.1 per cent in 1981. It was only 69.8 per cent in 1991. Even so, for a man whose later life's work was so totally devoted to the language, it is surprising that greater attention was not given to its role, and to the possibility of anglicization.

These comments, some implicitly critical, do no more than put the book into the context of the period in which it was written. But whatever the sociological antecedents on which it rested, whatever may be written in hind-sight, it was in itself totally innovative. Bell and Newby comment: 'at the time that Arensberg and Kimball were completing their study of County Clare, Alwyn Rees was embarking upon a study of the Welsh parish of Llanfihangel yng Ngwynfa in northern Montgomeryshire. Rees' study was much more of a pioneering work . . . Rees, rather than Arensburg and Kimball, can be considered the founding father of British community study – over the next fifteen years the prefaces of most studies acknowledge a debt to him . . .' (Bell and Newby, 1971, 137 and 140). Here was a study which for the fist time looked in the round, in a holistic fashion, at a British rural community and attempted to describe and explain its nature. It set up its own methodology for there was none to follow. The themes of Forde's 'habitat, economy and society' were woven together, but in no deterministic way. The intricate web of the relationships by which the community functioned and the impact of economic and social change on long-standing custom are delicately revealed. It is a study based on an incisive intellect and a sympathetic understanding; it was written with both mind and heart.

In the preface to *Life in a Welsh Countryside* it was indicated that it was initially intended to be but one of 'a series of such studies of selected com-munities in various parts of the Principality' (p.v). That intention had been undermined by the war, but between 1946 and 1949, the years immediately preceding the publication of the book, Alwyn was a member of the staff of the Department of Geography and Anthropology. That provided him with two associated opportunities. The first was to lecture to undergraduates, and for them he developed a specialized third-year course on 'The Social Anthro-pology of Modern Communities', so called to parallel a course offered by Walter Fogg on 'The Social Anthropology of Primitive Communities'. Alwyn was an

original and stimulating teacher and his course inspired a set of gifted students
to move into postgraduate research on Welsh rural communities, thus creating the second opportunity, to move his own work forward. Of the four
represented in *Welsh Rural Communities* (Davies and Rees, 1960), Tom Jones
Hughes was to establish geography at University College Dublin, to become
its first professor of geography and initiate a distinctive tradition of research
into Irish rural life; David Jenkins was to follow Alwyn into the Department
of Extra-Mural Studies and write a highly original book on *The Agricultural
Community in South-West Wales at the Turn of the Twentieth Century* (1971);
Emrys Jones was to become professor of geography at London School of Eco-
nomics and one of Britain's most distinguished social geographers; Trefor M.
Owen was to succeed Iorwerth Peate as director of the National Folk Museum.
Professor Gareth Lewis, a later student of E. G. Bowen, working in the same
general field, was to write a book on *Rural Communities. A Social Geography*
(1979) and now holds a personal chair in the University of Leicester. Professor Lewis has identified twelve studies carried out in Wales between 1940
and 1968. Of these, eleven were of communities in the north and west, in
what was later to be called 'Y Fro Gymraeg'. Not all the studies emanated
from Aberystwyth. Thus Jac L. Williams's doctoral thesis – a sociological study
of Llanddewi Aberarth – was presented to the University of London. Again,
not all Alwyn's students worked in Wales. W. M. Williams, later to become
professor of sociology and anthropology at University College, Swansea,
worked in Cumberland, and his book – *The Sociology of an English Village*
(1956) – marks a parallel but eventually diverging study. The result of this
short period of significant development, of real academic fervour, was that Bell
and Newby could write as late as 1971 that 'the University of Wales remains
the centre of British community study' (1971, 140).

That situation was to change quite drastically, and the stream of studies on
Welsh rural communities was to dry up. The reasons were both local to
Aberystwyth and general to community studies. Foremost in local terms was
the appointment of Alwyn Rees as director of the Department of Extra-Mural
Studies, for by leaving the Geography Department he removed himself from
direct contact with the undergraduate classes from which his research students
had been derived. But the local conditions reflected a much wider loss of
credibility in community studies in an atmosphere of consistent attacks by
sociologists.

The basis of most criticism was the impossibility of defining satisfactorily
what constituted a community. An American sociologist, G. A. Hillery (1955),
recorded ninety-four definitions but could provide no acceptable resolution.
A central work in this growing disillusionment was Margaret Stacey's paper,
'The Myth of Community Studies' (Stacey, 1969). She brought together all
the arguments against community studies: that they are merely descriptive;
that they are works of art, idiosyncratic and non-replicable – every critic recalls
the apothegm of Ruth Glass that community studies are the poor sociologists'
substitute for the novel; that they are of no use to a science based on the comparative method; that they are committed to a holistic approach to sociological
theory; that they are abstracted from empirical social reality at a point where
such abstraction is neither feasible nor useful (Stacey, 1969, 137).

It is possible to derive two dominant themes from most of the critiques.
The first is of some interest since it was an attempt by sociology to rid itself of

an unfashionable geographical shackle, and community studies in Britain had a clear geographical linkage. It was argued that there could be no territorial base to community. Thus R. E. Pahl, who had been a research student of Emrys Jones at LSE, wrote, 'any attempt to tie particular social relations to specific geographic milieu is a singularly fruitless exercise' (Pahl, 1966). Stacey contended: 'there is no good reason to suppose that everything is connected to everything else and there is even less reason to suppose that this should be the case in any locality' (Stacey, 1969, 138). There was, therefore, a total disbelief in the concept of a group linked in a variety of interlocking ways, kin, neighbourliness and so on, with no other non-conforming or external links, and all confined to a well defined territory. Such situations did not exist. Stacey attempted to substitute the term 'local social system' but it never was adopted and seldom appears. This rejection of community in the sense in which it had been used led to studies of a more restricted nature. Thus when the University of Wales Board of Celtic Studies began the publication of a series of social science monographs, the second of the series used the term community – *Community Action against Pollution* (Hall, 1976) – but it was concerned with the reaction of a residents' group to a specific incidence of pollution. The group, the so-called community, came together over a single issue and then dispersed. This was no holistic study of a 'community'.

The second dominant theme has already been introduced. Community studies, it was argued, were just that, a series of unrelated pieces of work, atheoretic and descriptive. There was no theory of community. At a time when social science laid emphasis on the science and when academic respectability demanded that theory came first and then from it came propositions which could be tested, preferably by the amassing of large data sets and their analysis by sophisticated statistical manipulation, then participant observation and description of the community, a concept which even lacked definition was deemed dated and naïve.

There was yet a third basis to the attack on community studies. The period of the development of a cynicism about them was the late 1960s, a time when the ethos of the decade stressed individual freedom to the point of anarchy. The interpretations of the rural community which had been published were seen as romantic, inventing a rural idyll where there was none – 'Sweet Auburn' before the enclosure movement. The reality of living in a Welsh countryside was better depicted in the writings of Caradoc Evans than in the academic studies; *pace* Ruth Glass, the novelist was the interpreter with the greater insight. Deconstructed, the community studies were part of the myth of a wholesome rural Wales which had been invented by nationally minded Welshmen. Pyrs Gruffudd writes: 'historiographical writing and academic research in the interwar period were both part of the process of remaking Welsh national identity according to cultural inheritance and geographical rootedness. Geographers located continuity and virtue in the countryside and theorized the social contribution of the *gwerin* and the organic communities it had formed' (Gruffudd, 1994, 74).

Actual life was very different. The individual, surrounded by the smothering constraints of a closed and inward-looking social system, was totally unable to exploit his or her potential. The urban world might generate anomie, but it also gave the freedom to experiment, or in the jargon of the 1960s 'to do one's own thing'. Community, therefore, was interpreted as constituting an illiberal, inhibiting environment, and the excesses of some of those who escaped only testified to the licence which followed liberation.

For all these reasons the sorts of studies pioneered by Alwyn Rees became highly unfashionable and ambitious academics steered well clear of their tainted reputation. 'The decade of the 1970s stands as a distinct phase in which little empirical community research was undertaken as community studies became "something of a lost art" (Crow and Allan, 1994, 15).

But after a period of neglect, of dismissal from the academic agenda, community studies have come back into fashion and into serious consideration. If Bradley could write in 1981 that 'reifying the traditional values embodied within rural communities is passé' (Bradley, 1981, 581), then Lewis could contend in 1986 that 'after a period in the doldrums the past five years have seen a revival of interest in rural community studies' (Lewis, 1986, 28). Or as Crow and Allan put it in 1994, 'the sociology of community is currently undergoing something of a revival' (Crow and Allan, 1994, xiii). But it can be contended that the revival did not come from a re-evaluation within the social sciences; indeed cynicism probably remains more prevalent than acceptance. Rather, concern with community has been brought into the public agenda by the consequences of economic and social change, and slowly, grudgingly, sociology has had to accept the continued widespread use of the concept and to attempt to assimilate it into its discourse.

There have been three sources from which concern with community has come. The first was the impact of counter-urbanization, or rural retreating, which was superimposed, in areas like rural Wales, upon the still extant process of rural depopulation. Discontent with urban living pushed people out into the rural periphery, seeking a more congenial life-style, and, as many would put it, 'community'. That their impact tended to disrupt the character of the localities into which they moved, that they were possibly seeking imagined rather than actual environments, these were only relevant in that they stimulated discussion as to how localities were affected by immigration, or in terms which have been widely used, how communities were changed.

Possibly most public debate has arisen in urban areas. It has long been accepted that the rural-urban continuum is flawed because of the existence of urban villages, the very word 'village' being borrowed from the countryside to describe closed and close communities within cities. This was especially relevant in coal-mining areas where a single and dominant occupation that was inherently dangerous engendered a high degree of interaction and solidarity in well defined areas (these were sometimes classed as 'occupational communities'). 'The notion [of community] is not solely a bourgeois or patriarchical invention. It has a long history as an authentic working-class counterpart, as a defensive weapon in the class struggle, and also as a vehicle for neighbouring solidarity and self-help' (McDowell, 1983, 151). Deindustrialization and the closure of coal-mines had a catastrophic effect upon the populations involved. The slogan of 'Save the mines' was seen side by side with 'Save our communities'. The whole concept of community as not *passé* but something of value, something to be preserved even at economic cost, was brought to the forefront of public debate.

A third context gave depth to the same public concern. Slum clearances replaced localities with long-standing traditions of neighbourliness and mutual support – relationships developed in specific environments – with large, impersonal housing estates. Established linkages between families were broken as the new estates were created. Most disastrous were the high-rise flat blocks. To romanticize slum life is as mistaken as to idealize rurality, but even so large populations have become aware of something lost, something they valued, something they called community. Moreover, the breaking of the constraints exercised by close communities, conceived as a liberation, has led to that rootlessness which Alwyn Rees wrote of in the closing paragraph of his book. Rootlessness and the sense of 'nonentity', of having no established place in a community to give meaning to life and of failing in the competitive world, have been at least in part responsible for the severe problems of social disintegration which characterize parts of contemporary Britain.

Finally, there is another sphere which has seen a revival of interest in community. Stein in his book *The Eclipse of Community* wrote: 'community ties become increasingly dependent upon centralised authorities and agencies in all areas of life. On the other hand, personal loyalties decrease their range with the successive weakening of national ties, regional ties, family ties and finally ties to a coherent image of oneself' (Stein, 1964, 329). There has been a growing reaction against that trend with a greater demand for power to be devolved down to the smallest unit, the community. Indeed, the civil parishes in Wales have been renamed communities. No one has argued more strongly for this process of change from a top-down system of government to one which is bottom-up that Ioan Bowen Rees (1971; 1993). He writes: 'the pioneers of the Parish Council in Wales were anything but parochial in their outlook. They saw Wales as the land of social cooperation and associative effort and saw her in that way, not from adherence to any theory, but as a result of Welsh conditions and the practical experience of ordinary Welsh people . . . The next reform of Welsh local government . . . could well result in a system built from the bottom up, on the basis of the communities.' (Rees, 1994). Here, then, is a demand for the community to be a primary building block in a system of government, and by that is meant something much more than a formally delimited territory.

For all these various reasons the whole notion of 'community' has become a prime issue in public debate. In spite of continued reservations academics have perforce had to reconsider its meaning and nature. This is not the place to embark on an extended review of contemporary community studies. The crucial arguments remain the same, and definition is as elusive as ever. Moreover, such a survey is available in Crow and Allan's book *Community Life. An Introduction to Local Social Relations* (1994). There, fifty-five community or local area studies dating between 1957 and 1990 are mapped. Strangely there is only a passing reference to Alwyn Rees and even more oddly the four studies in *Welsh Rural Communities*, published in 1960, are omitted. Welsh Wales, where community studies in Britain began, is a complete blank. Even so, with its extensive bibliography, the book is an effective review and a sure indicator that 'community' is again a concept to be researched. But still eschewing a territorial reference, investigation concentrates on networks rather than relationships in area.

It is entirely proper that the University of Wales Press should reissue *Life in a Welsh Countryside*. It is a classic in its own right. But more that that, it presents a challenge both to the academic world and to the public at large. To the academic it is a challenge to take up again the attempt to understand what constitutes community, what creates it, what sustains it and what are the implications which follow. To those outside the realm of academe it presents fundamental questions about ways and styles of life. Technological advance and material well-being have not produced contentment and security – rather the opposite. Everyone with views as to the source of contemporary malaise would do well to read *Life in a Welsh Countryside*.

REFERENCES

Arensberg, G. M. 1939. *The Irish Countryman. An Anthropological Study*. New York: Macmillan.

Arensberg, G. M. and Kimball, S. T. 1940. *Family and Community in Ireland*. Cambridge, Mass.: Harvard University Press.

Bell, C. and Newby, H. 1971. *Community Studies. An Introduction to the Sociology of the Local Community*. London: George Allen and Unwin.

Bowen, E. G., Carter, H. and Taylor, J. A. (eds.). 1968. *Geography at Aberystwyth. Essays written on the occasion of the Departmental Jubilee, 1917–18 – 1967–68*. Cardiff: University of Wales Press.

Crow, G. and Allan, G. 1994. *Community Life. An Introduction to Local Social Relations*. Hemel Hempstead: Harvester Wheatsheaf.

Davies, E. and Rees, A. (eds.) 1960. *Welsh Rural Communities*. Cardiff: University of Wales Press.

Frankenberg, R. 1966. *Communities in Britain. Social Life in Town and Country*. Harmondsworth: Penguin Books.

Gruffudd, P. 1994. Back to the land: historiography, rurality and the nation in interwar Wales. In *Transactions of the Institute of British Geographers*, NS 19, 61–77.

Hillery, G. A. 1955. Definitions of community: areas of agreement. *Rural Sociology*, 20, 111–23.

Jenkins, D. 1971. *The Agricultural Community in South-West Wales at the Turn of the Twentieth Century*. Cardiff: University of Wales Press.

Lewis, G. J. 1979. *Rural Communities. A Social Geography*. London: David and Charles.

Lewis, G. J. 1986. Welsh rural communities: retrospect and prospect. *Cambria*, 13, 27–37.

Linton, R. 1936. *The Study of Man*. New York: D. Appleton Century.

McDowell, L. 1983. City and home: urban housing and the sexual division of space. In *Sexual Divisions: Patterns and Processes*, ed. M. Evans and C. Ungerson, pp.142–63. London: Tavistock.

Pahl, R. 1966. The rural-urban continuum. *Sociologica Ruralis*, 6, 320.

Rees, I. B. 1971. *Government by Community*. London: C. Knight.

Rees, I. B. 1993. *Cymuned a Chenedl. Ysgrifau ar Ymreolaeth*. Llandysul: Gwasg Gomer.

Rees, I. B. 1994. *Government by Community 1894–1994*. Community Councils Handbook.

Shevky, E. and Bell, W. 1955. *Social Area Analysis*. Stanford: Stanford University Press.

Stacey, M. 1969. The myth of community studies. *British Journal of Sociology*, 20, 134–47.

Stein, M. 1964. *The Eclipse of Community*. New York: Harper Row.

Williams, W. M. 1956. *The Sociology of an English Village: Gosforth*. London: Routledge and Kegan Paul.

Wirth, L. 1938. Urbanism as a way of life. *American Journal of Sociology*, 44, 1–24.

Chapter I.

INTRODUCTION

THE civil parish of Llanfihangel yng Ngwynfa covers about fifteen-and-a-half square miles of upland country in northern Montgomeryshire. To the north and west of it are the high moorlands of the Berwyn, while south-eastwards the land falls towards the Vyrnwy and Severn valleys and the Shropshire Plain beyond. The scenery is typical of much of the Welsh uplands, with round-topped hills forming a gently undulating skyline broken here and there by a rocky summit. Between the hills, through deep steep-sided valleys, run the little tributaries draining the area into the River Vyrnwy which forms the southern boundary of the parish. Most of the hills in the northern half of the parish are over 1,000 feet, and the boundary deviates for a short distance to follow a ridge above 1,400 feet. The south is generally lower, the hills seldom reach the 1,000 foot line while the floor of the Vyrnwy valley falls below 600 feet. Rough grass, bracken and a little gorse form the natural vegetation of the hill-tops, and there is a little bog-land in some of the hollows of the north. The woods on the steeper slopes and along the banks of streams remind us of the forests that filled the valleys in olden times. But as one moves northwards across the parish the trees become fewer and the moorlands more continuous.

Nine-tenths of the inhabitants live in scattered farms and cottages, a few of which stand along the road-sides while the majority are well back among the fields and are connected with the roads and with each other by a network of rough tracks and footpaths. The remaining tenth of the population are in the three small hamlets of Llanfihangel, Dolanog and Pontllogel. The first, *Y Llan** as it is called locally, contains the parish church, a school and an old schoolroom which serves as a village-hall, together with eight dwellings—the rectory, the school-house, two shops, the post-office, the inn and two other cottages. Dolanog consists of a church, a chapel, a shop, a school and five dwellings. Pontllogel has a church, a vicarage, a school, a village institute, a smithy and a shop.

The pattern of settlement in the countryside around is broadly

*The hamlet of Llanfihangel is designated *Y Llan* throughout this book to distinguish it from the parish of the same name.

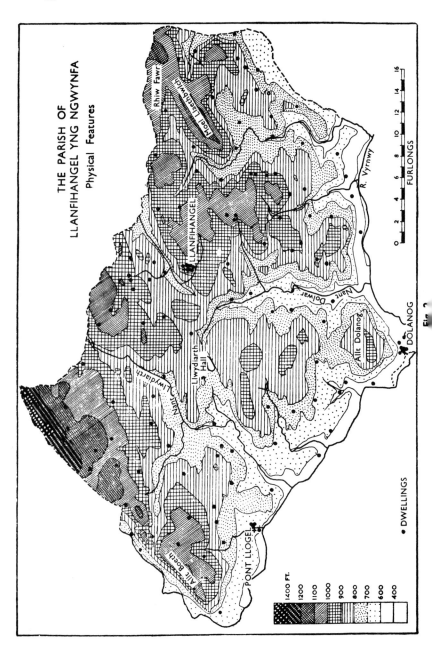

THE PARISH OF
LLANFIHANGEL YNG NGWYNFA
Physical Features

Rhiw Fawr

Moel Llechwedd

LLANFIHANGEL

R. Vyrnwy

Nant Dolwar

Allt Dolanog

DOLANOG

Llwydiarth Hall

Nant Llwydiarth

Allt Boeth

PONT LLOGEL

0   2   4   6   8   10   12   14   16
FURLONGS

• DWELLINGS

1400 FT.
1200
1100
1000
900
800
700
600
400

Fig. 2

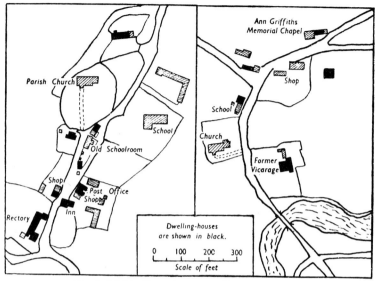

Fig. 3. (a) Llanfihangel. (b) Dolanog.

similar, consisting of scattered farms, with small hamlets gathered around churches as at Llanerfyl and Llangadfan, or at crossroads or bridges as at Y Foel and Pontrobert. Like those in Llanfihangel parish, these hamlets are, from the point of view of function, miniature towns rather than agricultural villages, and a few of those suitably placed have grown into market centres serving considerable hinterlands. The largest is Llanfyllin, a little town of less than 1,000 inhabitants about six miles east of the hamlet of Llanfihangel, which is the market-town for most of our parish. For the Dolanog district, the overgrown hamlet of Llanfair Caereinion performs some of the functions of a market-town, though in these days of greater mobility Oswestry, across the English border, tends to draw the whole area within its orbit.

In 1940 Llanfihangel had five hundred inhabitants most of whose ancestors, for generations, perhaps for centuries, had lived in the hills of northern Montgomeryshire and the neighbouring fringes of the counties of Merioneth and Denbigh. The parish of Llanfihangel and the eight parishes adjoining it[1] have a total area of

¹The small figures refer to Notes on pp. 171ff.

177 square miles, lying within a radius of eleven miles from the centre of Llanfihangel. About 85 per cent of the present house-holders and housewives of Llanfihangel were born within this area, as were 75 per cent of their parents. On the other hand, there has been much movement within the area. Farms change hands fairly frequently and removal to a new farm has often meant a change of parish. Thus, only about half of the heads of households were born in the parish itself, and the same was true of their fathers. Still fewer adult women are native to the parish, a little more than a third of the occupiers' wives and about a quarter of their mothers and mothers-in-law.[2]

Llanfihangel occupies an intermediate position in relation to the age-old trickle of population from high ground to the richer lowlands. The majority of newcomers hail from the moorlands to the north and west, whereas farmers and farm-workers who leave the parish usually move to farms on lower ground. The Shropshire Plain has a considerable number of Welsh-speaking farmers who have settled there in recent decades. In modern times, however, this older adjustment of the population to the dictates of its environment and social system has been completely overshadowed by the migration of the rural population to the industrial areas. In Llanfihangel, as in Montgomeryshire as a whole, the population reached a maximum in the census year of 1841, but after that date every inter-censal period has seen a considerable decline, except 1901-11 when there was a slight and short-lived increase. The population of Llanfihangel in 1940 was barely half its number of a hundred years before.[3] It should therefore be borne in mind throughout this study that we are dealing with a culture which has been impoverished by depopulation. On every hand there are cottages in decay, fields reverting to rough pasture and churches and chapels which are too numerous and too large for the present community.

The barrier of the Berwyn has tended to isolate this part of Montgomeryshire from the more vigorous Welsh culture of Merioneth and of north-western Wales generally, whereas the road to England lies wide open. But, although they are somewhat out of touch with current trends in Welsh life, the inhabitants of Llanfihangel are thoroughly Welsh in speech. I could count only a dozen English monoglots in the entire parish in 1940 ; the 1931 census records 22 (4 per cent). More surprising is the fact that more than half the inhabitants entered on their census forms that they spoke ' Welsh only '—a higher proportion than in any other

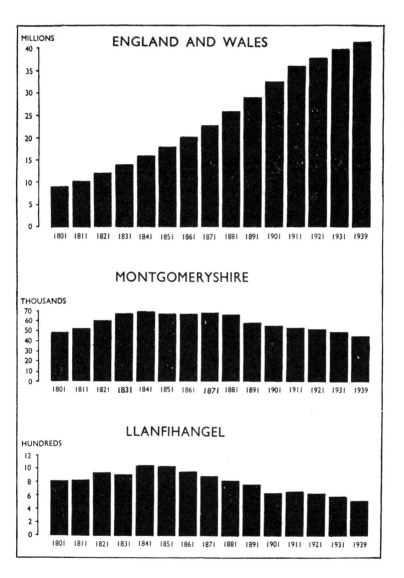

Fig. 4. Population changes, 1801—1939.

parish in Montgomeryshire.   In the parishes adjoining Llanfihangel
to the south and east the proportion able to speak Welsh becomes
smaller—70 to 80 per cent in Llanfair Caereinion and Llangynyw,
and 60 to 70 per cent in Meifod and Llanfyllin—and the same is true
to the north-west in Llanwddyn owing to the influx of English
workers to the Lake Vyrnwy Reservoir.   Towards the Border,
beyond Meifod and Llanfyllin, the percentage drops very sharply
to less than 20, and around Welshpool to less than 10.

II

Many cultural features in the landscape are of considerable
antiquity.   The dispersal of habitations goes back at least to the
Middle Ages, though their detailed distribution may have been
subject to many changes.   A church of Llanfihangel (St. Michael's
Church) existed in the thirteenth century,[4] and it may well have
been founded a century earlier.   Most of the parish churches in the
surrounding district, including the one at Llanfyllin, are dedicated
to Celtic saints and are thus still older foundations.   Llanfyllin
received its first charter in the late thirteen century,[5] and it remains
the only town with borough status in northern Montgomeryshire.

In medieval times the lands of Llanfihangel formed part of the
cantref of Mechain in the kingdom of Powys.   Mathrafal, the
principal seat of the kings, and one of the ' three royal residences of
Wales ', stood on the banks of the Vyrnwy within two miles of the
present boundary of Llanfihangel parish.   Meifod was at that time
the premier church of Powys and it remained the burial-place of
its kings until the middle of the twelfth century when the old
kingdom was partitioned.   The princes of Southern Powys then moved
their headquarters to Powys Castle, overlooking the Severn near
Welshpool, and Meifod was superseded by the Abbey of Ystrad
Marchell, also in the Severn Valley.[6]

Powys retained its independence until the conquest of Wales
in 1282, but its rulers were increasingly normanised in the twelfth
and thirteenth centuries, and in 1309 the Lordship passed by
marriage into Norman hands.   But, whereas Lord Powis was the
Lord of the Manor, the subsequent history of Llanfihangel is more
closely associated with the fortunes of the local Welsh family of
Vaughan[7] of Llwydiarth Hall, a family which was involved in the
rising of Owen Glyn Dŵr.   In the sixteenth century, and probably
earlier, the Vaughans were the chief landowners in the parish, and
also possessed great estates in Merioneth and Denbighshire.
They became one of the outstanding families of gentry in the

Plate I*a*. The hamlet of Llanfihangel viewed from the South

P   Inn   Rectory   Shop

Plate I*b*. A part of the hamlet of Llanfihangel

Plate IIa. The neighbourhood of Braich-y-waun

Plate IIb. A view in the Township of Dolwar

county, rivalling the Greys and subsequently the Herberts of Powys Castle and intermarrying with them as well as with the Vaughans of Glanllyn and later the Wynns of Gwydir. From their mansion, Llwydiarth Hall (Fig. 34), the family must have dominated the parish for centuries, as the great family pew, emblazoned with their ancestral coats of arms, dominated the chancel of Llanfihangel Church until it was rebuilt in 1862. But well over a century before this date the Vaughans had become extinct through lack of male heirs and their mansion had fallen into decay—to be rebuilt later as a farmhouse. Their lands passed by marriage into the hands of the Wynns of Wynnstay, Denbighshire, the biggest landowners in Wales, and were held by them until the eventual liquidation of the estate in 1946.

The countryside in and around Llanfihangel contains many other places of importance in Welsh history. Six miles to the north is Llanrhaeadr where (Bishop) William Morgan completed the first translation of the Bible into Welsh in 1588. A mile from the parish boundary stands Dolobran, the ancestral home of the Lloyd family, and the little seventeenth century chapel which bears witness to their activities as pioneers of Quakerism in Wales. Within the parish is the ruin of the little cottage of Dugwm, birthplace of John Davies who was one of the early Christian missionaries to Tahiti. But more distinguished than any of these places in the eyes of the average Welshman is the farmstead of Dolwar Fach, near Dolanog, the home of Ann Griffiths (1776–1805), who gave Wales some of its finest and best-known hymns.

Chapter II

THE ECONOMY

FOR centuries prior to 1946 most of the inhabitants of Llanfihangel were tenants of the Llwydiarth estate. This estate covered four-fifths of the parish and on it were 74 per cent of all holdings (including houses without land) as compared with 12 per cent owned by smaller landlords and 14 per cent held by owner-occupiers. When it was sold in 1946 nearly all the tenants bought their holdings and so a new period in their social history has just begun.

In all, the parish now contains 114 holdings of land.[1] Only 61 are over 50 acres, though they account for nine-tenths of the total area. A few of these cover several hundred acres, but nearly one-half of them are medium sized farms of 100–150 acres. Interspersed among the farms, sometimes in little clusters, are 53 smaller holdings, most of which do not exceed 20 acres. The *lle bach* (smallholding) sufficient for one or two cows, a few pigs and poultry, is an essential feature of the culture. There are only sixteen houses without land (*pen-tŷ*) in the entire parish and these include two vicarages, two school-houses and a country house. The remaining eleven are cottages, six of which were occupied in 1940 by tenants over sixty-five years of age, including two aged widows and two widowers living alone. Even craftsmen, shopkeepers and labourers generally hold some land whereas the cottagers are mainly people who are single-handed or too old to manage holdings.

The holdings (Fig. 5) form a patchwork of irregular shapes and the farmhouses are in most cases close to the boundaries rather than in the midst of their own fields. This patchwork has a long history which began with the scattered plots of the medieval land system, but only the last few stages of its evolution can now be reconstructed.[2] The first clear picture of the parish from this point of view is preserved in the Tithe Survey of 1842 (Fig. 6.) By that time the present pattern of compact holdings had already emerged on the Llwydiarth estate, though the remains of former habitations and also field-names such as *Cae yr Hen Dŷ* (the field of the old house) bore witness to fairly recent consolidation. In the remainder of the parish the holdings were much more fractionated than they are today.[3]

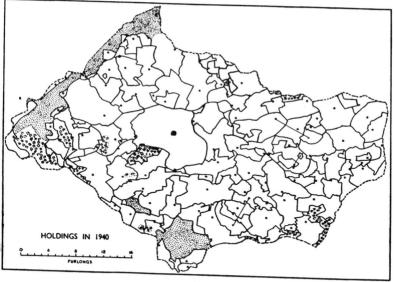

HOLDINGS IN 1940

FURLONGS

Fig. 5.

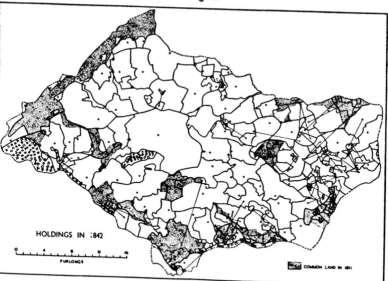

HOLDINGS IN 1842

FURLONGS

COMMON LAND IN 1811

The straight lines connect homesteads with their detached plots of land.

Fig. 6.

The Tithe Survey also contains evidence of the extension of farms by enclosing tracts of open hill-land, a practice which was general in eighteenth-century Wales. Most of the farmsteads stood on hillsides with relatively small enclosed fields around and below them. Above was the ridge or hill called *boncyn, moel, cefn, rhiw* or *ffridd*. Some of this was still unenclosed in 1842 but most of it was divided into large fields whose names revealed their newness. Thus, the holdings had gradually extended up the hillsides, and in some localities new holdings had been created out of hill-land. Nowadays *ffridd* means a hill-top roughly divided into large enclosures which are poorer than other fields but better than *mynydd* (open mountain).

In the late eighteenth and early nineteenth centuries a considerable number of smallholdings were established by squatters on the fringes of the surviving common. The Manorial Court Rolls[4] record interminable lists of small fines for encroachment and the erection of cottages ' on the waste ', and the inhabitants still point to many of the *tyddynnod* (cottages with land) on high ground as later dwellings erected on the sites of *tai unnos*. The latter were habitations built on the common in one night in accordance with the traditional belief that a squatter who could build a house overnight and have smoke ascending from the chimney by sunrise was entitled to the freehold of the site and of a piece of land whose limits were determined by the distance to which the squatter could throw an axe in different directions from his cabin door.

The tracts of common still remaining when an Enclosure Act was passed in 1811[5] have been marked on the map of holdings in 1842 (Fig. 6), and it will be noticed that the smallholdings are clustered in these areas. How much common land had already been enclosed without legal sanction cannot now be determined, but it is maintained locally that several smallholdings in other parts of the parish also began as squattings. Nearly all the squattings were eventually acquired by the estate, and many stories are told of how the agent would persuade the owners of these hastily erected dwellings to allow him to make improvements in exchange for a nominal annuity, thus depriving them of their freehold right. Another stratagem was to offer additional land at a low rent which was later interpreted as rent for the entire holding. Nevertheless an occasional free holding survived in the midst of estate-owned land, a memorial to the way in which so many of the *tyddynnod* came into existence.

The enclosure of new land had virtually ended before the

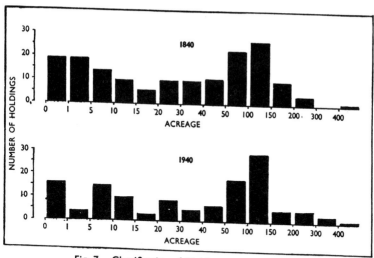

Fig. 7. Classification of Holdings, 1840 and 1940.

middle of the nineteenth century and most of the common still left in 1842 has remained to this day. From the 1840s onwards the population has declined steadily and by today a third of the small-holdings have disappeared including most of the tiny plots of 1–5 acres formerly held by married farm-labourers. There has been a corresponding change in the economy from subsistence farming supplemented by the sale of surplus stock to a specialised pastoralism. The intensity of stocking[6] has increased by a third since 1870—sheep have become two-and-a-half times as numerous. As the number of animals multiplied, the ploughed land receded. In 1842 over half the farm land was arable as compared with less than a quarter in 1939. The acreage of tillage crops was more than halved between 1870 and 1939, while the increase in clover and temporary grasses was very slight in relation to the greater number of animals to be maintained.[7]

The concentration of the present economy upon animal husbandry is in a way a reversion to the ancient mode of life in the Welsh hills after a long interval in which the plough was more widely used. Even during this interval the extension of tillage was not allowed to undermine the older and more fundamental side of the economy. In the hungry forties, when corn prices were soaring, much of the richer lowland was still retained as meadow and pasture

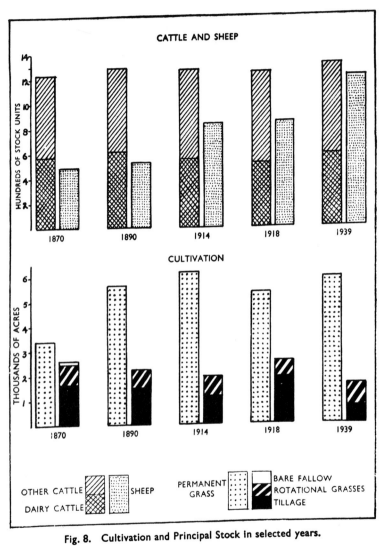

Fig. 8. Cultivation and Principal Stock in selected years.

while the newly-enclosed *ffriddoedd* were extensively ploughed. This was picturesquely described as *rhoi croen newydd ar yr hen ffridd* (giving the old *ffridd* a new skin). The response to the food scarcity of the two World Wars of the twentieth century has been broadly similar. The farmers have been readier to plough the poorer than the richer lands and, in Llanfihangel as elsewhere in Wales, it is the rough *ffriddoedd* and not the cultivated fields that have been given a ' new skin ' by the tractors of the War Agricultural Executive Committee.

II

The intermediate position of Llanfihangel between the mountains of the Berwyn and the lowlands of the Severn is reflected in the present farming economy which falls in between the two types described by agricultural economists as ' Cattle and Sheep (Poor land) ' and ' Cattle and Sheep (Better land)', respectively.[8] More than a quarter of the land is rough pasture, and farm rentals on the estate averaged only about 10s. 6d. per acre.[9] Many farmers described their farms as *ffermydd magu* (rearing farms) and stock-raising takes precedence everywhere over dairying and tillage. Practically all the cattle are bred locally, and their sale, mainly as *deunawiaid* (eighteen-month-old cattle), is usually the greatest single source of money income. Butter was the only important dairy product before the War, but since then the dairy herds have been enlarged on many farms and the sale of raw milk under the Milk Marketing Scheme has expanded rapidly.

With regard to sheep, Llanfihangel lies between the mountain sheep-runs which carry only a fraction of their flocks in winter and the complementary wintering areas around Meifod and Llanfyllin. With the exception of a few farms on high ground to the north-west, the parish is able to support its own sheep throughout the year. The complement of breeding ewes in 1939 was as high as 64 per hundred acres, but it has fallen since then owing to the new demand for tillage. Ewes are bought in from mountain farms and sold, normally as stores, after breeding for two or three seasons. Lambs, few of which are reared for breeding, are sold mainly in store condition, though a certain number are fattened. On farms which have a *boncyn sych* (dry hill) favourable for sheep, the income from the sale of lambs sometimes exceeds that brought by the sale of store cattle. A few pigs are reared, mainly for domestic use, and poultry is another sideline.

In 1939 four-fifths of the cultivated land was under permanent grass, a little more than a tenth under clover and temporary grasses and a little less than a tenth under tillage crops among which oats predominated. Large quantities of feeding-stuffs were bought to supplement these crops, costing in some cases as much as twice the rent. The unintensiveness of farming in the inter-war period is indicated by the small amount of labour employed. Taking all holdings over 20 acres together, the average number of male workers *including* occupiers, hardly exceeded two per hundred acres of cultivated land, and a considerable proportion of the farm-workers were, as we shall see later, youths in their teens. The average number of female workers, including housewives, did not exceed 1.6 even on farms over 150 acres.

Dairying is the chief activity on smallholdings, though some cattle are reared, both for sale and to maintain the number of milch-cows, and a surprising number of sheep are kept. The smallholder thus appears to model his farming as far as possible on the pattern of his larger neighbours. Twenty-three of the thirty-two occupiers of under 20 acres were men with other occupations—estate and forestry workers, roadmen, farm-labourers, craftsmen, shopkeepers and postmen.[10] Of the remaining nine, five were ex-farm-labourers in receipt of Old Age Pensions, two were widows in receipt of Widows' Pensions and the ninth was an aged spinster. None of them maintained a family on the proceeds of their holdings. Even on holdings of 20–25 acres, half the occupiers still had other occupations, but all seven holders of 25–50 acres were full-time farmers.

The yearly round of agricultural work still preserves something of the old Celtic division of the year into two halves—May to October and November to April. The calendar year opens with farming at a low ebb. Men and animals are largely confined to the farmstead by inclement weather. Implements are mended, firewood is cut and there is hedging to be done when the weather permits, while sheep left out on the hillsides require attention during snow-falls. Towards the end of February ploughing of leys for oats begins in earnest and continues during March. The seed is sown towards the end of March and the beginning of April, or ideally, according to the old saying, during *y tri deryn du a dau lygad Ebrill* (i.e. the last three days of March and the first two of April). At the same time lambing demands the attention of the farmer, and this period, with the cattle still indoors making extra work, is a peak period of activity. During April winter fallow is ploughed, harrowed and cleaned, and barley and rootcrops are sown at the end of the month, with the exception of swedes which are usually left until late in May to avoid blight.

By the end of April most of the ploughing and sowing has been done, lambing is over, the cattle are now left out at night, and the following six or seven weeks (from the beginning of May to the latter part of June) is a period of comparative respite. Now there is time for carting manure from the yard, and for fencing, ditching and tidying up generally. The latter half of June is the traditional time for washing and shearing sheep, and at the same time the crops need weeding. The farmer tries to do these tasks before the hay harvest starts at the end of the month. This busy period ends in July if the weather is kind, and there is a brief breathing-space during the first half of August before the corn harvest begins. Advantage is taken of this interval for dipping sheep and bringing in rushes and bracken for winter bedding. Then the tempo quickens again while the cereal crops are gathered in September, slackening off gradually during October and November when rootcrops are harvested and stubble is ploughed for winter fallow. In November the cows are brought in again and, with the main tasks of the year completed, the farmer and his household relax in the declining days of the back-end while the poultry is getting ready for the Christmas market.[11]

Thus, broadly speaking, the year consists of a short period of intense activity (March, April) followed by a short period of respite (May to mid-June), and then a long period of labour (mid-June to October), with a possible lull in early August, followed by the long inactivity of winter (November to February). The two periods of activity are also the chief periods of commercial transactions. March is the usual time for selling eighteen-month cattle, in April the smallholder who does not keep sheep himself is paid for wintering, and in May yearling calves are sold. Apart from intermittent sales of summer lambs there is a lull in money income during the mid-summer months until August when another spasm of commerce begins with the sale of the remaining lambs and wool, followed in September and early October by the sale of old ewes and some more eighteen-month cattle. May and October-November are therefore the months when the farmer pays his bills to craftsmen and tradesmen, and the six-monthly wages of his workmen. Labourers and maids are hired on yearly contracts ending on the first of May.

The rent, on the contrary, used to be paid half-yearly on the 24th of June and the 24th of December. Tenancies were on a yearly basis terminating on Lady-Day (March 25th), but since this occurred at the height of a busy season, the incoming tenant was entitled to the use of the land and to accommodation in the house and buildings from the 2nd of February so that he could get his ploughing done in time. But the outgoer could retain use of the farmhouse and buildings and a little pasture until the 12th of May.

The seasonality of agricultural activity is reflected in the social life of the community. Leisure and ready money mark out May and October-November as holiday periods. Farm-workers have a week's respite in May, and the few farmers who do go away for holidays choose either this month or the beginning of August. May and late October are the months of fairs in the neighbouring market-towns. Social events held in summer, such as preaching-meetings, singing-festivals, Sunday School tea-parties and sports, are fitted into the slack periods as far as possible. But the back-end is the main season for social activities, including the exchange of visits. As will be seen from Figure 9,[12] May-June and October-November

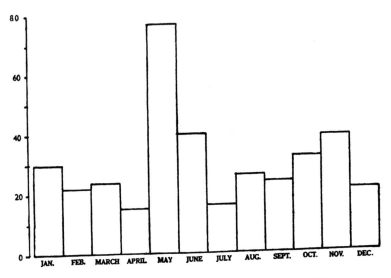

Fig. 9. Seasonal Distribution of Marriages (1885—1940).

are also the favourite months for weddings. May, when labourers and maids end their contracts and when the houses of farms which are changing hands become vacant, is particularly convenient, and the general belief that it is unlucky carries little weight in Llanfihangel.

III

The hundred years whose history on the production side has already been outlined was a period of gradual transition ‹from an economy primarily concerned with producing the requirements of the community to one depending upon the sale of a limited range of products and the purchase of consumption goods produced elsewhere. Back in the last century most of Llanfihangel's simple ' imports ' were raw materials and semi-manufactured commodities —iron and coke for the smith, flannel and cloth bought at fairs to augment the supply from local weavers, leather, glass, lime, slates and a few items of food, perhaps a little wheat, sugar, salt and spices. Ironwork of all kinds, from ploughs to nails, was made by the smith, carts and waggons by the wheelwright ; a carpenter in the Llan made furniture and clocks, there were local shoe-makers, tailors and dressmakers. Many other articles were made at home on the hearth on winter nights—the men would make shafts and handles for implements, rakes, traps, nets and baskets, while the women would be busy spinning, knitting and sewing.

Today, hardly any of these things are made locally. There are no tailors, shoe-makers, furniture-makers or even dressmakers. An occasional cart is still made, but generally speaking the function of the wheelwright and the smith has changed from making implements to repairing the products of factories—even horseshoes are imported ready-made. Some farmers still make their own gates and a few are very good at improvisation, but the old crafts of the hearth have almost entirely died out, and, as with the professional craftsman, making has degenerated to mending and patching. Thus, apart from certain important items of food, Llanfihangel ' imports ' practically all its requirements as finished goods, and its material culture retains little that is distinctive. In exchange it ' exports ' cattle, sheep, butter, milk, wool, eggs and poultry, whose production has also consumed substantial quantities of imported ' raw materials '.

Commercially, the parish looks towards the Borderland and towards England, the only important economic contact with the mountains of the west being the purchase of yearling ewes at autumn sheep-sales held at centres such as Dinas Mawddwy. Exportable stock is sold either to dealers who call round the farms, or is sent to marts held in Llanfyllin. Before the arrival of the railway, this town was a centre from which cattle were driven to England by drovers ....

and it remained the principal market-place and shopping-centre for the district until the inter-war period. Its position has, however, been gradually undermined by two modern developments. The first is the rise of busy little shops in the countryside itself to meet the day-to-day demand for consumption goods. There are two at the Llan and one each at Dolanog and Pontllogel. They are primarily grocery-shops, but their wares also include patent medicines, bandages, brushes, twine, rope, nails, lamp-wicks and paraffin, meal and chicken-feed, clothes, stationery—and indeed most of the usual contents of a packman's box. One of the shopkeepers at the Llan also deals in butter and eggs, while the other is the bus and hackney-carriage proprietor. The former takes an assortment of his shop's contents round the farms by car twice a week, and money is used only to settle the difference in value between the commodities bought from the shop-car and the farm-produce collected. He then sells this produce at Llanfyllin on market days to dealers from further afield. Again, in the 1920s a Wynnstay Farmers' Co-operative Society was formed to counteract the high retail prices charged for meal. It has its headquarters at the village of Llansantffraid, rather than at Llanfyllin, and there is a depôt in Llanfihangel. The majority of farmers buy at least a portion of their feeding-stuffs, as well as coal and lime, through this society, and there is at Llansantffraid a mill where they can have meal made from their own grain.

Secondly, improved transport facilities have made the larger market-town of Oswestry more accessible, and during the inter-war period an increasing amount of stock was being carried in waggons through Llanfyllin to its marts, and more shopping was also being done there. In more recent years transport restrictions and the establishment of Llanfyllin as a ' grading-centre ' for the district have helped to revive the economic life of that old town.

Generally speaking, the shopping-place varies with the commodity bought and also to some extent with social standing. It is more fashionable to buy at Llanfyllin than at Llanfihangel, and at Oswestry than at Llanfyllin. Most of the smallholders, and a few farmers, normally sell their dairy products and eggs to the local dealer and buy groceries and other oddments at the local shops. Before the War, the larger farmers and some of the smaller ones took their products direct to dealers in Llanfyllin or Oswestry and returned with the week's shopping, but with the introduction of rationing many of them preferred to register locally for groceries while continuing to sell their goods as before. Clothes, furniture and other household goods are usually bought at Llanfyllin or Oswestry, though the purchase of the more important of these will sometimes justify a visit to Liverpool. Agricultural implements are also obtained from Llanfyllin, or from Welshpool or Gswestry in the case of some of the larger machinery.

Notwithstanding the change-over to a money economy, pre-industrial conditions and values have partially survived and these account for much that is distinctive in the culture. To understand the tenacity with which the upland farmer has withstood economic depressions which would have destroyed an enterprise conducted on present-day business lines it must be realised that, unlike a modern factory, the farm remains a home and a means of subsistence as well as an instrument for making money. Thanks to his occupation the farmer is assured of a house, much of his fuel and many staple foods such as bacon, milk, butter, eggs, vegetables and fruit. Although flour and oatmeal are no longer produced, they are still not regarded as groceries. In trying to reconstruct a farmer's 1939 balance-sheet I asked him why he had omitted bread from his list of purchases. He explained that it was made from flour included in the estimate for ' feeding-stuffs '. The market-price of the farm-house and home-produced foods may not be very great, yet they are basic necessities which absorb an appreciable part of the average townsman's earnings.

The fare remains simple and inexpensive. Most households make their own bread, though baker's bread is now bought by some of the most accessible ones. Breakfast usually consists of porridge followed by a ' bait ' of tea with bread and cheese or cold bacon in the middle of the morning. *Cinio* (' dinner ') at noon is the main meal of the day and is most often made up of boiled bacon and a stew made of bacon broth and vegetables, followed by a pudding or tart made with home-produced lard and fruit. Bread and butter and cheese or jam are eaten for tea and this is followed at nightfall by a meal consisting of more boiled bacon, or porridge. Bread-and-milk is a favourite dish for supper. Many families buy butcher's meat for Sunday, which is the favourite day for entertaining friends, and there may be pineapple chunks, or some other tinned fruit, as a treat for tea. Bought food is considered more elegant than that which is home-produced, and the guest is frequently honoured with tinned salmon or *Spam*. On one occasion a farmer's wife gave me ham and eggs for supper apologising that she had ' nothing else in the house '. Eggs are produced for sale rather than for consumption, though the visitor will be offered a boiled egg for tea.

Apart from food, working-clothes and a little tobacco, the country-man's wants are very few. He generally buys clothes of good quality and a Sunday suit will last a surprising number of years.

Very few farmers in Llanfihangel kept accounts of any kind until obliged to do so by the Income Tax Regulations of the Second World War. Their measure of a year or a lifetime's profit was the amount of unspent money they had left at the end. This simple calculation took no account of the food and shelter provided by the farm, or of the money value of work performed by relatives. The extent to which this outlook differs from that of modern urban communities becomes clear when the farmer's calculations are elaborated to produce an up-to-date balance-sheet. Such an analysis of the financial returns of samples of farms from various parts of Wales has shown that the economic reward gained by the upland farmer and his wife for a year's labour was less than nothing during 1930–34, and only a few shillings a week per hundred acres during the more prosperous years of 1935–39.[13] In support of this, there was a consensus of opinion in Llanfihangel that the profits of the 'thirties were extremely meagre, and that in several years the farmer, despite his frugal way of life, was richer at the beginning than at the end. Many farmers maintained that farm-workers earned more than they did during this period.

Although very little money was made between the Wars, many families were regarded by their neighbours as *pobl gefnog* (people of means). But there were many others who, having no reserves, found it very difficult to make ends meet. Some even had to resort to the deplorable practice of ' halves '. That is to say, they borrowed their sheep from a dealer and were entitled to half the lambs as a reward for maintaining them. To protect their prestige, farmers forced to this extremity endeavoured to conceal their plight from their neighbours by pretending that the sheep were their own. Again, most of the reserves accumulated during the Second World War have been swallowed in purchasing the farms. A farmer whose judgment I believe to be sound estimated that one-third of those who bought their farms were able to pay for them, another third could pay a substantial part of the price, while the remaining third had to borrow practically the whole amount. As we shall see in a later chapter, this is about as near as one can get to knowing the amount of accumulated wealth possessed by Welsh farmers.

It is clear that from an economic point of view the countryman has continued to live in a world of his own, the standards of which differ from those of our modern industrial civilisation. His farming can hardly be said to have ' paid ' during this century except in war-time,* and he has been able to subsist only by accepting a standard of life which, measured in economic terms, has been lower than that of industrial workers. By relying on family labour, which, as we shall see, received no wages, by limiting his purchases to a bare minimum, and often by eating into precious savings, he has, in most cases, carried on, though some farmers failed even then and had to leave their farms. As the wage-rates of hired servants increased with the spread of industrial standards, they became more and more prohibitive to the small farmer, and he has been obliged to depend even more than formerly on the labour of his family and to reduce his scale of living in many ways.

To understand more fully why these farmers have clung to their traditional occupation even in adversity, other factors in community life must be considered. The solidarity of the family, the bonds of kinship, the connection with a chapel or a church and the individual's status among his neighbours, all tie him to his locality and make life incomplete elsewhere. A farmer with whom I discussed the disadvantages of country life quoted the proverb : ' *Cyw a fegir yn uffern, yn uffern y myn fod* ' (a chick reared in hell will want to remain in hell). But before we begin to examine these non-economic factors some attention must be given to the home-stead, the centre of so many social activities, and the chief thing in the material culture which remains, in its construction if not in its design, a local product.

*This passage was written in 1946. The period of agricultural prosperity inaugurated by Second World War still continues in 1950.

Chapter III

HOUSE AND HEARTH

M OST of the houses and farm-buildings of Llanfihangel are built of stone obtained from small quarries near their respective sites. There are, however, three partly half-timbered houses, but this type of architecture, characteristic of lowland Montgomeryshire, is comparatively rare in the hills. A few of the more recent cottages are of brick, which was for a time manufactured locally, and some of the newer outhouses are made of light timber obtained from the estate saw-mill. The majority of the farmhouses are substantially built, the older ones having walls two feet thick, but some of the cottages put up as recently as the nineteenth century had walls mortared only with clay, and a few had 'dry walls', the interstices filled with turf. Almost every house has an upper storey, or a loft of some kind, though many of the older ones were originally single storey dwellings.

The size of the houses varies considerably, roughly in accordance with the amount of land attached to them. The details of their plans also vary so much that it is difficult to find more than two or three that are exactly alike. Nevertheless, they may be divided broadly into two main categories, an older 'oblong' type and a newer 'square' type. The former ranges in size from the one-roomed cottage to the large farmhouse, but it is always one room deep over the greater part of its length. The living-room, in particular, stretches from the front to the back walls, while the other rooms, set on one or both sides of it, extend the house longitudinally. It can usually be entered only through the front and there is no vestibule or passage, each room opening directly into the next along the length of the house.

Pen-y-graig (Fig. 10, Plate IIIb) represents the most common type of oblong farmhouse in the parish (cf. Fig. 18, Plate IVa). This type consists of three main sections, the central and largest one being the *cegin* (living-room, lit. kitchen), with the *cegin gefn* (' back '-kitchen) on one side of it and a section divided into two on the other—a parlour in the front and a dairy or pantry in the back. The lean-to buttery in the rear of the house is also a characteristic extension. In the remainder of this chapter the conventional

Old Vicarage.
Cottages

School

Church

Plate IIIa. Dolanog

Plate IIIb. Pen-y-graig

Plate IV*a*. Cyfiau

Plate IV*b*. Y Fachwen Ganol

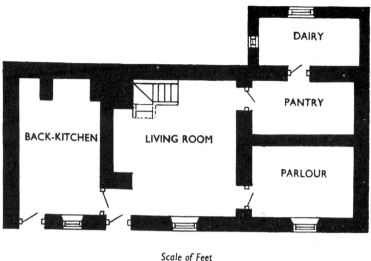

Scale of Feet

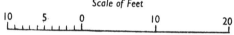

10   5.   0   10   20

Fig. 10.   The farmhouse of Pen-y-graig : ground plan.

terms ' upper end ' and ' lower end ' will be used to describe the
parlour and kitchen ends, respectively, though they are not in
use in Llanfihangel.

Originally, the only fireplace was the one in the living-room
with its back towards the ' back '-kitchen, but in all the houses of this
type which I examined an additional fireplace with a separate
chimney has now been built in the ' back '-kitchen, and in some
cases also in the parlour. The main entrance opens into the living-
room, usually where the front wall and the flanking wall of the
chimney form a little passage leading through a door into the
' back '-kitchen. Normally, the ' back '-kitchen also has its own
front-door with the 'back'-kitchen window between it and the
main entrance. The heavy axe-trimmed oak beams which support
the upper storey are seldom more than six or seven feet from the
floor, and upstairs the headroom is further restricted by the slope
of the roof. The narrow wooden staircase, boarded from the rest of
the room, is usually in the angle between the fireplace and the back
wall of the living-room. It divides near the top, the one branch leading past the chimney to the servants' bedroom(s) over the ' back '-
kitchen, and the other turning at right-angles to it to the bedrooms

of the family over the remainder of the house.   In one case there were two separate stairs, *stâr y dynion* (the men's stairs) in the 'back'-kitchen for the servants, and the family stairs in the parlour. Apart from this separation of the servants from the family, there is as little privacy upstairs as there is downstairs, each room opening as it does into the next.

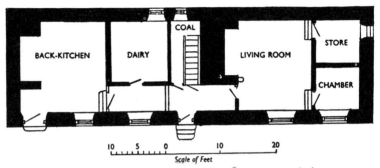

Fig. 11.   The farmhouse of Y Fachwen Ganol : ground plan.

Y Fachwen Ganol (Fig. 11, Plate IVb), which is the only one of its kind in the parish, represents another type of ' oblong house '. Like those already described, it has a ' central ' chimney with the living-room and two small rooms, now used as a store and a chamber at the upper end, and a ' back '-kitchen at the lower end.   It differs from them in that there are two other compartments in the middle portion of the house between the living-room and the ' back '- kitchen.   It stands on a site which slopes downwards towards the 'back'-kitchen end, and there are four different floor levels. The main entrance is four feet above the level of the ground and is approached by steps.   The house is in many ways reminiscent of the type of building comprising byre, and sometimes barn, as well as dwelling- house, with internal access from living-room to byre, which Dr. Iorwerth C. Peate has called ' the long house '.[1]   The ' back '- kitchen, which still has the granary over it, may well have been used as a byre in former times.   The coal-house occupies the position of the *penllawr*, the transverse threshing-floor at the entry, which is characteristic of such buildings, while the dairy may have been a barn or calf-box.

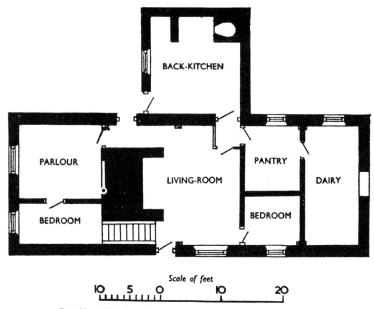

Fig. 12. The farmhouse of Dolwar Hall : ground plan.

The two houses *Dolwar Hall* and *Pen-y-parc* (Figs. 12, 13, Plate V) represent a third oblong type. In these the fireplace is at the *upper end* of the living-room, and its chimney also serves a small grate in the parlour behind. Moreover, instead of having two doors in the front of the house, each of these has a *back-door* at the chimney end of the living-room. At Pen-y-parc this door leads into a lean-to back-kitchen and thence into the open, while at Dolwar Hall it is a direct exit, there being a second back-door at the lower end giving access to the more recently-built back-kitchen. Dolwar Hall has the characteristic tripartite division into parlour, living-room and domestic sections, and there is a ' men's loft ' over the last with a separate outside entrance at first-floor level in the gable. At Pen-y-parc the lower end is occupied by the stable with a granary above it. It is characteristic of both that the chimney stands free from the long walls, a feature which is typical of the half-timbered houses of lowland Montgomeryshire.

Most of the cottage homes of the smallholders and labourers may be described as poor relatives of the oblong farmhouse. The most characteristic layout is that of *Tŷ-nant* (Fig. 14b), which is

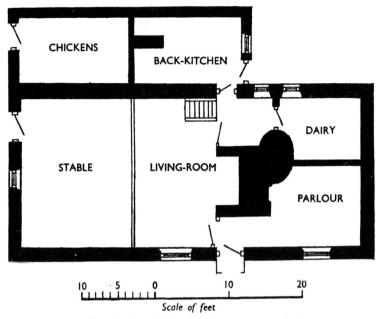

Fig. 13.   The farmhouse of Pen-y-parc : ground plan.

essentially the same as Pen-y-graig farmhouse, except for its smaller dimensions, and the absence of a 'back'-kitchen. This latter difference makes it two-sectioned and brings the chimney to the gable-end, giving the house the one-sided appearance of the *tŷ uncorn*.* The plan of a nineteenth century squatter's dwelling shown in Fig. 14a, is again similar in its essentials, but the bedroom occupies the whole upper end, giving in its simplest form the type known as *tŷ a siambr* (house and chamber). There is nothing in this deserted building to suggest that it ever had a staircase, but a small dormer window shows that the attic, probably reached by a moveable ladder, was used as a dormitory. Behind the chimney is a lean-to compartment which once housed a cow. This gives the building a sloping gable, a feature seldom found in the district.

The cottage shown in Fig. 14c, Plate VIa, is a still simpler structure, being a one-roomed cottage with a subsequently added dairy and loft. There are others in the surrounding district, but in most

*A house with a chimney at one end only.

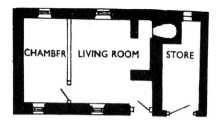

(a) Pen-foel

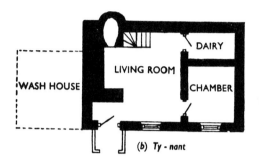

(b) Ty - nant

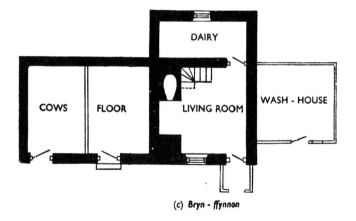

(c) Bryn - ffynnon

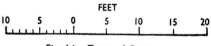

Fig. 14. Types of Cottages.

of them the entrance is opposite the chimney flank as in all the other dwellings which I have hitherto described. Cottages (as opposed to farmhouses) with ' central ' chimneys are rather exceptional in the district. The only one that I observed within the parish is Maes-y-gelynnen (Fig. 20, plate VIb). Kitchen and ' back '-kitchen lie on either side of the chimney as in most oblong farmhouses, but Maes-y-gelynnen lacks a parlour end. It therefore remains two sectioned, the place of the third section being occupied by the stable which has, of course, a separate entrance.

The history and distribution of house-types in Britain requires much more detailed study before any definite conclusions can be drawn as to the antecedents of those which characterise Llanfihangel today. Analogies may be referred to, but uncertainty as to the extent to which the medieval dwellings of Wales were distinct from those of England makes their arrangement in any evolutionary or devolutionary sequence highly conjectural. The arrangement of the rooms in the more usual type of oblong farmhouse is in some ways reminiscent of the later medieval manor house with a ground-floor hall.[2] Like the farmhouse the latter consisted of three sections. The hall, which was the common living-room, occupied the central section, with the domestic offices and servants' quarters flanking it at the ' lower end ', and at the other the solar or ' withdrawing room ' with the cellar beneath it. The entrance was at the lower end of the hall, as it is normally at the lower end of the farmhouse *cegin*.

Similarly, the lists of buildings at the medieval Welsh court always include the three household sections, *neuadd* (hall) *ystafell* (chamber) and *bwyty* (food-house, kitchen).[3] In addition, the hall itself consisted of three parts, the *uwch coryf, uwch celfi* (the section above the pillar and above the screen, where the king sat with the most honoured courtiers), the *is coryf, is celfi* (the section below the pillar and the screen, where sat the heir apparent with the other courtiers), and the *tal isaf* (the lower end where the chief of the household sat with the household officials). Once more the door was at the lower end, to the left of the chief of the household.[4]

The tripartitite division of habitations is therefore of considerable antiquity both in England and in Wales, and we shall meet it again in the lay-out of barns, but any simple derivation of the oblong farmhouse from the English manor-house, the three household sections of the Welsh court or the three parts of the Welsh *neuadd*, would carry us far beyond the evidence. As complicating factors it may be noted that at Dolwar Hall, probably the oldest house in

Llanfihangel, and at Pen-y-parc, the entrances like the fireplaces are in the *upper* part of the *cegin* next to the parlour. And these are not just local exceptions. Similar layouts could be cited from other parts of Wales as well as from northern England, Scotland and Ireland.[5] Again, the rectangular form of the farmhouses differs from the ⌐‾‾¬ shape of the typical manor-house.

Yet, whether their ancestry be English or Welsh or a marriage of both, all the oblong farmhouses belong to a stage in the evolution of the house which may be broadly described as the ' hall ' stage. The centrally-placed *cegin* is clearly a vestige of the hall, the common living-room and meeting-place, and, as will be described later, it has a traditional social significance which by no means justifies the name *cegin* (literally, kitchen). In fact, it is still called *y neuadd* (the hall) in some parts of Wales[6] and this term, in both its English and Welsh forms, survives in the names of many farmhouses in Montgomeryshire as well as in the names of most country houses.

The types of the cottages which I have described also have a very long history. In the one-roomed dwelling we have the house in its original simplicity, the common living-room, fire-room or hearth which is the nucleus around which all the more elaborate forms developed. The addition of the *siambr* (chamber) was already present in the oldest manor-houses and appears to have been general in England by the beginning of the thirteenth century.[7] Indeed, even the unfree Welshman's house, according to the Laws, had an apartment adjoining it called the *cell*, which may have been a chamber.[8] The chamber was originally the women's quarters, and it is significant that the equipment which a bride contributes to the setting up of a home is still called *'stafell* (chamber) in Cardiganshire. In Llanfihangel the chamber is now called *y rwm* (the room) when it contains a bed, and *y parlwr* (the parlour) when it does not. The division of this section into chamber and buttery also seems to have been a well-established practice in England, and evidence from other northern European countries suggests a similar arrangement.[9]

Very little evidence exists as to the age of the oblong farmhouses and cottages. A comparison of their shapes with those shown on the same sites on the Tithe maps of 1842 and on the Enclosure Award maps of 1811 suggests that most of them existed at the beginning of the last century, but it would be hazardous to assume that many are very much older than this. The ' hall ' plan, which survived even in England until well into the seventeenth century,[10] may have persisted in Wales until the end of the eighteenth century, while cottages of the kitchen, chamber and dairy type were still being built in Llanfihangel within living memory. On the other hand, dates on the timberwork show that the half-timbered house of Plas Dolanog and the farmhouse of Pen-ffordd were erected early in the seventeenth century, and slightly curved timbers in the long walls of Dolwar Hall, which may be the remains of crucks whose tops have been sawn away to facilitate the construction of an upper storey, suggest that this house may be even older. There is further evidence of crucks[11] in the remains of a farmhouse called Halfen Uchaf, and there are still four pairs of them supporting the outbuildings of Tŷ-brith just over the parish boundary. As opposed to these survivals, the map evidence shows that at least half the houses in Llanfihangel were built or thoroughly reconstructed after 1842.

The story of the evolution of the modern house-plan from the ' central hall ' plan, involving the contraction of the hall to a narrow corridor leading to the various rooms and containing the staircase, the conversion of the servants' kitchen into a winter parlour or dining-room, and the relegation of the domestic offices to the back of the house with a separate back-entrance, is too well-known to need recapitulation here.[12] There is little evidence of any stages of this development in Llanfihangel other than the addition of back-kitchens behind old houses. The ' square ' farmhouse, which is now the most prevalent type in the parish, was a nineteenth-century importation.

Y Farchwel (Fig. 15) is an example of this new type. It consists of four rooms on the ground floor—the living-room and the parlour in front and the back-kitchen and the dairy behind. Morphologically, the living-room is the winter parlour or dining-room, whereas the original Welsh cegin, the hall, has degenerated into a mere vestibule behind the entrance at the foot of the stairs. There is no central passage ; as in the oblong house, the living-room is the thoroughfare from the back-kitchen to the stairs, the parlour and the front-door. While this layout gives little more privacy than the oblong house on the ground-floor, the bedroom accommodation is much more satisfactory from this standpoint, and the headroom of both floors is much greater. Other examples of this type, with minor differences, are Braich-y-waun (Fig. 23, Plate VIIa) where the front-door opens directly into the kitchen as in the oblong house, and Ceunant (Fig. 22, Plate VIIb) which is one of the most recently built farmhouses in the parish. Y Fronheulog (Fig. 16,) built within the last two decades of the nineteenth century, is one of the

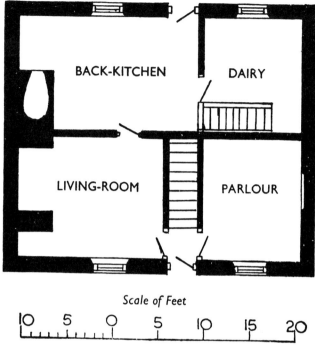

Scale of Feet

Fig. 15. The farmhouse of Y Farchwel : ground plan.

few cottages with a central entrance and stairs, and an outshot back-kitchen.

My translation of *cegin* as ' living-room ' requires a word of explanation since it accords more with the role of the *cegin* in the history of the house than it does with its present function. The oblong houses were built at a time when it was customary in most farms for the whole household, family and servants alike, to occupy the common living-room. Practically all the cottages and several of the farmhouses had no ' back '-kitchen, and where it existed it was called the *briws* (brewhouse), a place for washing, preparing food and other household work, but not a living-room. This lack of discrimination against servants differed from the relationship characteristic of the lowland farms of the Border, where the servants' kitchen was an old-established institution. In this, as in many other respects, the nineteenth century witnessed a widespread diffusion of lowland culture into the uplands. The new square house had a servants' kitchen entered by a back-door, and usually a separate staircase leading to the servants' bedrooms. This was copied when the older houses were reconstructed. Formerly, the servants and many of the farmers' sons had slept in the lofts of the outhouses above the animals. But when the roof was raised to accommodate an upper storey, the portion over the *briws* became the servants' bedroom, and a fireplace was put in the *briws*, thus making it into a servants' kitchen.

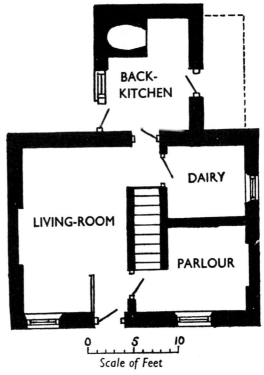

BACK-KITCHEN

DAIRY

LIVING-ROOM

PARLOUR

0 5 10
Scale of Feet

Fig. 16. The cottage of Y Fronheulog : ground plan.

But this distinction between family and servants has not been maintained. On the contrary, the servants and the family now live in the same room at every farm in the parish, but with the difference that it is now the back-kitchen itself that is occupied.

In the late nineteenth century every fair-sized farmhouse had one or two maids ; today there are practically none, and the housework, together with many other duties about the farmstead, falls on the shoulders of the farmer's wife, helped if she is lucky by a daughter. But the appearance of the *cegin* has not been allowed to suffer ; it is highly polished and spotlessly clean. To minimise the housework the family withdraws to the back-kitchen during the greater part of the year. In summer the days are long and the farmer and his family are busy until dark, leaving little time for leisure before retiring. The *cegin* therefore is used only on special occasions during this season. Even in winter the back-kitchen is the room mainly used in the daytime, but a fire is also lighted in the *cegin*, where the family and its friends gather during the long evenings.

Most smallholders and cottagers have no back-kitchens and the *cegin* remains their living-room. In many cases, however, a wooden or corrugated-iron wash-house has been built adjoining the house, which, in addition to serving as a work-room like the old *briws*, is often the place where meals are served during the summer. Thus even the cottager is beginning to regard the *cegin* as too good for ordinary use. It need hardly be added that a gradual withdrawal from the dining-room to the kitchen and from there to the scullery or a lean-to shed, leaving an ever increasing number of rooms as ornaments for prestige purposes, is an aspect of modern culture which is at least as typical of the urban working and middle classes as it is of country-folk.

The layout of the *cegin* is dominated by its large elaborate fireplace in relation to which everything else in the room is arranged (Plate VIII). This is the *aelwyd* (hearth) or *pentan* (fire-end), the ancient focus around which the Welsh household has gathered throughout the ages to converse and to exchange stories.[13] Formerly, the fireplace was a recess some three or four feet deep with the fire on the floor in the middle and seats on either side beneath the canopy of the chimney. This space has now been partly filled by a new grate and its appurtenances, but there is still room for at least a stool, a small chair or the end of a settle *o dan y fantell* (under the mantel) on either side, and it is such a seat that is invariably proffered to the guest. On one side of the grate is an iron oven, and on the other a boiler, their tops serving as hobs. This oven is, however, seldom used, for the baking is done in the large *tŷ-ffwrn* (built-in oven), heated by burning twigs in it, which is usually found in the back-kitchens of farmhouses and in the living-rooms of cottages.

Some of the equipment of the old open fire still remains along with the new grate.[14] There is always a chain over the fire from which the kettle is hung. This is in some cases suspended from a bar set across the chimney, and in others from a large metal crane. The hobs are adorned with brass or copper kettles, stewing-pots and a bed-warmer, and the chimney walls are hung with other brass and copper valuables, tongs, pokers, toasting-forks and an array of horse-harness brasses, all highly polished. The high mantelshelf supports a row of brass candlesticks and, perhaps, a pair of china dogs. A high-backed settle called the *screen* usually forms the fireside seat with its back to the door and this helps to keep the draught from the hearth. In some farmhouses, however, it has been relegated to the back-kitchen and its place has been taken by Victorian armchairs. The screen, which accommodates two or at most three people, originally fitted into the chimney recess. It is a feature of considerable antiquity and in various forms, sometimes itself being the jamb wall of the chimney, it has survived into modern times in many parts of Britain and Ireland.[15]

Beyond the immediate vicinity of the hearth the oak dresser is by far the most prominent piece of furniture in the *cegin*. This is almost invariably of local workmanship, and is usually an heirloom at least a century old. In former times its shelves and drawers probably had a practical use, but it now serves much the same purpose as the china-cabinet in the homes of the urban middle class. The shelves are loaded with crockery, the willow pattern being by far the most typical, and there are hooks along the edges of the shelves for cups and jugs. These vessels are seldom if ever used, except for the safe-keeping of bills, receipts and odd sums of money, but they are nevertheless valued family possessions. In particular they serve as a link between a family and its past. The history of every object on the dresser is known, and one will be told : ' My husband's mother had this dinner service from her grandmother as a wedding-present. These old jugs belonged to an aunt of mine— there was a complete set of them but she gave half of them to my sister. I bought these jugs at Tan-y-bwlch sale ; they belonged to old Mrs. —— ' and so on.

The remaining furniture in the *cegin* includes at least one corner cupboard, often containing the tea service used when guests are present ; a grandfather's clock, sometimes of Welsh workmanship ; a weatherglass; perhaps a harmonium, or, more rarely, a piano. There is a variety of pictures on the walls: Victorian pastoral scenes, Gladstone, Lloyd George, or an array of Nonconformist preachers, the ' young ' or the ' old ' Sir Watkin, past and present members of the family, and, perhaps, a little tapestry work or a pencil sketch by a relative or friend.

Originally, the *cegin* contained two tables, the *bwrdd bach* (small table) and the *bwrdd mawr* (large table). The former was often a round table and was light enough to be moved about. The latter was a long deal-topped table at the back of the room or under the window, with benches on either side. This was the servants' table. The head of the household and the womenfolk of the family, together with the honoured guest, ate from the *bwrdd bach* which was brought up to the seats by the fire. Other male members of the family ate with the servants. In a few farmhouses the two tables still perform their original functions, but they are now in the back-kitchen. In others the whole household now eats from the one long table and there is a tendency to deprecate the class distinction of the old system. The place of the two tables in the *cegin* has been taken by a large polished table set in the middle of the room as is typical of lowland farms, but efforts are still made to allow the guest to remain as near as possible to the fire during a meal. And there is no loitering at the table when the meal is over. Everyone is urged to 'turn to the fire'. In cottages the chair of the head of the household is usually between the table and the fireside so that he can eat without leaving his corner. This custom of eating by the fire goes back to tribal times in Wales and there is evidence that it was once general in north-western Britain and Ireland. The two tables were used in Yorkshire and Derbyshire[16] in exactly the same way as they are in Wales. The custom belongs, as Professor E. E. Evans has pointed out,[17] to the ' open hearth ' tradition of the western fringes of Europe as distinct from the ' oven tradition ' of central Europe where the social centre was the table and not the hearth. The large table imported from lowland England into the modern farmhouse *cegin* of Llanfihangel belongs, of course, to this second tradition.

The furniture of the back-kitchen consists of the bare essentials of a living-room, the long table with its benches as already mentioned, a kitchen cupboard for the crockery and other utensils in ordinary use, and a settle and a few wooden chairs around the fire-place. The latter, which also has a wide chimney containing a more recent grate, does not dominate the back-kitchen as the original fireplace dominates the *cegin*. It is an innovation occupying a corner or a narrow side of the room.

The layout of the parlour also lacks the distinction of the *cegin*. It was a bedroom until the relatively recent addition of a second storey and it remains as such in most of the cottages. Even in the farmhouses it has not won its place as a reception room. It is seldom used, and even in some of the larger farmhouses it is little more than a store-room. In others it is very simply furnished with an armchair on either side of the little fireplace, a small table under the window on which rests the family Bible (or a flower-pot), and a chest-of-drawers or a sideboard. Its most distinctive feature is the number of family photographs that adorn the chest-of-drawers and the mantelpiece. It is a kind of museum or sanctum—the repository of things which have, or which once had, an emotional significance : wedding-dresses and other old clothes in the chest-of-drawers—some of them belonging to the departed,—wedding groups in out-moded fashions along the walls, a cup won in an *eisteddfod* or agricultural show, a marble presentation clock which no longer keeps time, and the names of the family and some of its ancestors in the clasped Bible on the table. Its peace is seldom disturbed for any length of time save when a member of the family suffers a prolonged illness. Then some of its contents may have to be removed to make room for a bed, thus making it easier for the womenfolk to tend the sick person. The parlour may thus become the scene of death. On the other hand, it is not customary in Llanfihangel, as it is in many other parts of Wales, to bring the corpse of a person who has died upstairs down to the parlour to lie there until burial.

Chapter IV

FARMSTEADS

I T will be recalled that all the farmsteads of Llanfihangel and nearly all the cottages are separate settlements scattered over the countryside. Apart from those which originated as riverside mills and a few other exceptions, these settlements stand on hillsides, commanding extensive views of the surrounding landscape. Their distribution shows a marked preference for sunny southward-facing slopes (*bron-haul*), and the value of these sites is emphasised by farm names such as *Fronheulog* and *Haul-y-fan*. The houses almost invariably face down hill and towards the sun, though many of them are turned slightly south-eastwards in the direction of sunrise and away from the prevailing south-westerly winds. The advantage of a southerly aspect in the case of oblong houses, with living-room, back-kitchen and parlour all facing the front, is obvious. But it is interesting to note that the newer square houses have a similar orientation, though in these the back-kitchen, the room most generally used, is thus given a sunless northern aspect, while the less-frequented *cegin orau* (best kitchen) and the parlour face the sun. Both in the old and the new types, the parlour is usually in the eastern end of the house with the cool slate-benched dairy behind it, its small sunless window facing north or north-west.

The choice of sites has also been influenced by the need for shelter, steps or hollows in the hillsides being particularly suitable. At such places the slope immediately behind the site is relatively steep and trees have been planted on it to provide further shelter. Sometimes the land also rises on either side, but a large number of sites are sheltered on one side only. Others seem to have no natural advantages, a windbreak of trees being the only protection. Thus, while shelter was valued, as is illustrated by such farm-names as *Tŷ'n-y-twll* (house in the hollow) and such metaphors as *tŷ yng nghesail y bryn* (house in the armpit of the hill), it was by no means always found, and farm names indicative of shelter can easily be offset by others which show the lack of it, such as *Adwy-wynt* (wind-gap), and *Castell-y-gwynt* (castle of the wind).

It was still more important to have a convenient supply of water. Three-quarters of the holdings obtain water direct from wells, while it is piped to others from supplies a short distance away.

Four smallholdings depend on stream water only. The supply
from the well is usually augmented by roof-water collected in a cask,
and often by water from a nearby stream. At most of the farmsteads the well is immediately in front of or behind the house and is
covered over and fitted with a hand-pump. In the Llan some
houses have their own wells, whereas water piped to the roadside
tap supplies the remainder. Some wells have the reputation of
never being dry, but others fail in dry summers making it necessary
to carry water, sometimes for considerable distances. A reliable
water-supply thus contributes appreciably to the value and desir-
ability of a farm. Water-power is used only by the mill at Dolanog
and by two or three farms. A small hydro-electric plant supplies
light to Dolanog, and another was installed by local enterprise at the
Llan in 1949, but all the farmsteads and scattered cottages depend
upon paraffin lamps—a large one with an incandescent mantle
being kept in the living-room, but, in many cases, used on special
occasions only.

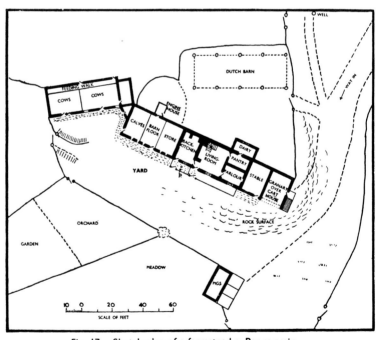

Fig. 17.   Sketch-plan of a farmstead :   Pen-y-graig.

Plate V*a*. Dolwar Hall

Plate V*b*. Pen-y-parc

Plate VI*a*. Brynffynnon

Plate VI*b*. Maes-y-gelynnen

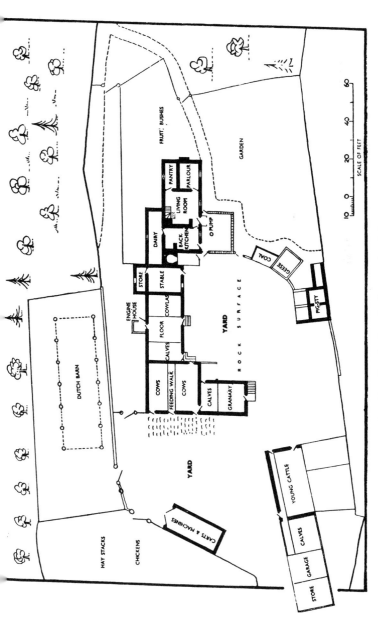

Fig. 18. Sketch-plan of a farmstead : Cyflau.

The layouts of the farmsteads are all different. Each one has its own distinctive character. Their original plans probably varied a great deal according to the possibilities of the individual sites, and they have been subsequently altered by the erection of new buildings from time to time and the reconstruction of old ones. Thus, in dividing them broadly into two main classes to facilitate description, it must be emphasised that the classification is based primarily

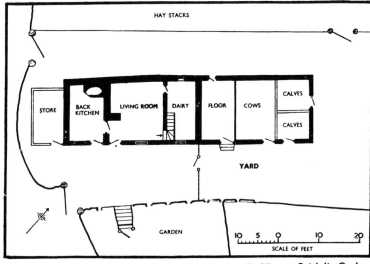

Fig. 19. Sketch-plan of the homestead of a Smallholding : **Brithdir Coch.**

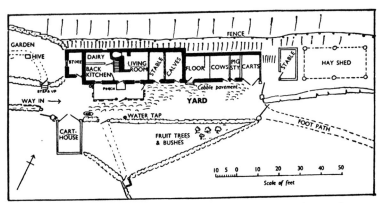

Fig. 20. Sketch-plan of the homestead of a Smallholding : **Maes-y-gelynnen.**

upon their present morphology, which is to a large extent fortuitous. In the first class the house *faces* the yard and is generally situated well back against the hillside. In some cases the hillside itself has been excavated and the back wall so embedded in the earth that one might easily step from the ground on to the roof. Frequently, the house and principal outhouses are attached, forming a single extended block, and the yard consists of a long track separating house and buildings from the garden or orchard below. The front of the house itself is usually separated from the actual farmyard by a wooden fence or, more occasionally, a stone wall, to keep the animals and the poultry from the door (See Figs. 17, 18, Plates IIIb, IVa). In some cases this simple layout has been modified by the erection of further buildings at an angle to the original block, or across the yard from it, but it can still be recognised by the orientation of the house towards the yard.

In the second type most or all of the farm-buildings stand apart from the dwelling-house. They are joined together into one or more blocks, and are usually so arranged as to form an enclosed or partially enclosed yard *behind*, or sometimes at the side of the house. The front of the house thus faces *away* from the yard, while the back-door (if any), protected by a rough-and-ready wooden fence opens on to it. An enclosed garden or green lies in front of the house

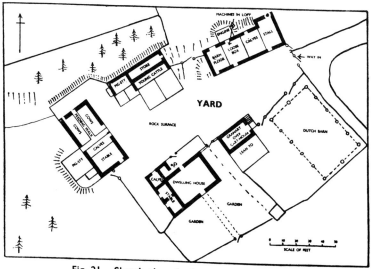

Fig. 21.   Sketch-plan of a farmstead : Y Farchwel.

traversed by a footpath leading from a wicket to the front-door. Nearly all the farmsteads with recent square houses are arranged in this way (Figs. 21, 22, 23, Plate VII) and so are a few of those with oblong houses (Fig. 24).

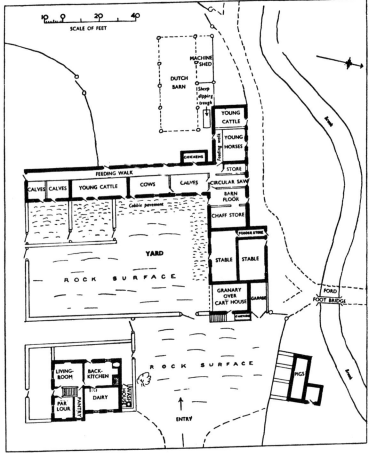

Fig. 22.   Sketch-plan of a farmstead : Ceunant.

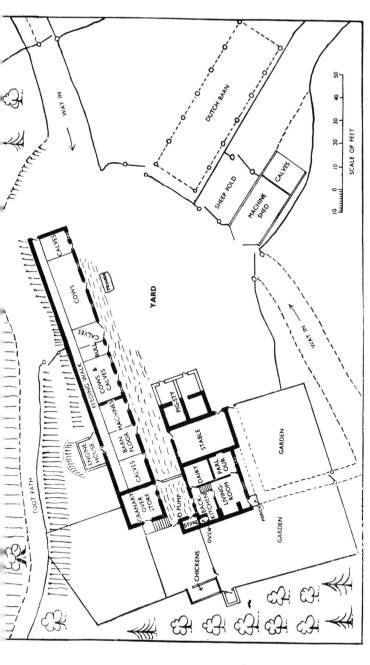

Fig. 23. Sketch-plan of a farmstead : Braich-y-waun.

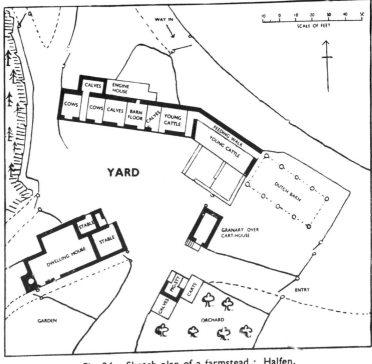

Fig. 24. Sketch-plan of a farmstead : Halfen.

The arrangement of the house and main buildings in one extended block in nearly all smallholdings as well as in many of the farmsteads with old houses suggests that the first type of layout described is older than the second, and this hypothesis is strengthened by the analogy of the ' long house ' which formerly housed men and animals under the same roof in so many parts of Wales. Nevertheless, such an arrangement is no proof of antiquity. For example, *Pen-y-graig* (Fig. 17, Plate IIIb), the best instance in Llanfihangel of a large farmstead of this kind, consisted of two separate buildings in 1842, located on the sites of the present house and cowshed, respectively. It is the more recent barn linking the house with the cowshed, and the stable and granary added to the other end of the house that have made it into a long unbroken row. Similarly, the house at Cyfiau (Fig. 18, Plate IVa) was not joined to the other buildings until the present stable was built in the latter half of the last century. Even on smallholdings the outhouses are often recent extensions built on to the gable ends of older houses.

The main buildings on a fair-sized farm comprise cowhouse, young-cattle shed, barn, granary, hay-barn, stable, carthouse, pigsties, poultry sheds, and sometimes a tractor-shed and a garage. On smaller farms the number and size of buildings are correspondingly less, while smallholdings have only the bare essentials—cowhouse, threshing-floor, pigsty, poultry shed, hay-barn and sometimes a small stable. In view of the dominant role of cattle in the economy one would expect the cowhouse to have pride of place in the layout of the farmstead, as is apparently the case in Ireland.[1] But this is not so, except on smallholdings which have few other buildings. The cowhouse is normally set at some distance from the house—whereas the pigsties are surprisingly near the back-door.

Most cowhouses are long buildings with one row of stalls facing a *bing* (feeding-passage) which runs along the back wall and is separated from the stalls by a low partition called the *côr*. Above the stalls is a *taflod* (loft) for storing hay. The floor of this loft terminates above the *côr* leaving a space, or it contains trap-doors through which hay can be thrown down into the *bing* as required. At some farms the cowhouses have a squarer plan which apparently is more recent, with two rows of stalls facing inwards towards a central *bing* (Fig. 21). The young-cattle shed is not divided into stalls, the animals having a free run of the shed and of the little yard in front of it. The manger is higher from the ground than in the cowhouse and there is a cratch for hay behind it.

The barn can be easily recognised by its large doors which rise to the eaves to facilitate the unloading of corn into it. It is divided into three sections, a carry-over from the days when corn was threshed with flails. The great doors open on to the middle section, the *llawr* (floor), and there is often a smaller door at the opposite side, used to create a draught for winnowing before the days of the hand-turned winnowing machine. The floor, which is a foot or two above ground-level, and in one or two cases has a dog-kennel beneath it, consisted originally of wooden planks, now replaced by concrete at some farms. A wooden floor is said to have been necessary in order that the flails might bounce on it, whereas it was raised above the ground to keep it dry. The construction of the floor, however, varied in different parts of Wales. Floors of slate flagstones are usual in Merioneth, while in South Cardiganshire the floor may be cobbled. It was customary to erect a temporary wooden floor over the cobbles when threshing, with spaces between the boards to allow the grain to drop through to the ground below.

On either side of the floor is a *cowlas* (pl. *cowlesi*, bays), one
on approximately the same level as the floor, and the other a step
below on ground level.   In olden days the former contained a
reserve of unthreshed sheaves which were served on to the floor
for the threshers, while the straw was cleared away into the other
cowlas as the work proceeded.   The ' straw *cowlas* ' was separated
from the floor by a wooden partition about a yard high which, in
addition to increasing the capacity of the *cowlas*, ensured that the
straw was *lifted* into it so that any grain that remained in the straw
might fall to the floor.   Unlike other buildings on the farm, the barn,
or at least the threshing-floor, has no loft, as a restriction of the
headroom would have interfered with the swinging of the flails.

Threshing with flails was still general among smallholders at
the close of the last century, and even today it is practised sporadi-
cally by a few of the older men. But, such survivals apart, the
process of threshing has passed through two stages since the days
of the flail.   The first began after the middle of the nineteenth
century with the introduction of small threshing-boxes into the barn.
The earlier ones may have been turned by hand, but those still
remembered were driven by turnstiles worked by one or two horses.
These turnstiles were placed behind the barn on ground levelled to
make a pathway for the horses, and their sites may still be seen as
circles of hachures on the 25 inch Ordnance Maps.   Such innovations
dispensed with the flails, but the three sections of the barn retained
their respective functions.

Then came the large mobile threshing-machine driven by a
steam-engine and later by a tractor. This is owned by an individual,   who   is   usually   a   farmer   himself,   and   hired   to
each farm for a day or two.   Threshing has thus become a periodic
event, requiring the help of neighbours to make full use of the
machine, and the barn no longer serves its original purpose.   On the
site of the old turnstile stands a shed containing a new source of
power, the oil engine, which drives the chaffing and kibbling machines
that now occupy the barn-floor.   The *cowlesi* are often used for
storing chaff, turnips or potatoes, to house a circular saw, also
driven by the oil-engine, or they have been converted into loose-
boxes for calves or young cattle.

The three-sectioned barn is not found on smallholdings, but
the threshing-floor, the nucleus around which it developed, is usually
there.   This generally forms a wide passage across the upper end of
the cowhouse, separating the cows from the gable-end of the dwelling-house (Figs. 14c, 19).   It is now used as a feeding-passage, but

is called *y llawr*, and is still occasionally used for threshing. At a smallholding called *Y Waun* in Llanfyllin parish, where the floor and byre are attached to the chimney end of the house (c.f. Fig 14c), there is a wooden lintel in the wall beside the fireplace showing that there was once direct access from the living-room to the floor. These facts point to the true significance of the *penllawr*, the transverse passage which separates the byre from the house-part in the Welsh ' long house '. It is the threshing-floor and not the ' head ' of the floor of the house as Dr. Peate translates it.[2]

It is considered an advantage to have the cowhouse adjoining the barn so that fodder and bedding can easily be carried to the cattle. The rick-yard, enclosing a large *helm* (dutch-barn), should also be as near as possible to the cowshed, and a favourite place is behind the barn. The granary is invariably an upper storey ; this helps to secure the grain from damp and rats. The space beneath it is usually a carthouse one side of which can be opened to ensure a circulation of air. The granary is approached by steps, which are generally, though not invariably, at the gable end. Sometimes the granary is a separate building, but more often it stands at the end of a row of buildings. Many of the existing granaries were not built until the second half of the last century, an older storage place being the loft of the house itself. A few houses still have the granary over the back-kitchen.

Every effort seems to have been made to bring the stable as near the house as possible. In some cases where there was already a barn at one end of the house, the stable has been built at the other end. If a new house has been built the old one has been turned into a stable (Fig. 22), and where there is only one outhouse attached to the dwelling-house it can almost be assumed to be a stable. Even the newer square houses which stand apart from the main outhouses often have a stable attached to them (Figs. 21, 23). At *Pen-y-parc* (Fig. 13) the stable is structurally a part of the house, separated from the living-room by only a matchboard partition. The movements of the horses in the stable rattle the dishes on the dresser which has its back to the partition. The same was true of *Maes-y-gelynnen* (Fig. 20) until the wooden partition was replaced by a brick wall about 1918, and it is said that the back-kitchens of some of the oblong houses were used as stables in the old days.

The local explanation of the nearness of house and stable was that the horses used to be the most valuable creatures on the holding, and that they should be within hearing distance because they might break loose and hurt each other at night. For the same reason, the waggoner, and sometimes other servants, used to sleep in the stable loft. But, valid as these utilitarian explanations may be, the partiality shown to the horse has a much older and more fundamental social origin. From remote ages, perhaps as far back as the spread of warriors from the steppes into Europe in the Bronze Age, the horse has been the noble animal of European tradition, the hunter and the fighter whose flesh must not be eaten as ordinary food, and until our own day the pride of the gentry. Mythology contains ample evidence that it acquired a similar significance in the Celtic lands in the distant past. The groom was a prominent official of the Welsh king's court. Horses were used in the Middle Ages for riding and to draw vehicles and harrows, but only oxen were subjected to the toil of ploughing. The Welsh Laws state categorically : ' Neither horses, mares nor cows are to be put to the plough '.[3]

The general substitution of working horses for oxen on ordinary farms in Wales dates only from the late eighteenth and early nineteenth centuries, and probably even later in some areas. The large number of stables built in Llanfihangel after 1842 points to a substantial increase in the importance of horses in the mid-nineteenth century, and their numbers continued to grow until the first World War.[4] Thus, whereas the horse has a long history in Wales, especially as a mount for the more privileged members of society, its prestige among Welsh farmers today springs very largely from the ' horse culture ' of the English and anglicised Welsh aristocracy of the eighteenth century. The social antecedents of the horse contrast sharply with those of the humble ox and the cow which have been basic to the rural economy from the remotest past. This contrast is well expressed in the vocabulary used in connection with the two classes of animals. Welsh words are used for almost everything relating to cattle, but a large number of English words have been introduced to describe horses and their appurtenances. Cows have homely Welsh names—Cochen, Penwen, Frochwen, with an occasional Beauty, whereas horses have English names, and aristocratic ones at that—Prince, Duke, Captain and so on.[5] Cows are spoken to in Welsh, but horses are treated as though they did not understand Welsh ; all the words of command addressed to them are English.

In adopting the horse the farmer acquired a whole complex of customs and attitudes which had been cultivated by the aristocracy for ages past. His horses became his great pride and their quality affected his status. It was only natural that the stables should be next to the house ; they occupied a similar position at Wynnstay, the residence of Sir Watkin Williams-Wynn himself. The best food was given to the horses, and a waggoner who was a good thief—who stole grain for the horses by boring holes in the granary floor—was considered an asset. The waggoner was the aristocrat among the servants. It was he who presided at the servants' table at mealtimes, and he very often supervised the work of the others. Even today on large farms with several brothers working at home, the eldest is always in charge of the horses, the second being the cowman and the third the shepherd.

Horses were seen in public more often than the other stock. They brought the traps and the waggons to town and held the place of honour at the shows. Farmers competed with each other, not only at the shows, but also for the privilege of taking the Sunday School for an outing or the choir to an *eisteddfod*. There was no question of payment, it was an honour conferred only upon the farmers with the best horses. These would be decorated with shining brasses and ribbons, the waggoner often staying up all night to turn them out well-groomed in the morning. Again, when the Yeomanry was established under the leadership of the Williams-Wynns it became essential to the prestige of a farmer's son that he should appear for training well-mounted.

Chapter V

THE FAMILY

A NY analysis of the structure of a community of this kind must begin with the family, which is not only the primary social group but also the unit of economic production. The family farm is the basic institution of the Welsh countryside. The 1931 Census revealed that in Wales generally farmers and their relatives accounted for more than sixty per cent of all persons engaged in agriculture,[1] and the proportion is very much higher in upland and

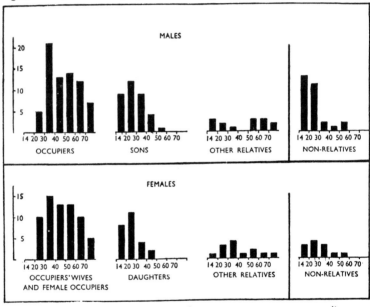

Fig. 25. Family farming. Labour on farms over twenty acres, according to Age group and Relationship.

moorland areas. On the farms of Llanfihangel, excluding small-holdings under twenty acres where all the work is done by the family, farmers and their relatives do eighty per cent of the male work, and farmers' wives or female occupiers and relatives do ninety per cent of the female work.[2]

Ideally, the occupational unit consists of father, mother, one or two unmarried sons in their youth or early manhood and perhaps a daughter. But this is only possible during a limited period in the history of any family, and in some families it does not occur at all. During the first period in the family cycle when the children are being born and reared, all the larger farmers are obliged to hire labour, and the same tends to become true again towards the end of the cycle when most of the children have married and left home. Yet, in spite of this and the lack of children in some families, only 34.6 per cent of the farms over 50 acres and 60.5 per cent of those over 100 acres employed hired labour in 1940, and, even so, several of the labourers were nephews or cousins of the farmer or of his wife. The great majority of the hired workers are youths in their teens and young men in their twenties. All of these are unmarried and they live under the same roof as the employer and his family and eat at the same table, except at one or two large farms where the ' two tables' have been retained. In fact, only four farm-labourers in the whole parish lived in dwellings of their own in 1940. Thus, the farmer whose sons are too young, or too few, or have married and left home, makes good the deficiency by hiring other people's sons.

The supply of labourers derived from the families of cottagers and smallholders is augmented by the custom whereby farmers with more children than can be usefully employed at home place some of them as labourers on neighbouring farms. Thus, in 1940, 27 per cent of the unmarried sons under thirty-five years of age from farms over 20 acres were employed as farm-labourers as compared with 52 per cent employed at home, 11 per cent farming on their own account and 9 per cent in non-agricultural occupations. Or, to go back a generation, a quarter of the present occupiers of such farms, who were themselves farmers' sons, worked as farm-labourers during some period of their youth as compared with the three-quarters who worked at home until they acquired holdings of their own.

As the size of the farm increases the likelihood of a superfluity of children in these days of small families diminishes, but there were in 1940 eight farms over 50 acres and four over 100 acres with children ' working out '. From the point of view of the majority there is nothing degrading in this. They will say that the lad learns a lot thereby. Since he is destined to become a farmer himself, his employer will teach him his craft and not just allocate tasks to him as he would to an ordinary labourer. But farmers of over 150 acres seldom have occasion to seek agricultural work for their children.

Moreover, they are inclined to copy the discrimination between farmers' sons and labourers which obtains in lowland areas and to regard it as below their station to hire out their sons.

As members of the household the employees can be called upon at all times and their duties and privileges are in many ways analogous to those of the family itself. Their working hours are not defined and there are no recognised holidays on Saturday afternoons or Sundays. As against this, it is not customary to expect them to work in the open on rainy days, and they are looked after and lose no wages when they are ill. Arrangements are made for them to have their share of religious services and to be released early to go to fairs and other social functions. It is also understood that all reasonable requests for opportunities to visit relatives and to attend weddings and funerals will be granted without deductions from wages. This ' give and take ' relationship conflicts with recent regulations, such as the Agricultural Wages Board's prescription of a 48 hour week in winter and a 52 hour week in summer with payment for over-time. In most cases employer and employee agree not to enforce their rights under regulations of this kind which seek to fit their relationship into an industrial mould. Under present conditions the employee usually receives more than the minimum wage and he weighs the privileges of the old system against the rights of the new one. Nevertheless, urban standards are spreading and many farmers complain that there is not the same interest and pride in work as in the old days.

Specialised workers, such as waggoners, cowmen and shepherds, are seldom kept nowadays, though middle-aged people remember them on all the larger farms. The responsibility for the detailed management of the farm now rests solely with the working occupier who allocates their daily tasks to his sons and employees. The normal practice is to hire a man for general farm work rather than for any branch of it, a young lad between fourteen and eighteen on the smaller farms, and a slightly older man, who may be assisted by a boy who has just left school (*hogyn*) on the larger ones.

Women and girls may be seen working in the fields during the hay and corn harvest, but on the whole they participate less in such tasks as planting, weeding and harvesting rootcrops than they did a generation or so ago. Normally, there is now a fairly clear division of labour between the sexes, the activities of the women being largely confined to the house and the farm-yard. The success of the family farm depends a great deal upon the resourcefulness of the farmer's wife. In addition to her household duties, she looks after the poultry, collects the eggs, makes the butter and sells all these products. In this she may have the assistance of a daughter or a domestic servant, but at nearly half the farms, as well as at the smallholdings, all the work was done by one woman.

From the sale of her domestic products—locally defined as the things taken to market in a basket—the wife derives the house-keeping money with which she buys groceries, clothes herself and the younger children and replenishes the stock of household equipment. The wife's budget is thus largely independent of that of her husband, and she is usually rather secretive about it. This separation of moneys is even more marked in some parts of southern Montgomeryshire where the farmer's wife starts her married life with a separate banking account based on a dowry of a few tens or hundreds of pounds according to the circumstances of her parents. As far as I could discover, no separate accounts were kept in Llanfihangel, but the wife was expected to manage as far as possible on the proceeds of ' the basket '. In this connection it is interesting to recall that under medieval Welsh law the wife of a freeman might dispose of her clothing, her meal, her cheese, her butter and milk ' without the advice of her husband ', while the wife of a *taeog* (serf) had far less liberty.[3]

Farmers' sons and daughters work for their keep, and handle only small sums of pocket money received at irregular intervals. This complete dependence of the rising generation upon their parents is perhaps the most striking feature of the family-farm. It is not unusual to see a young man of thirty or thirty-five years of age approaching his father at the market-town for money to buy some trifle he has fancied. The labourer's son on the other hand, has more independence. More than one farmer told me that he used to go to Llanfyllin Fair in his youth with a shilling or two in his pocket and had to select his pleasures very carefully, while farm-servants, who had just received their six months' wages, enjoyed themselves on a much more extravagant scale. The farmer's son has to serve a long apprenticeship, and it is my impression that the psychological effect of this prolonged boyhood may be observed in the reticent and subdued behaviour of farmers' sons as compared with labourers' sons as well as in an element of immaturity which seems to persist in the character of many an adult farmer.

On the other hand, this continued dependence is not resented by the young people. Wealth is a family possession, and a son is usually quite satisfied if the farm is prospering even though he reaps no separate personal reward. He knows that he will ultimately obtain his fair share. Indeed, it is when the sons have become old enough to work that the parents are able to build up a reserve of wealth to settle them on the land. No hired labour is then employed and the whole income from the farm can be devoted to this purpose. Again, sons and daughters who go into service are expected to save their wages so that they may have ' something by them ' when they start farming on their own. A fairly prosperous farmer with a number of unmarried sons will sometimes acquire another holding and place the eldest in charge of it, with a sister or other relative as housekeeper. But in such cases the final responsibility for the second farm rests with the father until the son marries. Only two farmers in Llanfihangel in 1940 had been able to anticipate the settlement of a son in this way. In the majority of families the time for subdivision arrived before adequate preparation had been possible.

The great change in status in the life of a farmer's son occurs at marriage when he is set up in a separate farm. Marriage marks the conclusion of his major obligations to his parents and the beginning of an independent existence. The transition is important enough to justify a change in the way in which the man is referred to and addressed. A married occupier of a holding is called either by his Christian name and surname together—Evan Evans, or William Jones—without any other appelation such as Mr., or else as *Gŵr-y-man-hyn-a'r-man* (the husband of such and such a farm ; c.f. *husbond* in medieval England). An unmarried son is never referred to in either of these two ways, but by his Christian name or one of its diminutives followed by the name of his father's farm. Even though he be an elderly bachelor farming a holding inherited from his parents, he is still *John Tŷ Uchaf*, or *Wil y Wern*. An informant from another district cited the case of a man who was called *Dai Tŷ Isaf* while he remained single and worked at home with his parents. He married and took a farm of his own and was then known as Dafydd Jones. His wife died and he returned to his father's farm and thus became *Dai Tŷ Isaf* once more. There is no conscious rule regarding this change of name, and people are unaware of their own practice until it is pointed out to them.

When a son marries, his father assumes the responsibility for setting him up in a farm of his own, and this is consciously regarded as compensation for the services he has rendered the family during his youth. Unless the farmer has already acquired the tenancy of a second farm, he will assist his son to secure one, and he may

Plate VII*a*. Braich-y-waun

Plate VII*b*. Ceunant

pay the first six months' rent. Until a holding is available there can be no independent existence of the new family. Therefore, when marriage takes place before the acquisition of a holding, the man remains at his father's home, and the wife continues to live with her parents. In 1940 there were six cases of a married son or daughter living at home awaiting a vacant farm, and in three cases the first child had already been born.

The major part of the stock and implements for the new farm are provided by the bridegroom's family. There is no rule as to the amount of goods transferred in this way, and it bears no relation to the value of the services the son has rendered. The father gives whatever can be spared, and if this is not enough to start with he may add to it by buying additional stock. The bride's family also makes its contribution and this usually includes a share of the stock as well as those domestic requirements which are the bride's particular concern. I could find no rule as to the extent and character of each family's contribution except that the bridegroom's family provides the bulk. This is a normal concomitant of patrilinear succession and male ownership, but it was explained to me as a recognition of the higher value of the bridegroom's services to his family.

There is no marriage bargain, as is the case in many other peasant communities, nor is there a formal meeting of the families to make the necessary arrangements. These matters may be discussed casually at a chance meeting or in the course of the wedding celebrations, but, in the meantime, the young couple themselves will have served as links between the two families so that each will know exactly what the other proposes to do. And despite the informal nature of the procedure both sides are fully aware of their obligations, and it is a matter of prestige that the contributions of one side should be proportionate to those of the other. The sanction of local gossip is usually effective enough to ensure fair dealing, and cases are known of farmers who have mortgaged their stock in order to deal honourably with situations of this kind.

Owing to the traditional preference for family labour and the need for creating a reserve before subdivision, the age of marriage is considerably higher than it is in Britain generally. For the same reasons farmers' sons marry later than the sons of labourers. On the average, present occupiers of over 20 acres did not marry until they were thirty. Taking all marriages of farmers' sons contracted locally between 1890 and 1940, the average age was 31.3, in contrast to 27.7 in the case of sons of other rural workers. Even the

latter is much higher than is normal in the country generally.
Marriage raises difficulties for labourers as well as for farmers owing
to the preference for workers 'living in ' and the scarcity of labourers'
cottages. The following figures show that in Montgomeryshire the
percentage of bachelors for each age-group increases as the district
becomes more completely rural.

Percentage of Bachelors in Male Age-Groups.

Age Group	Urban Districts 1931	Rural Districts 1931	Llanfihangel 1940
20 — 29	76.2	80.9	87.5
30 — 39	27.0	37.9	39.7
40 — 59	17.1	20.0	27.3

The marriage of farmers' daughters is not delayed to the same
extent. Their economic value to the family farm decreases rapidly
as their number increases, and since very few of the local farmers
are in a position to keep maids, many girls have to leave the parish
in search of employment. Some become maids at more prosperous
lowland farms while others enter service in the towns, and many of
these marry men from the localities where they work. Daughters
who remain at home are also freer to marry than their brothers,
because, as we have seen, a daughter's marriage causes a smaller
disturbance to the economic unit. Nevertheless, on an average,
the wives of present occupiers of farms over 20 acres did not marry
until they were twenty-six, and the average age of farmers' daughters married between 1890 and 1940 was 27.7 as compared with
25.5 in the case of daughters of craftsmen and labourers. It will
be observed from Figure 26 that the peak age of marriage for
farmers' daughters is between 25 and 30, in striking contrast to the
peak age of 21-25 for the daughters of other workers in Llanfihangel,
as well as for women in England and Wales generally. The bridegroom was at least four years older than the bride in almost half
the marriages recorded between 1890 and 1940, and at least eight
years older in more than a fifth of them[5]—a disparity which tends
to add to the authority of the father as head of the family and
manager of the family concern.

Figure 26 also shows that whereas the majority of farmers'
sons marry between the ages of twenty-five and thirty-five, the

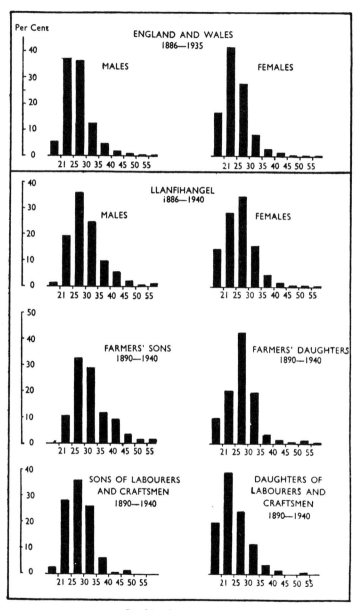

Fig. 26. Age at marriage.[4]

ages at which the remainder marry are spread over a very wide range. For every two who marry before they are twenty-five, three do not marry until they are forty or more. This postponement of marriage until late middle life can be understood only in the light of filial duty and the custom whereby the paternal hold ing and stock are inherited. The retirement of farmers on reaching old age is exceptional in Llanfihangel, and is mainly confined to those without children to succeed them. The majority remain in control to the very end, and family solidarity is normally strong enough to ensure that one son will remain at home to assist his parents in their declining years.

The duty of remaining at home generally falls on the youngest son, whose marriage is postponed until death breaks up the old family nucleus. When the parents die, he inherits the holding, since his older brothers are considered to have received their share of the patrimony when they married and left home. If the parents leave a substantial sum of money in addition to the stock, this, together with the furniture, is usually divided between all the children, with a special share for the succeeding son, who has given longer service. That is the normal procedure, but there are many aberrations as is shown by an analysis of the succession in 39 farms over 20 acres occupied by the same families for two generations.

Inheritance of Parental Holding.	*No. of cases.*
Succession by daughter, there being no sons ..	3
Succession by daughter although there were sons	3
Succession by an only son	7
Succession by youngest son	15
Succession by eldest son	7
Succession by an intermediate son	2
Joint succession by two bachelor sons ..	2

The son who is to succeed his parents must not marry while there are brothers at home, or while his mother is alive. There must not be two mistresses in the same homestead, and the mother will never surrender the management of the household to a daughter-in-law if she can possibly avoid it. In some of the exceptions cited in the table, the youngest son married before some of his elder brothers, and in that way forfeited his claim to the family hearth. Such a departure from custom is a source of disappointment to the parents, but the young man is rarely penalised. He is set up in a new homestead and given a start in life, while his position at home falls to an elder brother.

Again, the untimely death of one of the parents, can upset the normal procedure. If the mother dies before the father and only one son remains at home, the major obstacle to his marriage is removed. His wife can now be an asset in the management of the female side of the family concern. The presence of an unmarried daughter at home would, however, be a further complication, but in such circumstances the daughter will usually leave home to make room for her brother's wife. The survival of a widowed mother has the opposite effect. If the father dies when the children are still young, the eldest son assumes much of his father's responsibility. The others grow up and marry and in such cases it is the oldest and not the youngest who remains at home with his mother. The following examples of households in the last stage of the family cycle bear eloquent testimony to the way in which the system affects the destiny of the inheriting son.

Members of Household (ages in brackets).

	Family.	*Others.*
(1)	Widowed father (84) ; Bachelor son (56) ; Single daughter (40).	Labourer (25).
(2)	Widowed father (63) ; Single daughter (38) ; Daughter's illegitimate son (7).	
(3)	Widowed mother (66) ; Bachelor son (40).	Labourer (14).
(4)	Widowed mother (75) ; Bachelor son (42).	Labourer (24).
(5)	Widowed mother (72) ; Bachelor son (39) ; Single daughter (34).	Labourer (26). Maid (15).
(6)	Widowed mother (78) ; Bachelor son (44).	Labourer (17).

In many cases the succeeding son remains unmarried so far into middle life that he becomes a confirmed bachelor, and when his parents die he manages his farm with the aid of an unmarried sister or housekeeper. There were five bachelor households of this kind in the parish in 1940 in which the ages of the occupiers ranged from 36 to 45. Of the total of eighteen bachelors aged 40-60, nine were farmers' sons who were either actual or prospective inheritors of their parents' farms.

In many peasant countries[6] it is customary for ageing parents to retire from active management of the farm in favour of a married son, while continuing to live in a portion of the same farmstead. Three and even four generation households are thus quite common. In Wales, on the other hand, the elementary family consisting of husband, wife and children is the normal type, whereas three generation households occur only under exceptional circumstances. The 81 families occupying farms over 20 acres in Llanfihangel were composed as follows :

Husband and wife or parent(s) and child(ren)	58
Three generations · grandparent(s), parent(s) and child(ren)	13
Unmarried siblings .. .. ′	5
Bachelors or widowers : alone or with housekeeper ..	5

Even this summary exaggerates the number of three generation households because six of the thirteen cases were really temporary or makeshift arrangements. Two were cases of married daughters whose first child had been born before a farm had been secured for the new family ; two were cases of a widow and her children living with her parents in one case and with her parents-in-law in the other ; two more were really elementary families which included a daughter's illegitimate child. Apart from these anomalies, there were four cases in which a son and his family lived with an aged father, and three in which a daughter and her family lived with her aged father—and mother in one case. Two of the latter were not examples of a young family attached to an old one, but of a widowed father who had retired from his farm to live with his daughter. There was a consensus of opinion that in the absence of unmarried children, the appropriate place for an aged father or mother who has given up farming is with a married daughter. It is also quite usual to find other unattached relatives added to families in this way, a custom which complicates the simple picture given in the above table. Thus, of the 58 elementary families mentioned, nine contained an additional member, such as an unmarried sibling of husband or wife, an unmarried uncle or aunt, a nephew, a niece or a cousin.

The number of people constituting a household is now substantially lower than it was in the last century. In 1840 there was an average of over six persons per house ; in 1940 the average was less than four. This change is partly due to the smaller number of employees kept to-day, but its main cause is the decline in the size of families. Families were large in Llanfihangel until the beginning of this century. The parents of occupiers and wives over 45 years of age in 1940 had an average of six children. The parents of those aged 20-45 had an average of five. During the last two or three decades the decline has been much more rapid. Of the small sample available of 41 mothers over 45 years of age, those over 60 had an average of 6.6 children, as compared with 3.3 in the case of those aged 45-60. As far as I could find out, the use of commercialised contraceptives is extremely limited in the district, but this is more relevant to the discussion of extra-marital and intra-marital pregnancies. Recent demographic studies have shown that the use of these devices within marriage is generally very limited.[7]

Inhabitants with whom I discussed the decline in the size of families gave no definite reasons for it, except that it may be due to a change in the countryman's diet, or to the decrease in drunkenness. The latter suggestion is not without its point. Whereas increased sobriety may not be a major cause, it is a correlative, for, like the decline in reproduction, it reflects a more calculating and sophisticated attitude towards life. Whether the major cause is the smaller economic need for sons and farm-workers, or the infiltration of urban ideas, large families are no longer fashionable and are seldom found.

The roots of many of the customs described in this chapter lie in the social system of medieval Wales.[8] Unlike the English villager, who often handed on his holding to his successor during his own life-time with the proviso that he and his wife should be cared for in their old age, the Welsh tribesman retained control of his share of the land of the kindred until his death. Sons were entitled, as they are to-day, to equal shares of the moveable property when they left the family hearth, and after their father's day they inherited equal shares of the land itself. But the paternal homestead and the remaining moveable wealth were reserved for the *youngest* son.[9] Daughters were normally excluded from succession to land, but they were entitled to a share of the moveable property,

defined in Gwynedd as half a brother's share, and they had a right
to this whether they married or not.   On the other hand, the
present custom whereby a widow retains possession of a farm for
life, even when there are adult male heirs, does not spring from
tribal law.   The first step towards safeguarding the livelihood of
the widow was not taken until the modification of Welsh law by the
Statute of Rhuddlan after the Edwardian Conquest.   By this
Statute the widow was given the right to an assignment of a third
of the land held by her husband.   In addition, a bride became
entitled to a settlement made upon her by the bridegroom at the
church door with the consent of his father.   Both these customs
had long been practised in England.[10]

Although the old tribal society has long since passed away,
something of its spirit lives on in the cohesion and paternalism
of the present-day family.   This survival has been ensured by
the hereditary nature of the farmer's craft.   In the farming family
there is no relevant matter in which the son is more expert than his
father.   The latter is not only his son's guardian, but also his
teacher, employer and critic.   And it is from his father that the son
will eventually obtain the capital with which to exercise his craft
independently.

Chapter VI

KINDRED

IN a community the majority of whose members were born in the same locality, kinship naturally plays a larger part than it does in modern urban communities where kinsfolk are dispersed and a large proportion of those who live and work together know nothing of one another's antecedents. Yet it does not necessarily follow that a high degree of physical consanguinity will in itself create a familistic society. Biological blood-links as close as those of Llanfihangel may well be found in many an area which has been occupied for generations by the same stock, without a corresponding development of social relationships based upon them. Consanguinity provides only the physical basis for such relationships, and it is the latter that give it particular significance in Llanfihangel and throughout Wales.

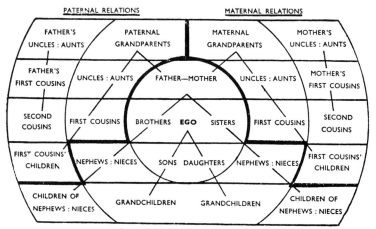

Fig. 27. ' Degrees ' of kinship.

For purposes of analysis we shall classify the complex relationships of kindred as indicated in Fig. 27. An individual's parents, siblings and children, contained within the innermost circle, will be described as his relatives in the ' first degree '. These are relatives who are or have been members of the same elementary family

73

as himself. The second circle brings in relatives of the ' second degree '—grandparents, uncles, aunts, first cousins, nephews and nieces, and grandchildren. The outer circle includes relatives of the ' third degree '—siblings of grandparents, cousins of parents, second cousins, the children of first cousins and the children of nephews and nieces. An awareness of affinity extends beyond the third degree, but the latter represents the limits within which the average person has knowledge of the genealogical connections. Those who fall outside these limits are usually described vaguely as ' distant relatives '. The thick lines divide the diagram into three sections. The one on the left contains the individual's kinsmen ' on his father's side ' and the one on the right his kinsmen ' on his mother's side ', while the middle section represents the elementary family into which he was born, together with its descendants.

All general classifications of kinship must necessarily be artificial in as much as they conceal the different and distinctive associations and feelings expressed in such words as father, brother, cousin, nephew. One hesitates to say whether the bonds which unite an individual with his grandchild are not sufficient to justify the inclusion of the latter within the first degree ; whether first cousins should be included in the same category as nephews and nieces. The countryman distinguishes very clearly between his 'mother's relations ' and his ' father's relations,' but he has no collective terms for relations of different generations corresponding with the ' degrees ' of the diagram. The difference in a person's attitude towards an uncle and a cousin, for example, precludes such designations. With these reservations, the classification will be used as a rough measurement of the closeness of kin ties.

Almost two-thirds of the families of Llanfihangel contain members who are related in the first degree to at least one other family, and one third contain members who are related in this way to at least two other families. More than three-quarters are so linked with at least one other family either in the first or the second degree, while one third have such ties with from five to twelve families. I did not attempt to explore the maze of third degree relationships, but this background has to be kept in mind since the countryman is aware of it. And even then the ramifications of kinship will not have been exhausted. In collecting material one had to revise one's picture of the kinship pattern continually in the light of chance references to remote relationships of which one was not previously aware. For example, a farmer, in criticising a neighbour, remarked rather guiltily : ' I say that although he is a relative of mine '. And, in response to a further query, he explained that the neighbour in question was the son of his mother's second cousin.

Second cousin relationships within the same generation are usually acknowledged, though people related in this way are not always sure of the genealogical details, and have to turn to the older members of the family for an elucidation of the facts. When we include relationships of this remoteness, it may be said of many parts of the parish that every household is bound to every other by kinship ties, and these consist very often of more than one strand. To quote a local expression, they are woven together ' like a pig's entrails ', and the aptness of the simile will be appreciated from a glance at the accompanying diagram (Fig. 28), even though this does not take account of the third degree. One can almost sense the isolation of those households which are not linked up with the others, although many of them are in fact connected on the second cousin plane. Moreover, it must be realised that the diagram tells less than half the complete story, and one must try to visualise the kinship network extending continuously across the artificial boundary of the parish and thereby tying up many of the ' isolated ' households in Llanfihangel with relatives in the wider neighbourhood.

To illustrate the environment of kinship in which the individual lives let us extract from Fig. 28 three individuals and their relatives who between them include a quarter of the households in the parish.

(1) William, a bachelor aged 33, lives alone at a holding which he has recently acquired. His widowed mother lives at the parental homestead a mile-and-a-half away with his two unmarried brothers and one sister. A neighbouring holding is occupied by his father's brother, and his father's sister is the wife of another neighbour. His first cousins are the occupiers, or the wives of occupiers, of seven other holdings in the same quarter of the parish, while a farm three miles away is occupied by his mother's first cousin. Thus, William is related within the second degree to eleven other households in the parish with a total membership of 43.

(2) Thomas, aged 63, with his family, occupies a farm ; he has also succeeded to the tenancy of his deceased brother's farm where he has settled a son and a daughter, both unmarried. A widowed daughter lives with her aged parents-in-law about three miles away, and another daughter and her husband live in one of the hamlets. A neighbouring holding is held by his mother's sister's

Fig. 28. Kinship. The lines join households containing persons related to one another in the "First" or "Second Degree."

widower and his family, and his youngest brother is farming in another part of the parish. His wife is the daughter of a farm just across the parish boundary ; her brother has a farm and her cousin a smallholding, both adjoining that of her husband. Thomas and his family are thus related to seven other households within the parish, with a membership of 21.

(3) James is a man of forty-six years of age who with his wife and children farms a holding. His aged mother and his bachelor brother farm the parental holding about three miles away. Another brother has a farm in the parish and so have two of his first cousins on his father's side. Another cousin and her husband occupy a smallholding. His wife is the daughter of a farm in another part of the parish and this is still occupied by her widowed mother and her brother. Her married brother farms another holding, and her father's sister is the wife of a neighbouring farmer. James and his family are thus related to nine other households within the parish with a membership of 24. One of the households mentioned contains relatives to both James and Thomas.

The bonds of kinship mark out for each individual a group beyond the confines of his immediate household who are ' his people ' in a very intimate sense. While still a child he learns to distinguish them from his other neighbours ; he is taught to call them uncle, aunt, cousin and so on. He finds that many of them have the same surname as himself, and that he and his brothers and sisters have been given the same christian names as some of them. As he grows older his kinsmen of the previous generation serve as an emotional link with his past. To him they are merely uncles and aunts, but they were brothers and sisters to his parents. He addresses them as *chwi* (you), but they were *ti a tithau* (thee and thou) to his parents. This awareness of the tightening of kinship bonds as one steps back a generation is revealed in the tendency to explain distant relationships in terms of the previous generation. Thus, instead of ' cousin,' we have ' his mother and my father were brother and sister ' ; there is no such term as ' second uncle,' but ' his father and my father's father were brothers '.

While the kinship group differs for every individual with the exception of unmarried siblings, there is a large measure of overlap whereby a still larger circle is loosely knitted together, thus : ' He is not actually a relative of mine, but his cousin married my sister '. And an individual who cannot be linked up in this way lives only on the fringes of the community. ' His people are not from these parts ; he is a stranger here ', and one life-time is not sufficient to overcome

this ' strangeness '. The gulf is bridged gradually as the newcomer's children and grandchildren grow up and, by inter-marrying
with the older families, are welded into the chain of kinship. The
countryman does not feel that he knows an individual fully until he
knows the stock from which he sprang. The question ' Who is
he ? ' is interpreted as ' To whom does he belong ? ', and the answer
is ' So-and-so's son ', or ' One of the Joneses ', or ' He is the same
sort of people as so-and-so (*yr un pethau â hwn-a-hwn*) '. Knowledge
of family connections extends far beyond the confines of the parish,
and individuals who are not personally known are identified by
reference to this background of kinship. To quote a middle-
aged farmer : ' I could walk from here to Llanfair or Llanfyllin
or Llanrhaeadr, and I should not be afraid of knocking at any door
on the way. I don't say that I know them all, but I could easily
explain who I was, and although they may not know me they would
almost certainly have known my father or one of my brothers.
My father came from Llanrhaeadr way, and there are some of the
old family still living there '.

Whereas no semblance of a clan system survives, the descendants of a common grandfather or great-grandfather are often
referred to collectively as ' the Joneses ' or ' the Evanses ', or by the
name of the farm where the ancestor lived. And the standard of
conduct and attainment expected from each person is at least
coloured by the reputation of the group to which he belongs. A
critical discussion of a neighbour's behaviour will often end with
some such summing up as this : ' Well, what do you expect ? His
father was very peculiar, and I remember my father saying that his
grandfather . . . '. After he has been placed in his genealogical
context there is nothing more to be said. Allowances must be
made, for after all the offender is one of the Thomases—*ac y mae
natur y cyw yn y cawl* (the nature of the chick is in the broth).

Thus, kin groups have their collective virtues and vices. One
is regarded as moody and self-righteous, another as outspoken
and quick-tempered while a third has a reputation for cunning.
Some have collective nicknames. The countryman's discernment
of family resemblances is keener than that of the townsman, and
it often dispenses with the need for formal introductions. ' You
are one of the Hugheses, aren't you ? John Hughes's son? I
knew your father very well. You are the very image of him '.
In addition to appearance, habits and gestures are recognised as
belonging to particular kindred groups. One of my informants
claimed that all his family had the habit of moving the skin of their

heads in conversation—a fact that I was able to verify in two or three cases—and that a stranger who knew his father had once identified him by this peculiarity!

There were some instances in the district of consanguine marriages, but they rarely involved first cousins. This again was regarded as a peculiarity of one or two groups of kindred rather than a general practice, a view which accords with the evidence which I collected. The purpose of such unions was ' to keep the money in the family '. Marriage within the kindred was popular in medieval Wales and was at one time common among most Western European peoples.[1] But it seems to have always stopped short of first cousins. Even Giraldus Cambrensis, who, as a good medieval churchman, severely castigated the Welsh for their ' incest ', charged them with nothing more than ' not being ashamed of marrying their relations, even to the third degree of consanguinity '.

The custom of naming children after older or deceased relatives persists on a considerable, though declining, scale. In particular, the eldest son is usually given the name of his paternal grandfather, sometimes combined with that of his maternal grandfather. This custom, which is by no means confined to Wales, appears to echo a former belief in a close affinity between alternate generations.[2] It also seems to have been customary to name the second son after his father, but this has been observed only in a minority of cases in Lianfihangel in the last two generations. The custom of naming the first and second daughters after their grandmothers likewise exists, but it is less regularly practised. There is no doubt that older people derive a considerable satisfaction from having children, as it were, dedicated to them in this way, and I have met instances in other districts of grandfathers being deeply offended when the custom was ignored. Generally speaking, the names of the dead, especially the prematurely dead, have priority over those of the living. A deceased maternal grandfather may take precedence over a living paternal grandfather, and time and again, in going through the evidence, I found that the normal practice had been waived in favour of an uncle or an aunt who had met an untimely death. In some families, on the other hand, the name of a relative with a distinguished career had been selected in preference to a more orthodox choice.[3]

The solidarity of the kindred is a constant source of surprise to the stranger. Relatives are expected to be loyal to one another, and there can be no more disparaging criticism than that a man has behaved shabbily towards a brother or a cousin. The kindred has an organic quality; what happens to the individual member is felt by the whole group. To offend one member is to arouse the hostility of a formidable section of the community—as many a tactless schoolmaster and minister in upland Wales has discovered to his cost. The saying goes in Llanfihangel that a neighbouring valley is like a dog. If you tread on its tail at one end of the valley, it will bark at the other end. The simile would apply almost as well to Llanfihangel itself. This ' clannishness ' performs a twofold social function. On the one hand, it gives the individual a sense of security, of belonging. On the other, it acts as a check upon violent and instinctive behaviour. The individual realises that the way he treats another individual will affect the attitude of a whole group towards him, and he will think twice before alienating a body of neighbours with whom he must continue to live.

Equally important is the control which the group exerts upon its own members. Not only do a man's actions reflect upon himself and his household, the reputation of his relatives is also involved, and there can be no stronger sanction in the countryside than the praise and particularly the censure of one's kinsmen. A person who gains the respect of his neighbours enhances the prestige of his kin group, and they are proud to own him as one of themselves (*arddel perthynas*) and to display his photograph in a prominent place in their homes. In the same way, a person who disgraces himself prejudices the good name of his kindred. Thus, not only is the individual's status coloured by the standards achieved by his ancestors and kinsmen, but he himself has it in his power to raise or lower the standards by which his contemporaries and his successors will be judged. And nothing humiliates a countryman more than to have the shortcomings of his relatives thrown in his teeth (*edliw perthynas*), with the implication that he comes of poor stock. The individual is expected to live up to the best traditions of his kindred, and if he falls short of the expected standards he will find it easier to regain the friendship of his neighbours and the affection of his immediate family than to win the forgiveness of his less intimate relatives whose pride has been wounded by his behaviour.

The emotional significance of kinship is a subject which could be dealt with more vividly in a novel than in a systematic description, because its presence as a factor underlying other relationships is far more important than its formal expression would suggest. It is a force to be reckoned with in every sphere of social life, in neighbourliness, in religious groupings, in marriage alliances and so on; it pervades everything, but it has few independent social expressions. These latter consist mainly of periodic visits in the case of relatives living far apart, while those who live in the same locality are able to express their solidarity in mutual help, in supporting one another in chapel affairs and in continual visits to one another's homesteads. But the consciousness of blood connections embraces a much wider group than is held together by these contacts. This becomes evident above all in funerals which bring together surprisingly large numbers of relatives from a radius of many miles, some of whom may not have had any contact with the deceased for a period of years, and may not have met one another since the last funeral of a common relative.

Like the solidarity of the single family, loyalty to relatives is a heritage from the tribal past. A tribal organisation of life continued in a modified form in Wales throughout the Middle Ages, in contrast to the feudal system of rural England. Every freeman belonged to a *cenedl*, a patrilineal clan, and within it he was bound by specific obligations and privileges to groups of his near kin. In a secondary way he also had rights and responsibilities with regard to his mother's kinsmen. Thus, the medieval Welshman, like his modern descendants, took cognisance of both his ' father's relatives ' and his ' mother's relatives '. Far more than is the case today, every person was responsible for and to his kinsmen, and a knowledge of pedigrees, even to ' the ninth degree ', was essential to the proper functioning of society.

Chapter VII

YOUTH

THE role of young people as members of their parents' families has already been described. In this chapter we shall deal with some of their activities outside the family circle, and with the approach to marriage. Owing to the demand for unmarried men on the family farm and the relatively few openings for girls, considerable numbers of the latter leave home to serve as maids on lowland farms or to find employment in the towns. Thus, the age-group 14–45 contains nearly two unmarried males for every one unmarried female. The young men are referred to collectively as *y bechgyn*, or *y llanciau* (the boys or the lads), but the inhabitants seldom have occasion to refer to the girls as a group.

Almost every evening from fifteen to forty young men gather at the Llan, leaving almost as many bicycles leaning against the hedge of the rectory garden, and similar numbers will be seen at Dolanog and Pontllogel. At the Llan they will sometimes play football or quoits in the Inn Field, and a few will take a drink at the Inn and play draughts or dominoes there. But the main centre of attraction is one of the shops, or, in fine weather, the enclosed pavement outside its open door which gives them a grand-stand view of the people passing up and down. Boxes are brought out of the shop to serve as seats, and there they will remain until almost midnight, drinking mineral water, eating tinned food, smoking, chatting, bantering and remarking on the passers by. And as night draws on they will sing hymns, ballads and popular songs.

These young men form a fairly definite youth group, the ages ranging broadly from about sixteen to thirty-five. Marriage brings association with the group to an end, and confirmed bachelors gradually pass out as they grow older. Some years ago the Rector and some friends endeavoured to give the young men better facilities. The Old Schoolroom was thrown open to them for one or two nights a week, and games such as table-tennis were placed at their disposal. But the young men were rather contemptuous of this well-meant effort to canalise their energies, and those who took advantage of the facilities proved unruly and rather destructive. During more recent years, an *Aelwyd Urdd Gobaith Cymru* (Branch of the Welsh League of Youth), has been more successful. It meets on one or two nights a week in winter and less frequently in summer, and is attended by girls as well as youths. But these are formal meetings organised for the young people by their elders, like similar meetings at the chapels. They do not replace the traditional society of the young men.

The youth group derives considerable amusement from ridiculing and embarrassing its elders and indulging in practical jokes. In such pranks they always act collectively and under cover of darkness so that no blame can be attached to any particular one of them, and they never give one another away if a joke leads to trouble. They resent interference from an older man, and are usually able to recall that no one was more mischievous than their rebuker in his own youth. People who really antagonise the young men lay themselves open to various forms of retaliation. Thus, one or two farmers who objected to the youths crossing their fields were mercilessly satirised in verses sung by the youths on the roads at night, and a person whose attitude is particularly unfriendly may be subjected to rather ungenerous jokes. His gates may be carried away at night, irregular shapes may be cut in his cornfields, a hen may be pushed down his chimney when there is jam stewing over the open fire, or his chimney may be stuffed with straw.

This behaviour is not as anti-social as it may seem. In many instances one certainly had the impression that the majority of the community secretly approved of the young men's action, although they never sanctioned it. Not far from Llanfihangel a middle-aged widow was being visited repeatedly at night by a young lad, and the youth group blamed the widow for enticing him. To break up the association they congregated around the house of the widow every time the lad was there, stopping up the chimney and throwing dead vermin and other obnoxious objects in through the doors and windows. In another district I was told of a married man, who was associating with another woman, being met by the youth group one night on his way home. They plastered him with cow dung and dragged him through the river.

The loyalty of the young men to their own group has its counterpart in a form of mock-hostility towards the youth of other localities. They are normally well-behaved at social gatherings in their own hamlet, but it is part of the fun to be rowdy and quarrelsome at such functions in other hamlets. Disturbances around the Old Schoolroom when a meeting is in progress at the Llan are generally attributed to youths from some other district. Hostility is expressed by the young men towards suitors from other neighbourhoods who come to court local girls, and such suitors have to put up with a great deal of horseplay. Turf may be thrown at the stranger from behind hedges, his bicycle may be hidden, or its tyres deflated or even torn, his pony may be driven away or a disturbance created outside the house he has visited. A favourite annoyance if he is found walking with the girl is for a group of lads to walk close behind him, talking loudly and disparagingly about him, kicking his heels or trying to trip him. If he accepts the challenge he is set upon by the whole group. When courtship has continued for some time the hostility ceases and the stranger is accepted on more friendly terms.

The behaviour is explained locally as an expression of jealousy, though it has to be admitted that in many cases none of the local group is particularly interested in the girl. They may also admit grudgingly that the suitor comes from a good family and is considered eligible by the girl's people. At first glance, therefore, the practice appears to be an example of ' consociation ', a device whereby an ambivalence of feelings is given expression in mock-hostility, excessive familiarity and joking[1]. But while this may account for the psychological satisfaction which the young men of today derive from the practice, the courtship customs of other European countries suggest another explanation of its origin. In Sweden, in Switzerland and other parts of Central Europe, the young men's guilds were the custodians of custom, and they imposed punishment upon those who broke the rules of courtship. One of these rules excluded suitors from another village,[2] and this tallies with the traditional preference in Wales for marriage within the kinship group. There is no doubt that in many parts of rural Wales a girl who accepts the advances of a complete stranger loses status and prejudices her prospect of marriage within the locality. This theory, which derives the young men's behaviour from what may once have been a recognised duty to enforce the observance of custom, might also explain the other instances I have given of the young men taking it upon themselves to teach people a lesson. Anthropological literature contains examples of other communities further afield in which the enforcement of custom is assumed by a society of the younger men.[3]

In a society where the family is the economic unit, the choice of spouse must be governed largely by economic considerations. Not only must the young wife be familiar with farm routine, but it is also important that her family should be able to make a proper contribution towards the establishment of the young couple in a farm of their own. For these economic reasons, and for the maintenance of prestige, which will be discussed in a later chapter, farmers' sons usually marry the daughters of farmers of comparable status. Nevertheless, the influence of parents upon the selection of spouses is of a negative and general character, and the actual choice is made by the young people themselves without consultation with their parents. Courtship is a secret to be concealed from both parents and neighbours for as long as possible. The parents will usually have heard of the courtship from third persons long before it is disclosed to them by the young people themselves, and, unless they disapprove, little will be said about it—particularly between father and son—until the wedding day has been fixed. The young man does not ask the girl's father for his consent until the marriage has been arranged ; it is left to each partner to secure the acquiescence of his or her own people.

One seldom sees unmarried couples going for walks together ; indeed custom offers few opportunities for couples to meet out-of-doors. It is unconventional for unmarried girls to go out unless they have some definite purpose, such as to attend a religious service or some other social gathering, or to perform an errand to a neighbouring farm or to the shop—and to go out to keep an appointment with a lover is not normally included in the list of legitimate destinations. A few years ago when a branch of the Welsh League of Youth had been constituted at the Llan the young girls suggested to the Rector, at the end of a winter's programme, that weekly meetings be held throughout the summer months, ' so that we can come out '. Thus, the ' youth movement ', which is justified as a means of ' keeping the young people off the streets ' in the towns, can have the opposite effect in a different culture.

Courtship is a private matter which has no public expression. Young couples usually behave nonchalantly towards each other in public and seldom acknowledge their friendship at social gatherings. At the end of such gatherings the young girls will set out for home in groups, followed at some distance by the young men, and they will not usually divide into couples until they are well out of public view. While the freedom of unmarried girls is in this sense restricted, young men are free to come and go as they will when their work is done, and no questions are asked as to how they spend their time. Indeed, it is this complete freedom given to the young men that makes meetings between the sexes possible. The most usual meeting-place is the kitchen in the girl's home at night, when the parents are in bed. In the case of established love affairs, these meetings may take place once or twice weekly, and it is usual to keep to the same night(s) of the week, referred to as *y noson* (the night). These meetings usually last until the small hours, or until dawn. During vigils with the Home Guard picket in 1940, traffic came to an end about midnight, and one could then rest until dawn when the young men would be going home on their bicycles or motorcycles.

Since the household is asleep when the young man appears on the premises, it is necessary to signal the girl, and this is done by throwing turf, gravel or dried peas at her window. Hence, the practice is called *mynd i gnocio* (going to knock). An appointment is not essential, a young man may go to knock up a girl to whom he has never spoken before. If he is lucky, she will come to the window, the young man will introduce himself, and if he is acceptable she will let him into the kitchen, and they may have a light meal or a cup of tea together. In Merioneth the custom is called *mynd i gynnig* (going to offer, or to try one's luck). Many jocular tales are told of men who have thrown gravel at the wrong window and have been chased away by dogs or gunshots. In another parish I heard the tale of an unwanted suitor who used to stand on top of a barrel of pig-swill which stood under the girl's window. Ultimately she succeeded in discouraging him by arranging the lid in such a way that he fell in.

The old custom of *caru ny gwely* (courting in bed) still survives to some extent, but it is difficult to judge how generally it is practised. The inhabitants are inclined to disown it, while admitting that it persists in neighbouring districts. Some of the observations made about this form of courtship suggest the former existence of certain safeguards, but I did not obtain any details of the local custom. Thus, an informant ' had heard ' that girls would tie the hems of their nightgowns into a knot, another knew of a girl who 'stitched herself up '. Mr. Rhys Davies[4] in a novel on the subject gives prominence to a stratagem which he regards as having been a general custom, whereby the girl laid a bolster between herself and her suitor, at least during the first period of courtship, and he maintains that it was a serious breach of etiquette to remove the barrier without the girl's consent. I have also heard natives of Cardiganshire refer to the bolster as a dividing line.

This method of courtship, known in English as *bundling*, had a wide distribution in Europe in former times[5], being particularly characteristic of Scandinavia and Central Europe. European mythology contains many examples of the motif whereby a strange lover enters a girl's room by the window and begets a wonder-child, and conventional literary forms such as the serenade and the *aube*, which deals with the parting of the lovers at dawn, appear to be related to it.[6] In many parts of Northern and Central Europe organised groups of young men would go out at night ' calling ' on a girl and would sit with her for a time joking and singing before leaving one of their number as her bed-fellow for the night. In some parts of Wales a suitor would take a younger boy with him as company,[7] and fourteenth century love poems refer to a *gwas caru* (servant in courtship), but there seems to have been no collective participation by the youth group.

The number of premarital pregnancies shows that sexual intimacy is frequent during courtship. Out of 243 marriages contracted between 1890 and 1930, 132 had no issue in the parish, while the first maternity occurred within eight months of marriage in 44 per cent of the remainder.[8] The corresponding figures in 1939 for England and Wales as a whole[9] were 22.7 per cent, and just over 29 per cent for north and west Wales, Cumberland, Westmorland and parts of Yorkshire. Although these figures relate to a later date than those obtained from Llanfihangel, the discrepancy is sufficient to indicate that the incidence of premarital pregnancies is appreciably higher in the latter than it is in the country generally.

The same is true of illegitimacy. During each decennial period from 1890 onwards the number of illegitimate births per thousand live births in Llanfihangel was more than twice the number for England and Wales, while the following figures for 1931-39 show a gradual increase as the area becomes more rural :[10]

England and Wales	 42	per thousand	live-births	
Montgomeryshire	 73	,,	,,	,, ,,
Llanfyllin Rural District	87	,,	,,	,, ,,
Llanfihangel	100	,,	,,	,, ,,

These facts must not be regarded as evidence of greater laxity in rural areas than in modern communities generally. Effective means of contraception, which are better known and more easily procurable in towns than in the countryside, have rendered statistics of this kind valueless for comparing the extra-marital sexual life of urban and rural communities. The incidence of illegitimacy per thousand unmarried women aged 15–45 in England and Wales as a whole fell by about one-half between 1890 and 1939, but it can hardly be said that this reflects a corresponding increase in continence.

More fundamental than any present contrast between the illegitimacy rates of urban and rural areas is the regional variation which existed in Britain when the population had been less thoroughly reshuffled than it is today, and when birth-control methods were not so generally known.[11] In the 1870's the incidence of illegitimacy in the north of England and Wales was generally higher than in the south, while it was much higher still in Scotland. The following numbers per thousand live-births will give some idea of the range : Essex 34, Wiltshire 49, South Wales, 45 ; North Wales, 69 ; Norfolk, 74 ; Cumberland, 76 ; most of Western Scotland, 65 ; North-East Scotland, 141. The detailed distribution admits of no simple explanation. Attempts at a straightforward correlation with 'Celtic' culture, partible inheritance, rurality, Protestantism, Nonconformity, illiteracy, or what not, all break down on the British evidence, whereas continental figures would further confound any such correlations. Even the very reasonable argument that a prolonged postponement of marriage for familistic reasons increases illicit sex relations and therefore illegitimacy is refuted by the evidence from Ireland, a country with a very low illegitimacy rate and a remarkable proportion of its adult population unmarried.[12] The only conclusion that can be reached without further study of the subject in its European context is that the traditional attitude towards illegitimacy in Britain must have varied considerably from district to district. For some reason or other, the social and moral sanction was much stronger in the south than in the north, in England than in Scotland, in South Wales than in North Wales.

In Llanfihangel, all extra-marital pregnancies were considered improper and extremely unfortunate unless the situation was saved by marriage. But public censure appears to be less severe than, for example, in the Welsh industrial communities of South Wales. The fact that such occurrences were frequent in their own youth ensures a measure of understanding and sympathy on the part of the older people, and criticism is often tempered with some such remark as : 'Well, things could be worse, she is not the first by a long way, and she will not be the last '. But condemnation is never qualified if the father of the child is a married man, which is rarely the case. If conception is not followed by marriage, a sum of money is paid by the parents of the man concerned to those of the girl, and unless paternity is doubtful this is usually settled without recourse to the courts. The child is brought up by the girl's parents and after a short while neighbours lose all interest in the matter. Subsequent social relationships do not betray obvious signs of a reduction in the girl's status, and while the possession of an illegimate child is undoubtedly a handicap, it by no means debars marriage to another partner.

In this connection it is interesting to recall the tolerant attitude towards illegitimacy expressed in the Welsh Laws, particularly in the North Wales Codes according to which illegitimates could be co-heirs with legitimate children.[13] It may also be significant that the seventeenth and eighteenth century Parish Registers of Llanfihangel almost invariably give the father's name in recording the baptism of an illegitimate child, while the mother's name is often omitted as it is in the case of a legitimate child. It seems that seventeenth and eighteenth century peasants, no less than seventeenth and eighteenth century kings, openly acknowledged their illegitimate offspring. The Registers also contain evidence of prolonged unformalised cohabitation. This again appears mainly in items recording the baptism of children, but there are also a few registrations of the burial of women described as the ' concubine ', ' trollop ' or ' rolik ' of so and so. The frequency of such entries varies with the handwriting, some rectors being more explicit than others.

In the absence of comparable data from other areas the significance of these records cannot be fully assessed, but it is relevant to recall Giraldus Cambrensis' assertion that the Welsh ' are not accustomed to undertaking the responsibility of marriage without previous proof of compatibility, and, above all, of fertility, through cohabitation and intercourse '.[14] It should be realised, however, that for Giraldus, as for the eighteenth century rectors of Llanfihangel, ' marriage ' meant a religious ceremony, which is nowhere mentioned as a necessity in the Welsh Laws, and did not secure legislative sanction even in England until the tenth century.[15] In sixteenth century England, and more recently in some districts, an informal trothplight still marked the beginning of conjugal life, the church marriage occurring some weeks later, or even after the birth of the first child.[16] Welsh marriage customs may not therefore have been radically different in this respect from those of England, but, like other customs, they survived longer in Wales than in most parts of England. In this connection life in the Border lands of Wales may be nearer to the original than in the more ' Welsh ' areas where Methodism, with its strict disciplinary action against sexual transgressions, secured a firmer footing.

Most of the traditional Welsh wedding customs, such as the concealment of the bride, the race of the bride and bridegroom on horseback to and from the church pursued by the young men, and the bidding letter, are now extinct in Llanfihangel, and such customs as prevail are fairly general in Britain. These include the firing of guns, the tying of old shoes to the wedding-car, the throwing of confetti and rice, and the holding-up of the procession by stretching ropes across the road or by tying the church-gate, with the customary payment for release. If the couple is popular with the local lads, an arch of evergreens will have been constructed over the church-gate the previous night.

The traditional *neithior* (feast on the wedding-night) has lost much of its former significance owing to the increasing popularity of the honeymoon, which had no place in the native Welsh wedding customs. Even now, in many cases, the honeymoon is restricted to one night at Llanfyllin or at the home of a relative, and a compromise is sometimes made between the old and the new custom by delaying the departure of the couple until the evening celebrations are in full swing. These are characterised by much boisterousness on the part of the young men outside the house before they are invited to enter and join the party. In the adjoining parish of Llanerfyl, the young men will sometimes bring out some of the stock of the bride's father and conduct a mock-auction in the farmyard. The extent of such roistering is a measure of the popularity of the couple and their families. Wedding-presents are received from friends and relatives, and when the couple have entered their holding their new neighbours will bring practical presents, such as a hen or two, and assist them with a day's work in getting their farm into order.

Chapter VIII

NEIGHBOURS

WHILE social relationships based upon consanguinity loom larger in rural Wales than they do in modern urban communities, or even in English villages,[1] they constitute only one pattern in the intricate social fabric. Kinship groups are interspersed geographically, and social relationships which give significance to physical proximity are interwoven with those associated with blood. And it is with this community life which links up neighbouring farmsteads, and the relation between it and the life of the hamlet, that we shall be concerned in this chapter and the one that follows.

Like consanguinity, physical proximity does not in itself determine social contacts. It only makes such contacts possible. If close proximity of residence were the only necessity the community life of urban and suburban localities would be stronger than that of the Welsh countryside, whereas the contrary is actually the case. Neither does a scattered habitat necessarily produce a strong community life based on locality. There are many parts of lowland Britain where distances between dwellings do not differ materially from those of upland Wales, yet the social interplay between the inhabitants of these dwellings is much poorer.[2] It is generally agreed in Llanfihangel that neighbourliness declines eastwards towards England and grows westwards towards the mountains, a view which is supported by the experience of upland farmers who have moved down to the plains.

What gives particular meaning to physical proximity in Upland Wales is the complex of social relationships based upon it. By friendliness towards his neighbours the countryman overcomes the isolation imposed upon him by his environment. By welcoming them to his home, by visiting them in their turns, by helping them in their troubles and by co-operating with them in the performance of certain kinds of farm work, he maintains a form of society which dispenses with many of the functions of a central meeting-place at a village or town. From his contacts with his neighbours the individual derives both companionship and assistance, but these are really but aspects of a single relationship. Offers of help arise naturally from companionship, and, conversely, co-operation promotes the growth of companionship and provides the occasions for its cultivation.

Except in cases of emergency, a farmer will not go to another's house in a ' business-like ' manner to request or offer a favour. He will call as though he were only paying a friendly visit, converse with his neighbour for an hour or two, and, perhaps, partake of a meal with the family. Then when he is on the point of leaving he will mention his mission as though it were an afterthought : ' O yes, I was wondering whether you could . . .' This custom seems to be fairly general in rural Wales. A town-bred schoolmaster in Radnorshire once described to me, with a mixture of amusement and annoyance, how after he had entertained a neighbour and his wife for a few hours he discovered about midnight that they had come to ask him to take a member of the family to hospital in his car the following day. But, strange as it may seem to the outsider, the custom is not just humbug ; it is a form of politeness. A favour can only be justified by friendliness, and friendliness means that one finds pleasure in the other's company and does not grudge spending time with him. Moreover, a practical errand can be used as an excuse for a visit as well as the reverse. One will hear the remark : ' I think I will call round to see so and so. Have you any message ?' A farmer from Merioneth tells me that in that county a visitor who feels that he should have a purpose to his visit may improvise an excuse—such as that he thinks he has seen one of his neighbour's sheep astray near his own home. But he will only mention it casually in the conversation, and his neighbour, who knows the ruse, will regard this as an invitation to pay a return visit.

Assistance in need is freely given and refusal to accept it is regarded as a sign of unfriendly independence implying an unwillingness to reciprocate. For, to assist a neighbour is also to impose upon him an obligation to assist you when the opportunity occurs. Neighbours are particularly ready to place at one another's disposal any special knowledge or experience they may possess. One may have exceptional veterinary skill, another may have a wife interested in nursing, the third can ' price an animal ', the fourth is a ' scholar ' who can help with form-filling, and so on. Illness brings many callers, and when someone is so ill as to require constant attention the neighbours are always ready with their offers to come to watch (*gwylio*) at night. Death brings further manifestations of kindliness. In the interval between death and burial the bereaved family leaves much of the housework to other people. In particular it is experienced neighbours who prepare the corpse for burial, and prepare food for those who have come a long way to the funeral.

A man who had moved from this kind of environment to a town described to me how on returning to his new home one evening he learnt that his next-door neighbour's wife had been ill for a week. Both he and his wife were very disturbed to think that neither of them had ' even been to the door to ask how she was '. He called at once before having his tea and was surprised to receive a brief matter-of-fact reply instead of being asked inside. Next morning his wife was washing the front door-step and, remembering the experience of the previous evening, they both spent some time deliberating whether it would be regarded as a kindness or as an insult if she were to wash the neighbour's door-step at the same time.

Co-operation in actual farm work includes the borrowing and lending of machinery, working for a neighbour with one's own machinery, giving a hand in the performance of some special job, or 'lending' a son or a workman for such a purpose. There is no formal contract, neither is there an exact measurement of benefits conferred as against benefits received. Such calculations would be alien to the spirit of friendliness which pervades the whole system. After all, you cannot fully repay a neighbour who has helped you to harvest a crop under threatening clouds until you find him in similar difficulties. Small articles of equipment which are only used occasionally, like ear-markers, scales, or veterinary instruments are extensively borrowed, and many a farmer would never think of buying a collar for a new horse if a neighbour had one of the right size without a horse to fit it. Articles of this kind are often borrowed for long periods and may pass through the hands of several borrowers before they are returned to their owners. Large-scale machinery is borrowed in the same way, though neighbouring relatives will sometimes own some of the more expensive machinery in common. Large farms are better equipped than others and their smaller neighbours depend on them a great deal. On the other hand, the large farm requires additional labour on many occasions, and in borrowing its machines the little farmer incurs the obligation to give a day's work now and again in exchange.

Before the advent of modern farm machinery co-operation was much more widespread than it is now, and tales are still told of the days when bands of neighbours would go out together to mow one another's fields with scythes. Nowadays, the main co-operative tasks are threshing, sheep-dipping, shearing, and, to a smaller extent, the hay and corn harvests. No one receives payment except those who cannot be repaid with services—and even their reward is often a present of tobacco or farm-produce rather than money. What is given and received varies according to need. Thus a small farmer may send a son to help with the hay and receive in exchange the loan of the larger farmer's mowing machine for his own fields, or a smallholder who grows no corn may give a day's work at threshing-time and receive a bag of corn for his poultry or a bull's service for his cows.

Local custom determines with which of his neighbours a farmer co-operates, and when a farm changes hands the newcomer accepts the same partners as his predecessor. The partners usually take the first step by offering to help him to get the farm into order, thus placing him under a lasting obligation. These customary arrangements do not divide the farms into separate co-operative groups. Each farm is the centre of a circle of co-operators which differs slightly from those of its immediate neighbours while overlapping with them, and in this way the whole countryside is covered by a continuous network of reciprocities. The number of partners varies with the size of the farm as illustrated in Fig. 29, which represents

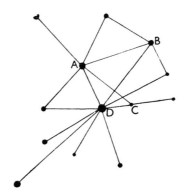

Fig. 29.

the spheres of co-operation of four adjoining holdings. A and D are large farms which co-operate with six and nine other farms, respectively. They assist one another and have three partners in common. B is a smaller farm which co-operates with A and D and with two others who are also partners to A and D, respectively.

C is a smallholding which co-operates with A and D, and with another smallholding with which none of the other three are concerned.

The system is further complicated by the fact that obligations have a different range for different tasks. The borrowing and lending of machinery is normally limited to a few of the closest neighbours, and the same applies to co-operation at harvest-time, and to sheep-shearing on the more low-lying farms. On the large moorland farms, on the other hand, shearing-day is an important event calling for the assistance of from half-a-dozen to a dozen neighbours. But on the majority of farms threshing is now the greatest single co-operative activity, owing to the need to make the best use of a hired machine. Although neighbourliness is the main basis of co-operation, kinship is also involved. A farmer's co-operative partners will often include one or two relatives from some distance. This is particularly true of shearing-days at the moorland farms, which are held on the same days from year to year, and bring together relatives from miles around. Shearing-day is essentially a ' farmer's day '. Labourers are not usually good shearers, and, even if they were, it would be an insult to send one to assist a neighbour or a relative. The farmer must go himself if possible, and, if he cannot, he must be represented by a grown-up son or some other near relative. In the same way, the farmer who is helped will have to spend a week or two going from farm to farm in return.

In addition to their practical value, these days of co-operative activity are important social events. Elaborate meals are prepared, the best rooms in the house are used, the best cutlery and china are brought out and every effort is made to give the guests a handsome welcome. The prestige of the family is involved in the lavishness of this hospitality, which is a concomitant of voluntary work the world over,[3] and any indication of niggardliness will be criticised among neighbours and ridiculed by the young men. All the co-operative tasks are ones where men work in groups, but shearing has the additional social advantage of being a relatively quiet task performed indoors. It is usually done on the barn floor, the shearers being seated on stools. They take great pride in the speed and skill with which they work and the opportunity for display and competition is not missed. When the evening feast is over they will gather round the hearth, and there will be long discussions on the events which have occurred in the district ' since we were here a year ago,' reminiscences of shearing-day at this particular farm in days gone by, with allusions to departed friends, and speculation as to ' how many of us will be here a year tonight '. And when these time-honoured topics have been reviewed, the discussion may be turned to a theological or a political subject.

Thus, every meeting of men for practical purposes has its wider social aspects. Even a business transaction is a social event, especially when the buyer and seller are old friends. The buyer may appear at the farmyard in the early evening, and, after a general chat with the seller and a walk round the buildings and the stock, he will mention the particular animal which he wants to buy, without revealing more than a passing interest in it. The owner may feign reluctance to sell, but eventually he will name a price far higher than he hopes to receive. The potential buyer will offer a price far lower than the creature's true value, and a great deal of jocular bantering will follow, interspersed with snatches of conversation on neutral subjects, and the prices will gradually move closer to one another. More often than not they will refuse to agree in the yard and will walk towards the house pretending that the matter has been finally dismissed. The farmer invites the visitor to the house, and the latter protests but is persuaded on condition that his host understands that he is no longer interested in the deal. They go in and talk of other things with occasional references to each other's stubbornness. The farmer's wife prepares supper, while the guest jokes about the preposterous price her husband has asked and pretends to solicit her support. The subject is dropped again while they eat, and may hardly be mentioned again until the visitor is departing. His host accompanies him to the yard, and there is a further parley during which the visitor pretends to walk away, or, nowadays, starts the engine of his car. At last the deal is made, but even then there may be further quibble over the amount of ' luck money ' to be returned to the buyer.[4]

Skill in bargaining has considerable prestige value, and a man who has been out-bluffed will endeavour to conceal his misfortune from his fellows. For this reason, farmers are usually reluctant to disclose the price they have received, and when they do so the figure is often exaggerated. ' Luck ' money, which is no more than a normal token of good will among the sheep-farmers of the neighbouring moorlands, is often used in Llanfihangel and the surrounding districts as a face-saving device. A seller who would never accept, let us say, £40 may nevertheless agree to conclude the deal for £45 and to refund £5 as luck money. Although he gains nothing financially by this manoeuvre, he receives a cheque for £45 with which to convince himself and his friends that he has made a good bargain.

Each individual has among his neighbours a few families with whom he is on intimate terms and whom he visits regularly. Their interests coincide with his own, and when the day's work is done he will call to see one of them, or they will come to him. No invitation is needed, and no arrangements are made ; the visitor just knocks at the back-door and walks in with a word of greeting. To wait until the door is opened might be regarded as a mark of unfriendliness rather than politeness. Interspersed with these unpremeditated calls come visits of a more formal nature by a man and his wife in response to invitations from friends scattered over a wider area. These formal visits are arranged more particularly in the back-end when the year's main tasks are over. Much time is devoted at such meetings to discussing the comparative success of various methods of farming used locally, new techniques as compared with the way ' the old people ' used to do things, market prices and the relative profitableness of various farm-products. The qualities of various breeds of animals, the training of horses and sheep-dogs, and their achievements, are subjects of perennial interest. References to mutual acquaintances lead to reminiscences about their ancestors. Tracing genealogy to ascertain exactly how ' so and so ' is related to ' so and so ' is always an absorbing pastime, and the conversation on all these topics is invariably enlivened with a wealth of anecdotes and stories.

The nature of these extra-utilitarian meetings on the hearth and the form of conversation will be discussed again in the chapter on recreation and entertainment, but as an essential factor in the social life of the homestead they have a direct bearing upon the theme of this chapter. Social intercourse and hospitality are inseparable in the Welsh countryside ; the hearth is the traditional meeting-place for all forms of social activity. Visitors are always pressed to partake of a meal before they leave, even when they arrive unexpectedly on an errand which need not occupy more than a few minutes. This hospitality is extended to strangers as well as neighbours. I never had to worry about food when going from farm to farm to collect information—except that I usually had to eat more than was good for me—and men whose work takes them regularly around the farms tell me that they are treated with the same generosity.

As a background to close relationships based upon mutual interests lies the neighbourhood, all of whose inhabitants are included in the countryman's social milieu. Many of them differ from him in capacities and inclinations, but he has known most of them and their relatives all his life, and this common experience ensures a wide measure of social intercourse. He is by no means uncritical of his fellows. The countryman is a shrewd judge of men, and there is usually a remarkable agreement among neighbours as to the character of each individual. Nowhere are the newcomer's qualities and defects more carefully weighed. But whatever the countryman's opinion of his neighbours may be it seldom precludes fellowship with them. He accepts them as they are, and their faults and their virtues, their fortunes and their misfortunes are all food for thought and conversation. When he meets them in the course of his day's work he seldom misses the opportunity for a few minutes' chat.

The bond between an individual and the general body of neighbours, irrespective of class or interest, is perhaps never so fully manifested as on the day of his burial. The funeral, which is almost invariably public, is attended by at least one representative from each household for two or three miles around, as well as by friends and relatives from still further afield. However busy the season, no emergency is allowed to deter people from paying their last tribute to the dead. The total attendance is seldom less than a hundred, and in the case of persons of exceptional popularity and prestige it is very much larger. A complete list of those present is published in the report of the funeral in the local newspapers, and a family that is not represented is the subject of comment and censure.

When the funeral rites are over, tea is served in the Old School-room or the Inn. Everybody, including school-children, are invited to partake of this meal. The whole afternoon is given up to the proceedings, and neighbours and relatives will remain in conversation over the ' funeral feast ' until five or six o'clock in the evening. The bereaved family consider it a duty and a privilege to provide this meal, and a minister from a neighbouring locality informs me that his suggestion of a public fund to bear the cost was met with general disapproval. In another parish a minister who disliked the custom tried to discourage it at one funeral by announcing that food would be available at the inn *for those who had come from afar*. But one of the mourners interrupted him with a whisper insisting that the invitation be extended *to all*. In Llanfihangel, as in many other localities in this area, it has been customary to pay the sexton by a collection at the graveside, called *offrwm* (offering) or *pres rhaw* (shovel money)—the sexton holding his shovel to receive the contributions. But during the past four or five years the custom has been discouraged by the incumbent, and the inhabitants no longer have the privilege of paying for the interment of a neighbour.

The social life of each of the three little hamlets is analogous in many ways to that of a group of neighbouring farms in the countryside. There is much borrowing and lending of household equipment, implements, newspapers and books. In addition, close physical proximity with its daily face-to-face contacts gives the social life of the hamlets a communal character which is absent in the countryside. The Llan is one of the most sociable and friendly places imaginable. The houses are small and ill-ventilated with the result that the doors are nearly always open, and neighbours are continually passing to and fro between one house and another. The community has many of the attributes of a large family, and if a member does not turn up during the course of the day his absence is noticed and questions are asked : ' Where is X keeping ? I haven't seen him all day '—and this applies to the rector and the schoolmaster no less than to the shopkeeper, the postmistress, the postman and so on. Some houses do not lock their doors at night, and the shop, which has no closing-time, is a hive of activity between ten and eleven o'clock at 'night.

The daily work of the inhabitants of the hamlet consists of services to one another and to the surrounding neighbourhood, but apart from this practically everyone has some additional social function. A shopkeeper interests himself in cures and his advice is sought in case of illness. He also takes a lead in the organisation of sports, and coaches the local teams, while his wife plays the piano and has now succeeded her father as church-organist. The latter, a retired blacksmith and part-time postmaster, was very well read, and good use was made of his literacy not only by his immediate neighbours, but also by the inhabitants of the surrounding district. The postman makes walking-sticks in return for which farmers give him presents of tobacco, and he is also the church bellringer and organ-blower. Every person counts as a part of the social organism, and when one dies or leaves the hamlet he is missed by the whole community. A sense of incompleteness lingers on as though an organism had lost a limb.

Leaving the relationships between the hamlet and the surrounding countryside to the next chapter, let us conclude with a brief reference to the background from which the country society has derived some of its most distinctive characteristics. A medieval writer has observed that the Welsh ' do not live in cities, villages or castles, but inhabit the woods like anchorites '.[5] The freemen of medieval times, like their modern descendants, lived in scattered dwellings and visitors to Wales in all ages have been impressed by the lack of visible signs of community life. This reaction arises from the assumption that social isolation is inevitable where people do not live close together, or where they are not within easy reach of a village or town. But there exists in upland Wales a diffused form of society which is not only able to function without a unifying social centre but seems to be opposed to all forms of centralisation. The hearth of the lonely farm itself *is* the social centre. The farms are not outlying members of a nucleated community, but entities in themselves, and their integration into social groups depends upon the direct relationships between them rather than upon their convergence on a single centre. The traditional social unit does not consist of the environs of a town or village ; it is *cefn gwlad*, the neighbourhood in the countryside.

In medieval times every man of substance kept open house and hospitality was the basis of community life. ' Beggars are unknown among this people, for all houses are open to everyone alike. Liberality, especially in the form of hospitable entertainment, is deemed by them to be the chief of virtues '[7] Throughout subsequent centuries the home has retained its hospitality and social significance. It has been the place at which people gathered for a *noson lawen* (merry evening), for religious devotions, and above all for conversation. It has been the repository of the arts and crafts which were also ' uncentralised '. The bards, musicians, storytellers and craftsmen of former times wandered from place to place carrying their arts and crafts with them to the homes of the people. Even today many cultural institutions such as the *Gymanfa Bregethu* (Preaching Festival), the *Gymanfa Ganu* (Singing Festival) and the *Eisteddfod*, both local and National, still continue this peripatetic tradition. These festivals can no longer be brought into the homes, but the doors of the homes remain wide open to welcome those who have come from afar.

Chapter IX

NEIGHBOURHOODS AND HAMLETS

THE primacy of the diffused society of *cefn gwlad* is implicit in the territorial history of this part of Montgomeryshire, and, indeed, in the very name Llanfihangel yng Ngwynfa. *Gwynfa*, or possibly *Gwnfa*,[1] was the old name of the countryside in which the church was founded. The church thus became known as St. Michael's Church in *Gwynfa*, the reverse of the more recent nomenclature whereby a tract of country takes its name from the church and becomes 'the parish of Llanfihangel'. When reference is made to 'the parish of Llanfihangel yng Ngwynfa' to distinguish it from other Llanfihangel parishes, the name has the confused meaning of 'the territory of a church in a territory'.

Before the end of Welsh independence *Gwynfa* was a part of the *cwmwd* (commote) of Mechain Uwchcoed,[2] one of the commotes forming the principality of Powys Wenwynwyn. This commote embraced most of what is now the parish of Llanfihangel together with a portion of the parish of Meifod. Adjoining it was the commote of Mechain Iscoed in which Llanfyllin developed. Both these commotes, like most commotes in Wales, derive their names from natural features. They were territorial entities and not environs of nucleated settlements. The settlements were settlements *in* Mechain Uwchcoed or Mechain Iscoed. Even at that time Llanfyllin was certainly larger than any other hamlet in the area, but it remained a settlement *within* Mechain Iscoed, rather than a town around which the life of the commote was orientated.

Compact settlements of freemen with special privileges, like the Norman boroughs, were foreign to the native Welsh. In their society it was villeins who inhabited compact settlements. It is true that a prince of Powys granted a charter to Llanfyllin shortly before the end of Welsh independence,[3] but in so doing he was merely emulating the Normans. After the Edwardian Conquest normanisation proceeded more rapidly. The commotes became known as 'manors', and in some cases lesser units within them were given the same status. Not only was Llanfyllin's charter confirmed, but the land around it was incorporated in the 'Manor of Llanfyllin'. Thus it was under alien influence that the town developed as the administrative centre of a territory.

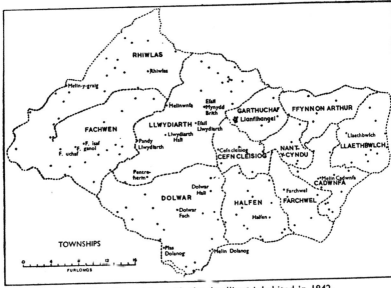

Fig. 30. Townships with the dwellings inhabited in 1842.

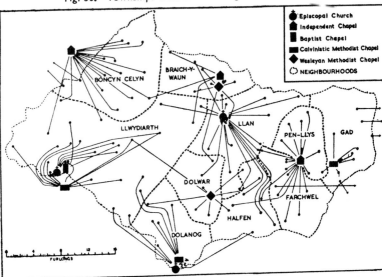

Fig. 31. Neighbourhoods and Places of Worship. The continuous lines indicate the places of worship attended by members of each household.

The next step in the unification of England and Wales brought a corresponding extension of this territory. By a statute to re-organise the administration of Wales after the Act of Union of 1536, the whole of Mechain Uwchcoed, a part of Mechain Iscoed and other territory, comprising in all seven-and-a-half parishes, were included in the Hundred of Llanfyllin. The same occurred in other parts of Powys and throughout Wales.[4] Where towns existed they became the centres of the new Hundreds, and it is instructive to contrast the territorial names of the old units—Llannerch Hudol, Deuddwr, Cyfeiliog, Mawddwy, with the urban designations of the Hundreds of Llanfyllin, Llanidloes, Machynlleth, Newtown, and so on. In the same way the *land* of Powys became the shire of *Montgomery*, deriving its name from the little castle-*town* which a Norman baron had christened after his ancestral home in Normandy. Subsequent administrative developments have further enlarged the environs of these towns. The Petty Sessions Division of Llanfyllin covers ten parishes, and there are twenty in the Llanfyllin Rural District. The town, being a borough, has no jurisdiction over the Rural District, but it is the meeting-place of the Rural District Council and the centre from which the District is administered. ' Llan-fihangel *in* Gwynfa ' has become ' Llanfihangel *near* Llanfyllin ', or, as the postal address has it, ' Llanfihangel, Llanfyllin '.

The manors, successors of the commotes, were composed of smaller districts called ' townships', which were probably the same as the *trefi*, the rural townships into which the commotes were sub-divided.[5] There were twelve of these townships in the parish of Llanfihangel, and, like the commotes, they took their names from topographical features (Fig. 30). Significantly enough, there were no townships of Dolanog, Pontllogel, or even Llanfihangel, though a *Tre-llan* (church township) did emerge in connection with some of the older churches in the surrounding district. In Llanfihangel parish the church and the little hamlet associated with it lie in a corner of the township of Garthuchaf. The hamlet may have originated as a *taeogdref* (bond vill), or a *maerdref* (a vill occupied by the king's villeins), or it may have grown up freely around the church, but in any case it was a subsidiary settlement in the wider landscape of scattered habitations.

Until comparatively recently everything which normally makes a village seems to have been scattered. The millers, the craftsmen and the inn-keepers lived in lonely dwellings and combined farming with their trades, as is shown by the names of several present-day farmsteads and smallholdings—Pandy Llwydiarth (the fulling-mill

of Llwydiarth), Melin-y-graig (the mill of the rock), Melinwnfa
(Gwnfa mill), Melin Cadwnfa (Cadwnfa mill), Hen Dafarn (old inn).
The farmstead known as Efail Lwydiarth functioned as an inn in
the last century, and Melinwnfa after ceasing to be a mill became
a lonely shop.

Figure 31 shows the areas recognised today in ordinary conversation as *ardaloedd* (localities), or *cymdogaethau* (neighbourhoods),
whose inhabitants are distinguished as ' the people of Pen-llys ',
' the people of Dolwar ', or whatever the locality may be. The
boundaries are those adopted when a task involving a visit to every
house, such as collecting subscriptions for the District Nursing
Association, is delegated to representatives from each locality.
If the map is compared with that of the townships it will be seen
that at least six of the latter are still recognisable as neighbourhoods
—Rhiwlas, Llwydiarth, Dolwar, Halfen, Farchwel and Llaethbwlch
—though some have changed their names and some their shapes
and sizes. But there have been several significant regroupings.
Both Dolanog and the Llan have now become the centres of neighbourhoods, the former at the expense of Dolwar, and the latter by
absorbing Garthuchaf, Cefncleisiog and much of Ffynnon Arthur.
As Llanfyllin won its environs out of the commotes, so, centuries
later, these two hamlets are gradually winning their environs out
of the townships.

The growth of the hamlet as a centre has not, however, been
a continuous process. In fact, it is only now recovering from the
reverse suffered through the revitalisation of the countryside by
Nonconformity. Before the Methodist Revival the parish church
at the Llan was the only place of worship. Nonconformity destroyed this unity. By dividing the community into a number of
religious sects, and by re-emphasising family devotions, it dispersed
religious observance throughout the countryside, thus bringing it
into harmony with other aspects of social life. Little more than
a fifth of the families now worship at the parish church, and these
together with the members of the two district churches at Dolanog
and Pontllogel account for only one-third of the total. The remainder are divided between nine Nonconformist chapels, seven
of which are within the parish and two a short distance outside it.
Thus, this population of just under five hundred is split up into
twelve religious groups.

The parish church remains the only place of worship in the
hamlet of Llanfihangel, the nearest chapel being over half a mile
away. Both Dolanog and Pontllogel have a chapel and a church,

but in both cases the chapel was built before the church. All the other seven chapels stand away from nucleated settlements. It is the same in the surrounding districts : although chapels will sometimes be found in, or, more frequently, on the outskirts of church hamlets, the majority are scattered. There are some practical reasons for this. In the first place, the hamlet with its long-established church, its resident clergyman, and its Church school and resident schoolmaster, was a centre of ecclesiastical influence and therefore was uninviting to the Dissenters. Even today the people of the Llan are all church-goers whereas the countryside remains the home of Dissent.

Secondly, the landowner has always been a staunch Churchman and, while his attitude towards his Nonconformist tenants was more tolerant than that of many of his kind, he did not favour the raising of chapels at the Llan where they would be a direct challenge to the authority of the Church. For example, when an Independent congregation began to meet there about 1832 Sir Watkin and the incumbent sought to refuse them land on which to build a chapel within a radius of two miles of the Llan. They were outwitted by a Dissenter who managed to buy a cottage in the Llan from another owner and threatened to build a chapel on its site at the church-gate. To avoid this, Sir Watkin hastily presented the Independents with the piece of ground, about half a mile away, for which they had originally asked.[6]

Nevertheless, it is probable that these obstacles would have been overcome if the farmers had been accustomed to regard the hamlet as their natural meeting-place. Behind the immediate reasons for the dispersal of the chapels is the independent tradition of the scattered farms. In Llanfihangel, as elsewhere in Wales, the Nonconformist congregations began their existence as groups of people meeting in one another's houses. Denominational histories mention more than a dozen homesteads in Llanfihangel, the living-rooms of which were used for preaching-meetings and Sunday Schools long before the chapels were built, and it was natural that the location of the chapels should be influenced by this background. The House of God became an isolated building like the houses of His people, and the community was subdivided into a number of smaller communities with different geographical centres.

A comparison of the map of neighbourhoods with that of the old townships will show that the identity of several of the latter has been emphasised by the possession of a chapel. This is parti-

cularly true of Dolwar, hemmed in as it is between the new neighbourhoods of Llan and Dolanog.   In Pen-llys the chapel has merged
the greater part of two townships into one neighbourhood and has
weakened the boundary between them and a third township. The
story of Llwydiarth, the township of the Vaughans, is somewhat
complicated.   Its northern extremity was the scene of considerable
squatting in the eighteenth and early nineteenth centuries, and two
chapels were built there among a cluster of smallholdings. From
these beginnings the area developed into a neighbourhood of Braich-
y-waun, distinct from Llwydiarth, and including a strip of territory
to the north of the parish boundary. With the establishment of
chapels, a church, a school and a shop at or near Pontllogel, the
remainder of Llwydiarth tended to look more towards this hamlet,
and it has become merged with the township of Fachwen into one
neighbourhood. Yet, this neighbourhood is more than the environs
of Pontllogel. The influence of the hamlet at one end is balanced
at the other by that of Llwydiarth Hall which remains the greatest
einzelhof in the parish.

While the chapels strengthened the social self-sufficiency of the
countryside, other modern innovations have had the effect of draw-
ing it more into the orbit of the hamlets The three elementary
schools, being Church schools, are located in the hamlets along-side
the churches, and therefore the parish consists of three main school
areas centred upon the hamlets.   As previously noted, the increasing
dependence upon ready-made products has enhanced the importance
of the hamlet shops, and the growing functions of the post-office and
the telephone are multiplying the occasions involving a visit to the
hamlet.   And there are other less utilitarian attractions.   A small
group of farmers and smallholders, sometimes jocularly referred to as
' The Committee ', repair fairly regularly to the Inn at the Llan on
Saturday nights, and, as we have seen, the hamlet is the principal
meeting-place of the young men.

Again, the present weakening of sectarianism, to which we shall
return in the next chapter, has enhanced the significance of the
hamlet as a centre where all may unite for non-denominational
activities.   The Old Schoolroom is available for these functions at
the Llan, and at Llwydiarth a ' village institute ' was built after the
First World War.   The land and some of the materials for the latter
were provided by the landlord and the remaining cost covered by the
proceeds of a bazaar and a few other efforts.   At Dolanog the little
school itself has been the only available room, but schemes to erect
a ' village hall ' have often been discussed during recent years.

Whereas these modern factors are gradually increasing the links between the countryside and the hamlets, a certain obliviousness to advantages possessed by close settlement and centralised services still lingers. Both the smithy which serves the Llan district and the more recently-erected garage are lonely buildings and, as opposed to the concentration of the shops in the hamlets, the depot of the Farmers' Co-operative Society stands apart in the countryside. A recent official scheme to build new cottages at the Llan was opposed by some farmers who would have preferred them about half a male away in the countryside, and similar reactions could be quoted from other parts of the county. Even in the raising of Pontllogel Institute the initiative seems to have come from some young wives who had married into the neighbourhood. ' The men felt that they could manage with the little schoolroom as they had always done, and they still joke about the Institute '. Again, notwithstanding the growing popularity of hamlet functions, no social activity has been more successful in the area, as in Montgomeryshire generally, during recent years than the ' fire-side chats ' arranged by the County Agricultural Organiser for groups of neighbours meeting at one another's homes. This, rather than the youth club at the Llan, is the true *aelwyd* (hearth).

There is a trace of aloofness in the attitude of the larger farmers towards the Llan, and they are not very often seen within its precincts. One or two of them are even reluctant to include 'Llanfihangel ' in their postal address, preferring to give the name of the farm followed by Llanfyllin. The larger farmer tends to look past the hamlet to the market-town, and it is significant that errands to the hamlet are usually delegated to the younger members of the family, while the farmer and his wife seldom miss the opportunity to go to Llanfyllin or Oswestry. These have long been the recognised centres for the transaction of business and for meeting friends and relatives from a wider district. But even here what really matters is not the town as such but the mart and the company of other farmers who congregate there or at the inns and in the streets. The cinema at Oswestry may attract the younger people occasionally, but, on the whole, the town has little to offer the farmer by way of society and entertainment, and it does not pay to run a bus there except on market-day. Even then there is little incentive to stay when the auction is over and the shops are closed, and the countryman is usually home for tea. Not many even of the younger men make a habit of going to Llanfyllin for an evening, except on special occasions, such as the night of the fair or a singing festival when other country people are present.

Thus, generally speaking, the native way of life in upland Wales has retarded the growth of nucleated settlements, despite their antiquity in a great many cases. A few of those which happened to be conveniently situated developed into small market-towns, but many failed to grow at all, and there are many *llannau* where the church, the vicarage and the church-school stand alone in a neighbourhood of scattered farms. As we have seen, modern inventions are tending to increase the importance of the hamlets, but they have not displaced the rural neighbourhood. The standards are still set by the lonely farm whose very building, simple as it is, stands in striking contrast to the tiny cottages of the hamlet.

The growth of towns is a still more recent phenomenon in Wales. The residences of Welsh rulers did not give rise to permanent towns. The rulers, like their humbler kinsmen, lived in homes and not burghs. Mathrafal, the seat of the Principality of Powys, and Sycharth the hall of Owen Glyn Dŵr, are now unfrequented mounds, while Aberffraw, the seat of the Venedotian princes, is only a village. The great majority of the pre-industrial towns of Wales owe their origin to Norman fortifications, and many of them continued to be islands of alien influence throughout the centuries. The native towns, some of which originated as *maerdrefi*,[7] are little more than overgrown hamlets which have gained commercial and administrative functions, but have never acquired ' the culture of cities '. They draw their inspiration from the countryside and have the appearance of being alive on market-days when the country-folk are there, but there is little in their intrinsic culture to distinguish them from their rural environment.[8]

Wales has no civic heritage. The essentially rural culture of Wales, like that of the Balkans, had crystallised before the introduction of towns by aliens, and after the Conquest the distinction between country and town became largely a distinction between Welsh and English. In these days of centralisation, this diffuse, centreless social tradition is revealed in the rivalry of small municipalities still competing for the status of county towns, and in the distribution of county administration in some cases between two or more of them. It also helps to explain the absence of a recognised capital city, the dispersal of the University and other national institutions, and the disunity of Welsh life.

Chapter X

RELIGION

I

THE beginnings of most of the culture elements hitherto described are hidden in antiquity. Similarly, there are no
contemporary accounts of the original conversion of the Welsh
to Christianity. The re-emergence of religion as a supreme interest
in Welsh society, on the other hand, is a phenomenon of the last
two centuries, the history of which is abundantly documented.
This reorientation was achieved by the great religious awakening
of the eighteenth century, and renewed by lesser revivals in the
nineteenth and the first decade of the twentieth century. A consideration of the teachings and writings of the Revivalists would, however,
take us beyond both the scope of this study and the competence
of its methods.

With regard to the ' deep-seated psychological elements within
culture ', a distinguished American anthropologist writes : ' Until
we arrive at a more complete understanding of them, no study of
culture in terms of its overt expressions, history, or the obvious
functions of its elements, can really penetrate below the surface.
The ultimate realities of culture are still hidden from us, but it is
possible to draw a few superficial conclusions as to its processes '.[1]
Indeed, anthropological science cannot explain the bias of any
culture. ' Why one society fixed its attention upon a particular
series of interests and the other upon another is an unanswerable
question . . . Such interests remain an unexplained and un-
resolved element in all cultural equations, and their presence fore-
dooms to failure any purely mechanistic approach to the problems
of culture and society '.[2]

In dealing with such phenomena the historian too abandons
the usual modes of description. Professor R. T. Jenkins asks
himself ' What was the Methodist Revival ?', and replies ' Not a
protest, not a matter of doctrine, not a matter of morality, but
spirit and power '. Of its consequences for Wales he writes :[3]

' It took hold of a mute nation and made her articulate ;
it set upon her lips the rich language of the fine Tudor Bible
which Griffith Jones and his followers taught the people to

109

read. It took hold of a thoughtless nation and taught her seriousness ; although much of the thought and the seriousness was dissipated upon Calvinistic Scholasticism, yet much remained to be applied to better things. It took hold of a nation shallow in her joy and sorrow ; it shook her to the depth of her nature ; it opened her eyes and sharpened her hearing ".

Some of the most profound hymns of the Revival were actually composed in Llanfihangel yng Ngwynfa by Ann Griffiths (1776– 1805), whose name has immortalised the farmstead of Dolwar Fach where she lived her short life of twenty-nine years.[4] Her schooling can only have been of the most elementary kind, yet, in expressing her religious experience she used not only a wealth of scriptural imagery but other figures of speech which are paralleled in the works of mystics of other lands and ages.

For her, as for so many who shared her experience, it was as though the heavens opened and a land, or a city, beyond the clouds of time came into sight. A ' way ' beyond the experience of the physical senses led to this land, and yet the way was essentially the same reality as its destination. Means and ends merged into one. It was a ' way ' of life contrary to nature, a path to follow and, in itself, an eternal resting-place. The ' way ' was also a rock of refuge, streams of living waters, a person of incomparable beauty, Christ, the Cross, a spouse, a sea of wonders without shores, without ebb. It was a sea in which to live one's life, to ' swim ' without ever reaching beyond it, a sea in which one might rest for ever.

A glimpse of this reality aroused in the seer a consuming desire to dwell in it, and at the same time a profound sense of unworthiness and of the worthlessness of earthly things. So enchanted was Ann Griffiths with this revelation that, in the words of Robert Gittins,[5] the talented shopkeeper of Dolanog :

> 'The beauty and excellences of the Rose of Sharon had so completely swallowed up her affections that the heather flowers before her and the blush of the earth around her did not enchant her muse nor draw music from her holy harp.'

Possession of the promised land by mankind was made possible by the Crucifixion, 'the way,' 'the door.' Ann Griffiths is overwhelmed by the mystery of this sacrifice—the death of the Creator of life, of Him in whom the creation moved, the burial of the Resurrection. And she cannot find words adequate to express her gratitude for an historical act of redemption which was also a ' way ' trodden before the existence of time. The hymns as they stand, rather than torn to pieces in this manner, are wonderful attempts to express the inexpressible. It is small wonder that anthropological technique cannot find its way inside this ' aspect ' of culture.

These hymns are the work of an exceptionally gifted poet, but the experience which they endeavour to convey was possessed in varying degrees by a considerable proportion of the Welsh people for the best part of two centuries, and its reality was believed in by the majority of the remainder who did not directly experience it themselves. Like its counterpart in England, the Revival in Wales did not give rise to new doctrines, but it gave the traditional Christian theology and cosmology a new relevance, and laid particular emphasis upon the depravity of man and upon the Atonement as the means of salvation. Doctrines which had formerly been accepted without question, but also without great interest, now became subjects for thought and discussion, and attempts to resolve their paradoxes and to rationalise the experience of religious conversion reanimated and often embittered many a time-honoured theological controversy.

For reasons that need not be recounted here, Calvinism became the dominant theological system, but neither this nor any other specialisation of doctrine passed in its entirety into the realm of unquestioned universals. *Bod yn iach yn y ffydd* (being sound in the faith) on such matters was always something to be watched and guarded. Gradually, as the vision itself faded, the controversies became increasingly scholastic and lost their appeal. A more recent stage was the spread of Liberal theology among educated Welshmen. Interest passed from the rationalisation of *experience* to the rationalisation of *beliefs* by bringing them into line with scientific theories and pseudo-scientific dogmas. Today, the growth of Neo-Calvinism, not to mention the return of an occasional Nonconformist to the mother Church, suggests that this also was a passing phase.

The hymns penetrated more deeply into the culture core than the theological arguments and have become the common property of all denominations, including the Episcopal Church. They are an essential part of the heritage of all Welsh-speaking people, and their enchantment persists in these more secular days when theology is neglected and when even the scriptures are less familiar than they used to be. Welsh culture is, of course, by no means the only one that has preserved the essence of its religion in its hymns.

All the most noteworthy flowerings of Welsh culture in modern times owe a great deal to this religious impetus. The development of a distinctive kind of radicalism in politics, to which we shall return later, the zest for education and indeed the versatility, the

' culture ', of the common people, what makes the connotation of the term *gwerin gwlad* qualitatively different from that of its English equivalent, *country folk*—none of these things can be understood except as extensions of the interest originally aroused by religion to new but related fields of thought and activity.

I have opened this chapter with a short statement from within the culture because in religion, more than in any of the elements already described, the latent meaning is far greater than can ever be established by an objective analysis of its overt expression in institutions and behaviour. For the remainder of the chapter we shall return, in Linton's words, to the surface. Three aspects of the religious life of the parish will be considered : (1) the sociological implications of denominationalism, (2) the forms of services conducted by the Nonconformists, (3) the influence of religion upon conduct. The more secular activities of churches and chapels will be described in Chapter XI.

II

In Llanfihangel, as throughout Wales since the Methodist Revival, the people are split into two major religious classes, Church people and Chapel people, a dichotomy which goes much deeper than the further subdivision of the latter between the four main sects of Welsh Nonconformity. In 1940 the Chapel people were roughly twice as numerous as the Church people, though the latter remained the largest single denomination.

Religious Persuasion

	Families	Chapels or Churches
Episcopal Church	42½	4
Independents	38	3
Baptists	2	1
Calvinistic Methodists ..	26	3
Wesleyan Methodists ..	16½	2

(A church and two chapels outside the confines of the Parish draw a proportion of their congregations from Llanfihangel ; these places of worship have been included in the Table).

The Independents and the Baptists are early Puritan sects which spread from England, while the Calvinistic and Wesleyan Methodists are, respectively, products of the Welsh and the English Revivals of the eighteenth century. With a few outstanding exceptions, Upland Wales retained its adherence to the Episcopal Church until the Methodist Revival[6], and there is no evidence that the Independents and the Baptists represent an older stratum of Nonconformity in Llanfihangel. Yet, thanks to their proximity to the Border, the inhabitants must have known many Puritans before the Revival; Independent Congregations had been formed at Llanfyllin and at Meifod in the seventeenth century, and the Quakers were meeting at Dolobran, a mile to the south-east of the parish, and even at Llanwddyn to the north-west of it.[7]

This early contact with Puritanism helps to account for the fact that in the early nineteenth century, after the Revival had instilled new life into the old sects and had created the new denomination of Calvinistic Methodists, it was the Independents and the Baptists who built the first chapels in the parish.[8] The subsequent history of these two denominations was, however, very different. The old-established congregation at Llanfyllin was a source of strength to the Independents of the surrounding countryside and the town had been for a time the home of an academy for the training of Independent ministers.[9] On the contrary, the Baptists suffered through the emigration of a number of their staunchest adherents to America soon after their chapel was built in 1823, and the group never regained its strength.[10] The chapel was finally closed in the early nineteen-forties.

The erection of Calvinistic Methodist chapels in Llanfihangel did not begin until 1830, though the congregations had existed for several decades as *seiadau* (societies) meeting in the homes of members. Wesleyan Methodism, the product of the English Revival, was introduced a little later as a result of the missionary activity of Welsh Wesleyans from Border towns, particularly Wrexham, and the first of the Wesleyan chapels of Llanfihangel was not built until the eighteen-forties. To summarise: the chapel-building age in Llanfihangel extended from 1810 to 1854, and during this period its people had a hand in the erection of no less than ten meeting-places. The eighteen-fifties also saw the erection of the two district Episcopal churches of Dolanog and Pontllogel, and the parish church was rebuilt in the following decade.

At that time the average layman, no less than the denominational leaders, was vitally interested in such questions as whether the Atonement was made for the whole of mankind or for the elected few; whether the Fall of Man was ordained in the Divine Plan;

whether it is possible to Fall from Grace ; whether adult baptism by total immersion is a prerequisite of salvation. So important was it in Llanfihangel in 1842 whether one was an Independent or a Wesleyan that the two sects were at work at the same time building chapels for themselves within two hundred yards of each other.

But today the inhabitants have little knowledge of the historical reasons for their religious groupings. Such terms as Calvinism and Arminianism are unintelligible to most of the younger people, and their elders can go little further than to say that the one stands for predestination and the other for the possibility of universal salvation. Unlike the other three denominations the Calvinistic Methodists have a written creed, the ' Confession of Faith ', but it is little used in the preparation of young people for membership, and very few, even of the leaders, are really familiar with its content. The fact that the Independents and the Baptists were predominantly Calvinistic in their original beliefs has been completely forgotten. They no longer subscribe to any creed, and the only differences between them, of which the ordinary member is aware, are that the Independents practise the christening of children whereas the Baptists practise adult baptism, and that the Independent communion is open to all believers while the majority of Baptist churches confine theirs to the baptised.

Nevertheless, sectarianism remains an established part of the social structure. Every child is born into a particular denomination and is nurtured in its lore. As he grows up he becomes familiar with its organisation, with the details of its services, with the hymn-tunes in the denominational hymnbook and the way they are harmonised. He knows, with varying degrees of intimacy, the ministers and leaders of his denomination in the surrounding districts, and he is familiar with the names and reputations of its celebrated preachers in other parts of Wales. As often as not, a Gallery of the most distinguished of them has looked down on him from the walls of his father's house as he grew up. Indeed, even his knowledge of Welsh place-names is intimately linked with the names of great preachers who have made these places famous within the denomination, and his knowledge of world geography is related to the missionary work of his sect. The Calvinistic Methodist has heard a great deal about the Khasi Hills in Assam, the Independent about the South Sea Islands. All this gives two people of the same sect a range of conversational topics with which they are both familiar, while a change of denomination involves a break with this background and the acquisition of a new body of lore.

Again, there is the emotional link between the individual and a particular chapel which is also attended by many of his kinsmen and by neighbours whom he has learnt to know better than others through meeting them there. Some of his forefathers may have been founders of the chapel or ' pillars of the cause ', and, in so far as he is prepared to be religiously active, he feels an obligation to continue their work. Again, each chapel has its elected leaders, from two to four deacons or elders or leaders, a secretary and a treasurer, a ' leader of the singing ' (precentor) and an organist. While these offices are not sought after as they used to be, they continue to give their holders power and prestige both within their own congregations and in the community generally. Nor is the ordinary member without significance. He is, in most cases, a close relative of one of these functionaries, and the group is small enough to give him a real sense of belonging to a society in which he is valued. Thus, such allegiance as survives is an allegiance to a particular group and its chapel, and this would be largely undermined if the chapel were closed and the group merged with another. To attempt to unite two moribund Nonconformist churches would be like trying to create a new living organism by grafting together two dying ones. In one locality the Independents and Calvinistic Methodists do in fact co-operate to the extent of meeting alternately in their respective chapels. But they preserve their separate identity, playing the parts of hosts and guests in turn.

Notwithstanding the power of denominationalism, the advantage of having a place of worship near at hand often outweighs traditional loyalties, particularly in the case of families which have moved into the parish in recent decades. A change of district often coincides with marriage and the foundation of a new home, when many other social adjustments have to be made, and in such circumstances the allegiance to a sect is often overcome by new ties of neighbourhood. On the other hand, a glance at Figure 31 will show that many families still walk considerable distances to the church or chapel where they were brought up.

Not only is the individual's immediate social circle partly determined by the sect to which he belongs, it also affects his contacts with the inhabitants of a wider district. Each chapel is linked with a group of others for co-operative activities. Thus, the Independents have a Quarterly Meeting which is held in the various chapels of the county in turn. At this meeting the ordinary members of the local chapel have the chance of meeting the ministers and lay leaders of the denomination from other areas.

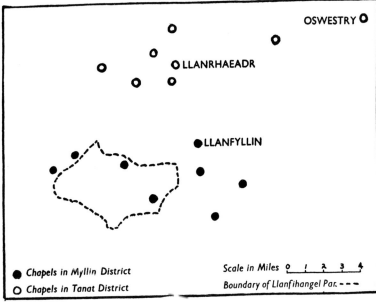

Fig. 32. (a) Independent Chapels.

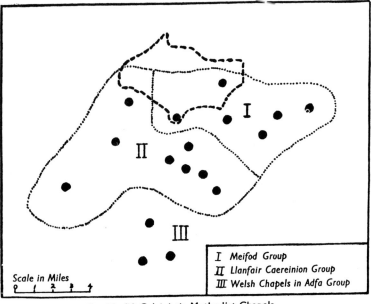

Fig. 32. (b) Calvinistic Methodist Chapels.

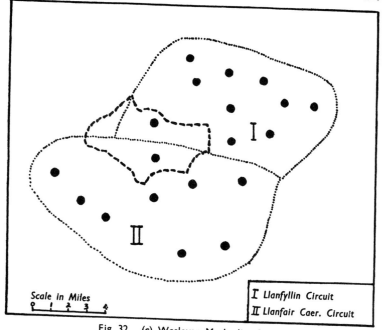

Scale in Miles

I Llanfyllin Circuit
II Llanfair Caer. Circuit

Fig. 32. (c) Wesleyan Methodist Chapels.

The same applies to the Group Meetings and Monthly Meetings of the Calvinistic Methodists and the Circuit Meetings of the Wesleyans.

Again, there is within each denomination a system whereby the work of the Sunday Schools is examined. From five to ten chapels are grouped together for this purpose and periodic meetings are held in each one in succession. These meetings are attended by members of the local Sunday School and by representatives from every other Sunday School within the group. The ways in which the chapels are grouped for this purpose is shown in Figure 32, but not all of them now participate, as we shall see later.

Each denomination also has an annual *Cymanfa Ganu* (Singing Festival) which unites all the chapels marked on the respective sketch-maps. Every little congregation practises the hymns and anthems contained in the *Cymanfa* programme for some months before the event. Buses are engaged to take them to the festival and between the meetings, which occupy the whole of one week-day, food is available and there is an opportunity to meet friends and relatives who belong to the same denomination and to renew acquaintances made at the last *Cymanfa*.

A comparison of the three sketch-maps (Fig. 32) will show that the three Nonconformist denominations tend to draw their adherents in different directions. Generally speaking, it is only the Independents who are likely to meet relatives from Llanrhaeadr at a Cymanfa. The Calvinistic Methodists will have more contacts with localities to the south of the parish, while the Wesleyan Circuits divide the parish into two, the one centred on Llanfyllin and the other on Llanfair. The Independents have also an annual County Preaching Festival (Cymanfa Bregethu), which occupies two week-days. From eight to ten sermons are delivered by celebrated preachers in the course of the Festival, and it usually draws a gathering of over a thousand people. It is held at a different centre every summer, and I have met people from Llanfihangel at this Cymanfa when it was being held at Llanbrynmair about thirty miles away.

These denominational festivals remain exceedingly popular. Apart from the opportunity for social intercourse there is the pleasure of listening to the eloquence and observing the artistry of accomplished preachers, and the emotional satisfaction of singing in a large choir under a competent conductor. But the individual chapels are not the going concerns that they were. As we have seen, the Baptist Chapel at Pontllogel has already closed, and there are others where the congregations are extremely small. Not only has the population decreased to half its size since the chapels were built, but during the last two decades there has been a remarkable decline in religious observance. Practically all the inhabitants have retained their membership of chapels and churches, but only half of them attend services regularly. There are a few who go only on special occasions, such as Harvest Thanksgiving Services, many are content if they are represented at a meeting by one member of the family, while only a minority attend more than once on a Sunday. Judged by urban standards these are still very high proportions, but in an area where there is a separate place of worship for every 12 — 15 families it means that several of the weaker churches have an average congregation of less than a dozen. The stronger congregations, on the other hand, may number as many as twenty or thirty at ordinary meetings. A falling off in religious observance has occurred in all parts of Wales, as in Britain generally, but in Llanfihangel, and indeed in most parts of Montgomeryshire, it has proceeded further than, for example, in Merioneth and Cardiganshire.

It is one of the basic tenets of Nonconformity that ordinary men and women are competent to work out their own salvation in matters of religion. Emancipation from the hierarchical Mother Church implied the assumption of responsibility by laymen. To the Dissenters a church is a society of people who believe and practise Christianity, and not a place of worship or a religious authority, and there can be no priesthood other than the priesthood of all believers. Among the Independents the ministers are the employees of the democratically organised congregations which they serve (*gwasanaethu*), a relationship terminable by three months' notice. A candidate who has undergone training for the ministry is not ordained until he receives a ' call ' from a particular congregation to enter *their* service. And the congregation is responsible for his salary, apart from nominal grants made to weak churches from a small central fund maintained by voluntary subscriptions.

The Calvinistic Methodists have a stronger central organisation and a more substantial fund from which the salaries paid by weak churches are brought up to a modest minimum, while in the Wesleyan system it is the central body that pays the ministers from a pool to which the individual churches subscribe. But, the Wesleyans apart, the Nonconformist denominations of Wales are more loosely organised than the corresponding ones in England, and the responsibility of the individual churches is greater. Such independence and self-government presupposes a people who actively participate, not only in the devotional side of chapel life, but in its administration and maintenance. The effects of any weakening of this participation become visible sooner than in the case of churches administered and financed from above.

Llanfihangel, and Wales generally for that matter, is living on its religious inheritance rather than enriching it. This is evident even on the material side of chapel life. The amounts of subscriptions vary with means and generosity, but the bulk of them fall within the limits of ten to thirty shillings per annum per member. Such contributions are large as compared with the quota to which members of the Ecclesiastical Church have been accustomed, but, significantly, the scale has risen very little since the First World War, members being content to give as their fathers did. Owing to the fall in the value of money this is proving increasingly inadequate to meet modern requirements. A minister who moved from the district a few years ago was receiving from three churches a total salary of £130 per annum, together with the periodic gifts of farm produce, such as vegetables, with which ministers are customarily presented in the Welsh countryside. Under modern conditions this sum would have to be doubled to bring it to the level of a farm-worker's wage.

It is not surprising therefore that ministers are becoming scarcer in the Welsh countryside and that little churches are finding it increasingly difficult to ' fill their pulpits ' on Sundays. And this is happening at a time when the proud claim to the priesthood of all believers is becoming more and more academic. Welsh Noncon-formity came into existence at a time when religious experience was vivid and general enough to enable its founders to dispense with the traditional forms of church authority, priesthood and ritual. With a new vision gained through the Revival, and certain of its destination, it left the protection of the old nest, despising the weak-lings who remained behind. Now, with its powers spent and its sense of direction uncertain, its survival is conditional upon a fresh glimpse of ' the land beyond the clouds of time '.

III

Ideally, the Nonconformist's Sunday should include two preaching-meetings, or a prayer-meeting and a preaching-meeting, and a Sunday School for both children and adults. In addition, there should be two weeknight meetings all the year round, a prayer-meeting and a *cyfeillach* or *seiat* (society), and, in winter, a *Cyfarfod Darllen* (reading meeting), Bible Class or Literary Meeting for the young people, and a Children's Meeting. In Llanfihangel today there are no regular weeknight meetings of any kind, and even the Sunday School has been discontinued in at least three of the smaller chapels. The ideal pattern is nevertheless relevant to our study for two reasons. Firstly, the middle-aged and the old inhabitants were brought up at a time when it was more strictly followed, as is shown by their scriptural knowledge and the number of hymns they know from memory.

Secondly, the ideal pattern is still recognised as the right one although the gap between it and practice continues to widen. Irregularity in attending meetings (and this applies to Church as well as Chapel people) will be confessed guiltily : ' Indeed, I should go oftener. When I was a boy I always went three times every Sunday and once or twice in the week '. Several people when questioned about weeknight meetings at their chapels said that regrettably there had been none for several years, *fel y mae mwyaf o gywilydd inni* (the more shame to us). The only explanation given for their discontinuance was ' lack of faithfulness on the part of members ' and old men would maintain that they ' kept the door open as long as they could '. In several cases the suspension of meetings occurred during an interregnum when there was no regular minister to shepherd the flock, and some people hoped that they might start again when a new minister came along.

The preaching-meeting is the central institution of the Non-conformist Sunday. Its climax is the sermon, while the lesson, the extempore prayer and the hymns, the simple counterpart of the Church service, is significantly described as *dechrau'r cwrdd* (starting the meeting). The contents of the sermons vary considerably with the interests and points of view of different preachers. Some are simple and evangelical, some didactic and practical, some subtle and theological. They are generally well conceived, the traditional plan being an introduction, three main headings and a conclusion, exhortation or peroration. Even in these days of religious in-difference a good, well-delivered sermon remains a treat to be ' enjoyed '. Its merits will be discussed by groups outside the chapel and on the way home, and its main points summarised for members of the family who were not present.

Without claiming that they are in any way representative, the following summaries of two sermons, to which I listened at ordinary meetings on the same Sunday in different chapels in Llanfihangel, may give some indication as to the content of two very different styles of preaching. But it should be borne in mind that they were meant to be *uttered in extenso* rather than *written* in précis form. The first endeavours to extract three simple moral lessons from the Gospel narrative of the healing of the centurion's servant. The relevant chapter from the Gospel according to St. Matthew was read in 'starting the meeting' so that the narrative was fresh in the minds of the listeners. The sermon was delivered with great eloquence and gusto and illustrated with a wealth of word-pictures. Several of the listeners commented after the meeting that it was ' nice ' to have an ' old-fashioned ' sermon of this kind from time to time.

Text: Matthew VIII, 13. And Jesus said unto the centurion, Go thy way ; and as thou hast believed, so it shall be done unto thee. And his servant was healed in the self-same hour.

The sermon began with an imaginary account of the centurion's background. He had been brought up in a pagan country to worship lifeless gods. But he had become dissatisfied with the religion of his fathers and had begun to ask questions : ' Why should I worship gods that are lifeless and therefore less than I am ' (Here followed a

digression on the value of questioning on the part of young people).
And he came to Capernaum and heard of the living God. His idea of
a living god was something in the same image as the lifeless ones to
which he was accustomed, that is in the image of man. He saw the
Prophet and believed in him.

There are three things in the character of this centurion that I
should like to have in my own life :

(1) Brotherliness. He was a wealthy gentleman. His servant
was ill, a slave that he had bought. He could easily have turned him
out and bought another. But he ministered unto him. This world
will not become right until we all possess the centurion's brotherliness.
Plans and conferences will not avail without it.

(2) Humility. He was brought up a gentleman, people bowed
to him. He said to one, ' Go ', and he went, and to another, ' Come '
and he came. Yet (a) he threw himself at the feet of the young
Physician, and (b) he became a servant to his servant.

(3) Belief. He had heard of the Healer and went in search of him.
He delivered his message and Jesus offered to go with him. But he
declined the offer. Who of us would be satisfied if the doctor did not
come along and examine the patient and give him medicine. But this
man was confident that if Jesus only spoke the word his servant
would be healed.

Jesus praised his belief. ' I have not found so great faith, no, not
in Israel '. The Christ gave him a pat on the back ! Jesus Christ
himself gave him a cheer ! What has become of the cheers in our
churches, friends,—not for the preacher, but for the Gospel ? There
are three things in the character of this centurion that I should very
much like to have in my own life, Brotherliness, Humility, Faith.
May God help us all to possess them.

The second sermon is more theological and profound, what is
usually called ' a deep sermon '. It endeavours to convey to the
understanding the same mystical principle as is enacted in the
communion ritual of the more traditional churches. The setting
for the sermon was evoked by a lesson read from the first chapter
of the Prophecy of Isaiah.

Text : Hebrew IX, 14. How much more shall the blood of Christ, who
through the eternal spirit offered himself without spot to God, purge
our conscience from dead works to serve the living God.

The problem of every religion is the separation between God and
man. But they differ in the way in which they deal with the problem.
False religions endeavour to reconcile *God* to man through sacrifices.
This was true even of the Old Dispensation. They brought offerings
to the temple to try to appease God, and one can imagine their think-
ing on their way home :   ' What shall we take to Him the next time ? '
Ultimately, God, who could no longer tolerate this unworthy attitude

expressed through Isaiah his loathing of offerings brought by people who persisted in sin. The glory of Christianity is not that it reconciles God to man, but that it reconciles *man* to God. We shall consider three aspects of this reconciliation.

(1) The nature of the reconciliation. God approaches man. It is not the first fruits of man's flock that lie on the altar. The Lamb of God is on the altar. God through the sacrifice brings about a change in man by purifying his conscience. What is conscience ? There are many definitions, but we can say this : it has to do with the essence of man. The Old Dispensation emphasised the purification of the flesh, the natural man. The priest required clean hands ; if he defiled himself, as by touching a dead body, he had to withdraw from the temple rites for a long time. Christianity purifies the inner man ; it appeals to his reason and purifies his conscience. It is concerned with the Good, not with what is easy and comfortable. (Here followed a digression on the emptiness of chapels owing to the choice by men of the easy and comfortable way).

(2) The means of reconciliation. Through His blood, the blood of God, not of man. Blood is the life of the body. Similarly, the means of reconciliation is the life and character of God's Son. God could have forced man into reconciliation, but he has chosen to do so through his conscience (refers to text). It is the blood that *draws*. 'And I, if I am lifted up from the earth will *draw* . . .'

(3) The duration of the reconciliation : for eternity. The sacrifices of the Old Dispensation had only a temporary efficacy. This blood is of incomparably greater significance. It is given, not only as one act in history : it is eternally given. This is the ' Lamb that was slain before the foundation af the world .' It is the promise of *eternal* inheritance (refers to the verse following the text).

The sermon ended with an exhortation to believe in Him, in His sacrifice, in His blood.

The prayer-meeting and the society-meeting have the same general pattern as the preaching-meeting, commencing with the introductory parts and ending with the Benediction. In the prayer-meeting the place of the sermon is taken by two or three extempore prayers by laymen, while the society was originally a meeting where personal religious experiences were related by members. Subsequently, the latter degenerated to the recitation of verses from the Bible and impromptu talks on religious subjects by those who could speak in public. It still persists as such in many parts of Wales, but not in Llanfihangel.

None of the chapel congregations of Llanfihangel has been large enough to support a full-time minister of its own. They share the services of a minister with one or two other churches of the same denomination in neighbouring parishes. This means that there is normally only one preaching-meeting per Sunday, the other being a prayer-meeting conducted by the members themselves. In order that this arrangement should work it is essential to have in each congregation a few people who can ' take part ' in public worship. In the past practically all the deacons, as well as a number of ordinary members, were capable of this. Young people learnt to pray at the *allor deuluaidd* (family altar), the custom, now rarely observed, of beginning and ending each day's activity in the home with religious devotions. New leaders were also trained in the Young Men's Prayer Meeting, and at least one congregation is still benefiting from the attention paid by a recent minister to this aspect of his work.

Those taking part in this way are expected to address themselves to God in their own words rather than through the medium of set prayers, an essential difference between the Nonconformists and the Church people. It is interesting to recall a verse, written by a mid-eighteenth century native of Llanfihangel, which says that he will have no truck with either Roundhead or Quaker, ' people who have ceased to say their *pader* (paternoster, set prayer').[12] Among the Nonconformists of the following century set prayers were still taught to children, but adults offered a *gweddi o'r frest* (prayer from the heart). Gradually, however, the extempore prayer itself took on a fairly definite form and much of it now consists of a selection of well-worn phrases. During recent years the number of people prepared to pray in public has been falling. As the older ones die, hardly any new ones come forward to take their place. One chapel has only two, another three, and when these are absent the meeting is turned into a singing practice for the *Cymanfa*.

The essence of this kind of religion is a matter of inner experience unsupported by outward forms, and it is the weakening of such experience that accounts for its present decay. Apart from personal and family devotions, the principal means of inducing this experience is through listening to sermons. This is unconsciously symbolised by the central position of the pulpit in front of the congregation. Around it, and usually a step above the floor of the building, is the *sêt fawr* (big seat) or *scwâr* (square) occupied by the elders. What stands out before the congregation is not an altar but men who, ideally, are more experienced in religion than others. The walls of the chapel itself are devoid of pictures, but if there is a vestry its walls are usually adorned with photographs of *men*, founders of the cause or past ministers. Similarly in the homes, the religious pictures are predominantly those of celebrated preachers.

Christening, marriage and burial retain only the barest essentials of ritual, though hymn-singing and funeral orations make the last a somewhat lengthy service. The communion is administered monthly after a morning, afternoon or evening preaching-meeting. It is a simple act of commemoration described as the Ordinance of the Lord's Supper and contains no more than a suggestion of mystery. New Testament accounts of the Last Supper are read by the minister and a blessing is asked. The elements are served from an ordinary table which stands within the ' big seat ', and members remain in their places to receive them from the deacons. Whereas the minister is not attributed with any of the special qualities of a priest, laymen do not administer the communion, though this is permissible, at least among the Independents. In the Wesleyan Methodist and some of the Calvinistic Methodist churches the minister communicates before the elements are distributed to the congregation, but even this vestige of priesthood does not remain among the Independents ; the introduction of individual communion cups has made it possible for the whole congregation together with the minister to partake of the elements simultaneously.

Welsh Nonconformity has always set a high value upon scriptural knowledge, and in this the average person in Llanfihangel is much better versed than is generally the case in urban communities. But this again is declining, and it is unlikely that the rising generation will be as well taught as their parents, who acquired their knowledge at week-night Bible classes as well as at the Sunday School. At the chapels where it is still held, the latter is attended by people of all ages, and the school is divided into classes for children and adults of various age-groups. The older classes provide the teachers for the younger ones, while they themselves are normally tutored by experienced elders. In the lower classes Bible stories are related and the children are taught to read Welsh, which was completely neglected in the day-schools until recent years. The older classes read a prescribed ' lesson ' from the Bible verse by verse round the class, and discuss doctrinal and ethical problems arising from it, the teacher stimulating thought by the use of a Socratic method of questioning. The memorisation and recitation of verses and passages is also a feature of all classes. In some chapels, as well as in the episcopal churches, books are distributed annually to children as prizes for good attendance, and every summer there is a tea-party, or a trip to the sea-side—events

in which neighbouring chapels of different sects are able to colla-
borate in these days of wider tolerance.

The services of the Episcopal churches follow the Welsh translation of the Book of Common Prayer and their ritual is that of a
Low Church in England. Sunday morning and evening services
and a Sunday School for children are held both at the Llan and at
Pontllogel, and the rector of Llanfihangel conducts an afternoon
service at Dolanog. There are nowadays a few annual occasions
when the Llan draws the parishioners together, irrespective of sect,
as it did in former times. Thus, although the Nonconformists have
their own harvest thanksgiving meetings, they help to fill the
parish church to the door on the evening of its harvest festival.
Again, a music festival called *Y Blygain Fawr* is held there on the
second Sunday of the New Year. It consists of the singing of
Christmas and other carols by parties and soloists from Llanfihangel
and from neighbouring districts. In 1940, prayers by the Rector
and a hymn by the congregation were followed by a programme of
thirty-six items. There were seven parties from various neighbourhoods in the parish and from centres as far afield as Llanwddyn,
Llanfyllin and Pentre'r-felin. When the long service was over,
supper was provided for the visitors in the Old Schoolroom.

IV

Faithful attendance at religious services and the practice of
personal and family devotions are only a part, though a fundamental
part, of a wider pattern of ideal behaviour covered by such terms as
buchedd rinweddol or *ymarweddiad glân* (a virtuous life, or un-
blemished conduct). This moral ideal is essentially the same as
that of the English or American Puritan, though its inspiration in
Wales springs mainly from the experience of the Methodist Revival.
Detached from that experience it becomes as negative as the Ten
Commandments. An English writer's observation that : ' No
movement as fruitful as English Nonconformity ever nourished
itself mainly on negations ',[12] might also be applied to Wales. The
negations were not, however, the real nourishment. They were the
by-product of a positive experience. This may be illustrated from
one of Ann Griffiths' hymns in which she portrays the Christ as a
person of inestimable beauty who arouses in her a profound love.
In comparison with Him the poor idols of the earth have no value
and she testifies that the world and all its toys will never again
satisfy her affections. The negations of the Puritanical code seem
to be the counterpart of this. Earthly desires and pleasures are

futile distractions, and the very capacity to enjoy them is evidence
of spiritual poverty.   The positive content of this experience could
not be transmitted through precepts, but the negative corollary
could be perpetuated as a series of ' Thou shalt nots ', enjoining
restraint in all things except religious observance and work.

Economy in pleasures and in ostentation reduced expenditure
and, when conditions were favourable, led to the accumulation of
moneys which strengthened the traditional independence of the small
farmer.   These savings helped to build and maintain the chapels
and made possible the purchase of the religious books and the
harmoniums which so many families in Llanfihangel have inherited
from their forebears.   Money should be spent only on substantial
things, and this helps to account for the present high evaluation of
money in the Welsh countryside and the low evaluation of the
luxuries and ephemeral pleasures it might buy.   Nonconformity
produced a close correlation between prosperity and virtue, which
led to the recognition of upright, diligent, successful and abstemious
elders as paragons of moral excellence. Their photographs and life-
stories, published for the edification of the young, may still be seen
in old religious periodicals in many a home in Llanfihangel.

This puritanical ideal has lost its sharpness during recent decades, and most of its stricter taboos are honoured in the breach
more than in the observance.   But its influence may still be
recognised both in the absence of certain forms of amusement and
in the restraint with which pleasures formerly prohibited are
enjoyed.   There is no dancing in the Parish of Llanfihangel, and,
in spite of the prominence of competition in the traditionally Welsh
forms of recreation, there is very little gambling, even on football
pools.'

Instilled by a vigorous temperance movement in the later
nineteenth and early twentieth centuries, abstinence from intoxicants
was made a major tenet of the Welsh Nonconformist code, and the
Calvinistic Methodists still require an affirmation on this subject
from newly-elected elders.   Even the communion ' wine ' is
generally non-alcoholic.   Abstinence is practised by a large proportion, probably the majority, of men in Llanfihangel as a matter of
principle, and indulgence by women would be considered extremely
degrading.   There is practically no drunkenness in the parish,
and the proportion of Churchmen who are even moderate
drinkers is now probably as low as it is the among Nonconformists.
Yet, the attitude of churchmen to drink is different from that of
chapel-men.   The old ' Thou shalt not ' still casts its shadow over

chapel-men, and those who indulge realise that their behaviour is disapproved of by many of their fellows and by the minister. It is proverbial that they look around before entering a public-house, while the Churchman, for whom intoxicants were never tabooed, shows no such concern. Nonconformist ministers are expected to be adamant on the subject, even by those who indulge themselves, and if they fell short of total abstinence their positions would become quite untenable. Yet, division between those who drink and those who do not is less pronounced than it is in many other parts of Wales. The inn-keeper is an abstemious farmer respected by all sections of the community.

Premarital chastity and faithfulness within marriage are universally accepted as ideals. But in practice deep-rooted customs transmitted from older to younger youths have prevailed against the former, despite the public censure and temporary excommunications of the recent and more puritanical past. Within marriage, on the other hand, cases of unfaithfulness appear to be extremely rare and broken marriages are almost unknown. In view of the opportunities for separation allowed under medieval Welsh Law and the survival of at least some unformalised cohabitation until the eighteenth century, the strict interpretation of marriage commitments in the present society must owe a great deal to the puritanical sanctions of the nineteenth century.

Again, the Puritan Sunday, or the ' Welsh Sunday ' as it is now often called, remains both as an ideal and in practice. No work is done on Sunday, even by those who no longer attend services regularly, apart from such essentials as feeding the stock, milking—and cooking the Sunday dinner. A large farmer who broke this rule by carrying hay on a fine Sunday in a wet summer was generally criticised for his shamelessness, and neighbours agreed that no good would come of it. Indeed, it is in the sphere of recreation rather than of work that the sanctity of the Sabbath is likely to suffer first. Motorcycles and motor-cars have made it possible for young people to spend an occasional Sunday afternoon at the seaside, but as yet the number who do so is extremely small.

These negations, however, give only a one-sided picture of the influence of Nonconformity upon Welsh culture. Although Nonconformity was largely a town religion in England, social conditions in rural Wales proved particularly conducive to its growth. Through following the injunction to read the scriptures, the Welsh peasant found in Hebrew literature a picture of a tribal society in many

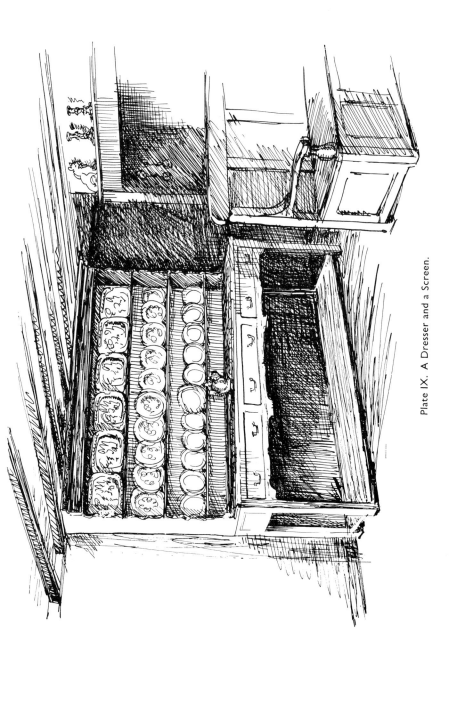

Plate IX. A Dresser and a Screen.

Plate Xa. The Parish Church
To the right of the illustration is Ann Griffiths' Memorial

Plate Xb. Pen-llys Independent Chapel

ways reminiscent of his own.[13] Its pastoral economy, its patriarchalism and its idealisation of filial piety all found sure points of contact, and such stories as those of Jacob and Esau, Joseph and his brethren, and the prodigal son had a direct bearing upon life in a familistic society. Again, a people devoid of urban culture could fully share the contempt of Old Testament prophets for the extravagances of the cities of the plain.

In this way Nonconformity strengthened some of the older foundations of Welsh culture. It decentralised religion and renewed the life of *cefn gwlad*, the dispersed neighbourhood. And although the chapel, a communal meeting-place, was something new, much of the informality of the hearth was transferred there. The meetings, both religious and secular, were conducted for the most part by members of the audience in turn, the leaders inviting and encouraging the others to take part and audibly confirming (*porthi*) their utterances in speech and prayer. Religious discussion, hymn-singing and prayer-meetings gave a new content to the fellowship of the hearth itself, and the need for entertaining ministers, and others who had come a long way to a meeting, gave hospitality a new purpose.

In stamping out dancing and play-acting the new movement was in fact expelling elements whose roots in Celtic culture seem to have been shallower than in England.[14] On the other hand, many an ancient custom, and perhaps a whole body of folk-tales, were also blotted out.[15] The new lore drove out the old, the preacher and the deacon supplanted the *dyn hysbys* (seer, wizard). Yet several old arts lived on in the service of religion. For example, the preacher in his long sermons, made vivid by a wealth of narrative, imagery and gesture, adapted the art of story-telling to a new saga. Again, the enjoyment of singing in harmony rather than in unison, which had come down at least from the Middle Ages[16] but had found only limited scope in the services of the Church, was given full rein, and there is no doubt that many of the popular hymn-tunes are old folk-tunes to which sacred words have given a new life. Thus, through its tonic sol-fa classes, its *ysgol gân* (singing practice) and its singing festivals, Nonconformity perfected and sanctified an ancient art.

Furthermore, in a land where not only the aristocracy but many of the clergy and the educated classes generally had become agents of anglicisation, Nonconformity gave the native language a new status by making it the language of religion. Throughout the nineteenth century when state-aided schools used English as the medium of instruction and discouraged Welsh, the people were taught to read Welsh in the chapels, and an abundance of reading material was produced in the way of religious books and periodicals. Llanfihangel had many a monoglot English schoolmaster during that time, but the children received a free education in Welsh at the Sunday Schools and the Children's Meetings. Thus, the religious awakening, in spite of its negations, ensured the continuity of many of the most essential elements of Welsh culture by harnessing them to its own purposes.

Chapter XI

RECREATION AND ENTERTAINMENT

I

IT has been emphasised that the hearth is the traditional scene of recreation and entertainment in rural Wales. This aspect of social life is largely linked with practical work, but there is also an appreciable amount of visiting purely for purposes of fellowship. At these little informal meetings the primary form of recreation is conversation. It is not without significance that the Welsh word for conversation, *ymddiddan*, is essentially the same as the word for entertainment, *diddanu*, and that in South Wales the dialect word *wilia* for conversation is derived from *chwedleua*, story-telling. This is undoubtedly one of the oldest forms of entertainment.

The art of conversation in Llanfihangel reveals some interesting traditional features. For example, it is customary to approach subjects which are in any way personal in an extremely circuitous manner, and direct questions play a much smaller part than in modern life. The usual method is to lead the conversation round to a point where the desired information is relevant to the discussion, perhaps as a confirmation or a contradiction of the view expressed by one of the company. When collecting material for this study I was seldom asked outright the purpose of it. The curious would sometimes suggest some explanation themselves and leave me free to agree or to disagree, or to follow their own practice of avoiding an issue by joking about it. A few would approach the subject jocularly by accusing me of some preposterous motive, a method which they used among themselves as a means of eliciting information. The story is related in the parish of a man who once asked another point-blank the price he had received for a certain animal. The other replied : ' *Wel, fachgen Diawl, cymer dipyn o rownd* ' (' What the Devil, man, go round a little ! ') This is the modern counterpart of the rule which made it incumbent upon the medieval Welshman to entertain a stranger not only, as in Homeric Greece, until he had regaled himself, but for three days, before he was free to ask him who he was and where he came from. ' But on the third day it is permissible to put the question politely '.[1]

In keeping with this round-about way of dealing with others there is a certain reluctance on the part of the countryman to commit himself. He is more interested in knowing what the other man thinks than in making pronouncements. Even obvious statements of fact are habitually qualified with the phrase *'byca gen i* (most likely in my estimation). So ingrained is the indirect approach that it is often not totally absent when feelings are expressed frankly, as in the story of a farmer who countered a preposterous offer made by a dealer for his sheep with the words : ' If I were to say what I think, I would call you a bloody rogue! ' My informant commented : ' He did not *say* he was a rogue, did he ?'

Another characteristic reminiscent of the reputation of the medieval Welshman is the amount of humour that runs through ordinary conversation.[2] Much time is devoted to teasing and bantering, and the stratagem called *taro'r post i'r pared glywed* (striking the post for the wall to hear) is a popular method of conveying inoffensive criticism as well as a means of innocent amusement. In its simplest form it involves twitting one of the persons present without alluding specifically to him, thus, ' It is surprising how some people . . . ' But it can be made into a fine art involving the use of metaphors, puns and other devices.

The average countryman is very modest and even self-effacing regarding his own qualities and possessions. Yet competitive boasting, usually half jocular, is a traditional means of entertainment. This has given rise to a series of humorous stories of the *celwydd glân golau* type (clear obvious falsehoods), in which the setting is usually the hearth of some farmstead in the district. Thus, a group of farmers gathered round the fire were extolling the virtues of their sheep-dogs in an endeavour to draw an old fellow known to glory in his own possessions, while he sat sullenly in the corner trying to devise a story that would silence them. At last he told them of the occasion when he asked his men to get up early next day to fetch the sheep from the mountain for shearing. They did so, but as soon as they had left the farm they met the sheep coming along the lane with the dogs behind them. 'The dogs must have heard me talking to the men the night before !'

There are several men in the district who amuse themselves and their friends by composing verses. When friends drop in, the discussion invariably turns to poetry. The host may have composed some new verses which must be recited to the visitors and they must express their opinions about them. The merits of the winning poem at a recent *eisteddfod* may be discussed, or the talents of some neighbouring *bardd gwlad* (country poet). A few have learnt the intricate rules of *cynghanedd* (assonance) and can compose *englynion* (stanzas of four closely alliterated lines used more particularly for epigrammatic description). And tales are still told of the contests of wit (*ymryson*) in which local bards of a generation ago used to satirise each other to the amusement of the countryside.

In the same way other homes are known as centres of theological argument, music or, nowadays, card-playing, while one or two are outstanding as places where young men habitually congregate. In former times there seems to have been much more specialisation. Some houses were used more than others by women and girls holding a *noson weu* (knitting night) ; an expert basket-maker would attract friends to his house to learn to ply the craft. And there was one home where people gathered annually to celebrate New Year's Eve. Moreover, the culture of the hearth lies behind all formal meetings such as concerts and *eisteddfodau*. In preparation for a public performance songs and recitations are learnt, the young visit more experienced elders for instruction and choirs rehearse in the homes.

II

Before the ascendancy of Nonconformity the yearly round of social intercourse and entertainment on the hearth was punctuated by periodic festivals at the Llan, such as the fair and the *gwylmabsant* (saint's day). Itinerant traders and entertainers visited these festivals bringing new fashions in wares and entertainments, and thus made the Llan a point of contact with the world outside. The fair, held on the ninth of May, still survived as a stock-sale until the first decades of the present century, but the *gwylmabsant*, presumably held on St. Michael's Day (29th September), was discontinued long before living memory, and there is no local evidence as to its character. Every parish had its *gwylmabsant* in the eighteenth century, and its general characteristics were probably much the same everywhere.

' The festivals were generally held on Sundays, but often began on Saturday and continued until Tuesday. The proceedings included contests in leaping, running, hurling, wrestling, cock-fighting and foot-ball playing. In the latter contest, players of two parishes would be opposed, and the losers had to supply the winners with beer. Relics of the Saints were carried in procession in some places . . .Intoxication and fighting seem to have been general at these meetings in the eighteenth century . . . Rivalry and competition were prominent elements in the

Gwylmabsant, which is the reason, perhaps, that to this day there is little chance for anything—religion, education, literature, music, drama, art or sport—to thrive in Wales except on lines of competition '.3

Bull-baiting and bear-baiting, wrestling with a bear, dancing and the performance of dramatic interludes also appear to have been customary. The *gwylmabsant* came to an end early in the nineteenth century, but this brief reference to it is relevant as a background to many of the activities of the present-day.

While the fair at Llanfihangel has been discontinued, spring and autumn fairs are held at Llanfyllin, and, on a smaller scale, at Llanfair Caereinion, and a considerable proportion of the people of Llanfihangel take a day off to attend them. In addition to the auction, which is the major attraction for the men, there are street-stalls selling a variety of merchandise like clothing and china, and a small pleasure fair which is visited by everybody, though participation in the competitions and the joy-rides is left mainly to the young people.

The neighbouring hamlet of Llanerfyl has an annual event more reminiscent of the *gwylmabsant*. It is known as *Ffair Ffyliaid* (Fool's Fair),4 and is held on the first Tuesday in May. It differs from other fairs in that it is a pleasure fair which has had no economic function, at least within living memory. People, drawn from many miles around, begin to congregate at Llanerfyl about three o'clock in the afternoon, but the crowd is not at its densest until between ten and eleven o'clock and the last do not leave until three in the morning, or later.

In the war and blackout year of 1940 when I visited the fair there were fewer people present than in normal times, but even so they numbered something between six and eight hundred. Everyone at the fair agreed that there was nothing there ' except people '. Actually, there were two china-stalls at the roadside selling by auction, the auctioneer entertaining the crowd with jokes. There was a less frequented clothing stall and an ice-cream cart, while the local shop did a flourishing trade in refreshments. A yard, off the road, contained swings, a shooting-booth, a coconut-stall, a gaming table and slot machines, but none of these seemed to be popular. The main enjoyment was to be found in moving up and down and meeting in little groups in the thickly crowded highway. Young people formed the majority of the crowd, but there were many older people and some of these remained until after midnight. The crowded road had an atmosphere comparable with that of a dance or a large party. All were sociable and an introduction was unnecessary as a preliminary to a chat. Old acquaintances were renewed and coming across neighbours at the fair also held a certain novelty justifying the exchange of a few words.

For the young men the opportunity of meeting girls from other districts was a major attraction. They were specially groomed for the occasion, and the girls smartly dressed. Small parties of each sex moved about accosting one another and forming little conversational groups. Later at night there is usually a fight or two between young men from different districts. The pretexts for such battles vary, but most of them are fought over girls. It is the custom for the lads of Llanerfyl in particular to challenge anyone who ventures to escort a local girl to her home, a custom that has already been discussed in Chapter VII.

Old-established social gatherings of this kind are, however, only minor features of the recreational life of rural Wales today. For more than a hundred years the chapel has been the major centre for all kinds of pre-arranged recreation. It is true that in its early enthusiasm Nonconformity stamped out the *gwylmabsant* and discouraged all kinds of secular entertainment, substituting the prayer-meeting for the *noson lawen* (merry evening) in the home, and the preaching festival for the pleasure-fair as an occasion to draw the crowds. But from the beginning the chapel was not only ' The House of God ', it was the *Tŷ Cwrdd*, the meeting-house of a society. As this society grew out of its extreme puritanism, it took over many of the less reprehensible elements in the old amusements, as well as education, and rendered them compatible with its own standards. Many activities are held in chapels which would nowadays be considered too secular for the parish church, but by being brought in they are, as it were, sanctified. Even lectures on the most lay subjects are frequently preceded and followed by hymns.

A regenerated version of the spirit of *gwylmabsant* survives in the Sunday School tea-parties which are followed by open-air sports, and competitions are prominent in other chapel functions, though they are now contests of wit and versatility, and not of physical prowess. Again, although the disguise, the pretence and the mimicry of play-acting were originally condemned, a mild variety of drama, known as a *dadl*, has long been popular at Sunday School Quarterly Meetings, forming a link between the old interludes and modern plays. A *dadl* is a drama stripped of costume, stage and acting, what remains being an exchange of long speeches between the two or more persons who take part in it. Even gestures are reduced to a minimum and such exits and entrances as are essential consist of movement in and out of the area encompassed by the ' big seat '. In performing the parable of the prodigal son, the lobby becomes the ' land of the pigs and the husks '. The subjects are scenes from the Scriptures, or some other episode with a moral. Thus, a *dadl* for two women, the one believing in witchcraft, and the other condemning it, was written and published by a farmer from Llanfihangel a few decades ago.[5] This like most *dadleuon* ends with the conversion of the misguided and the singing of an appropriate hymn.

Most secular and semi-secular chapel activities were held until recently under the auspices of the Young People's Society. The organisation was left to the younger members who thus learnt how to conduct meetings and keep accounts, whereas the functions were attended by people of all ages. These functions included the *darlith* (a kind of lecture which combined instruction with entertainment), musical evenings, debates and the reading of papers by members of the Society. The winter's programme was punctuated by little festivals such as a *cyfarfod bach* and an *eisteddfod*. A regular programme of this kind is no longer followed at Llanfihangel, as it is in many other parts of the county, but the *cyfarfod bach* and the *eisteddfod* are as popular as ever. As in the strictly religious sphere the week to week activities have suffered but the special events still flourish.

The *cyfarfod bach* is a miscellaneous meeting in which concert items are interspersed with competitive ones. The former consist of solos, duets, choral parties and recitations, and the latter include competitions in reading an unpunctuated paragraph, telling funny stories, making impromptu speeches, composing a last line for an unfinished limerick, or again a general knowledge or spelling test, *codi tôn* (choosing a tune to suit the metre of a given verse), sight-reading tonic sol-fa, or reciting proverbs from memory. In most of these competitions, the competitors, who are, of course, members of the audience, are sent out to the lobby and brought in to be tested in turn.

Again, each chapel usually holds at least one small *eisteddfod* in the course of a winter and the following programme may be regarded as representative :

Recitation (children under eight)	Whistling Duet.
Solo (children under ten)	Spelling Bee.
Recitation (children under twelve).	Carol (trio).
Solo (children under fourteen).	Memory Test.

Recitation (children under fifteen).

Pencil Sketch (children under fourteen).

Duet (children under fourteen).

Reading an unpunctuated paragraph.

Unison recitation for four.

Pencil Sketch (open).

Solo (open).

Recitation (open).

Limerick.

Impromptu Speech.

Octet.

The proceedings at both a *cyfarfod bach* and an *eisteddfod* are conducted by an *arweinydd* (conductor, compère) who manages the competitions, pursuades people to take part in them, keeps the audience in good humour with witticisms and humorous stories, and prevents the meeting from flagging or from getting out of hand. Local ministers or schoolmasters, or anyone with specialised knowledge, act as adjudicators. The chapels are always crowded on these occasions, and, while most of those who participate are from the locality, the *eisteddfod* usually attracts some competitors from neighbouring parishes. Both types of meeting give the young people practice in public-speaking and in performing before an audience. They are also a means of educating the audience. By listening to a number of competitors singing the same song or reciting the same poem they learn them themselves, and their critical faculties are exercised in the endeavour to select the winner and sharpened by listening to the more expert opinions of the adjudicators.

The standard of the little *eisteddfodau* in Llanfihangel may not be very high, but they encourage the better competitors to try their luck in larger ones at neighbouring centres and to pass through them to County Eisteddfodau, the Powys Eisteddfod and perhaps ultimately to the supreme court of the National Eisteddfod of Wales. And the adjudicators and the *arweinydd* can distinguish themselves in the same way. Conducting a large *eisteddfod*, lasting from eight to ten hours, in an orderly manner is an art in itself and considerable skill is often required to handle the heckling of the young lads at the back. The time-honoured method of dealing with them is to shame them with ridicule or to defeat them in a contest of wit. For example, at an *eisteddfod* at a large hall in a neighbouring parish the *arweinydd* held up the winning book-stand in a woodwork competition, calling out the pseudonym of its maker and urging him to come forward to receive the prize. The person concerned was not present but a voice in the back shouted : ' Here I am '. Again the conductor called ' Who made this book-stand ?' to which the same voice cried ' I did '. The conductor replied : ' There is enough wood in your head to make another one ' (Loud laughter).

The inhabitants take practically no interest in horse-races nor in the achievements of football teams, but the success of a local competitor at a large *eisteddfod* is a source of satisfaction to the whole neighbourhood. While this work was in progress prizes were won by competitors from Llanfihangel both at county *eisteddfodau* and at the National Youth Eisteddfod, and considerable pride was manifested recently when a native of the parish became an *arweinydd* at the National Eisteddfod.

The Parish Church *as such* has no recreational life corresponding to that of the chapels, but in the Old Schoolroom, which is church property, many activities are held in which the rector, the schoolmaster and church members play a prominent part. These meetings have no official connection with the Church, they are formally nonsectarian, but all the inhabitants of the Llan are Church people and it is they that normally take the lead. During the first three decades of the present century Llanfihangel was fortunate in having both a rector and a schoolmaster who were accomplished musicians, and under their leadership the hamlet became the musical centre of the parish and of a wider neighbourhood. The adult choir, conducted by the rector and consisting mainly of parishioners of all sects, was augmented by music-lovers from within a radius of over nine miles. In addition to sweeping the boards at local *eisteddfodau*, it won many times at the Powys Eisteddfod and in one year competed successfully at the National Eisteddfod.

The Children's Choir under the leadership of the schoolmaster also became one of the best in the county. The success of the choirs aroused local pride, and the rivalry between them and those of Llanfyllin, together with the enjoyment of journeys to distant *eisteddfodau* and concerts, added to their appeal. The rector gave up the work at the beginning of the nineteen-thirties and the schoolmaster retired soon afterwards. The choirs had come into existence in response to their personal leadership, and after their time they rapidly disintegrated in spite of attempts to keep them together.

When the choirs had passed their heyday, the young women and girls found a new interest in a Women's Institute which was established at the Llan. It had twenty-seven members in 1940, twenty-two of whom were unmarried women and girls of various ages. It was an institution introduced into the locality from outside and the lead during its first and most successful years was taken by the rector's daughter, the schoolmaster's wife and one or two of their friends among the wives of neighbouring farmers. The meetings, which were held monthly at the Old Schoolroom, consisted mainly of demonstrations and lectures on domestic crafts followed by a chat over a cup of tea, the members taking their turns as hostesses.

The Women's Institute still survives but it has been largely superseded by an *Aelwyd* (' hearth ') of the Welsh League of Youth (*Urdd Gobaith Cymru*). This *Aelwyd*, which was founded at the Old Schoolroom in 1942 and is a branch of a national organisation, has a subscribing membership of thirty young people of both sexes, while its special functions are attended by a much larger audience. The rector of the parish plays the part of Youth Leader, though the majority of the members belong to the Nonconformist chapels. As we have seen, the maintenance of Young People's Societies became impossible in the individual chapels during recent years owing to the fewness of numbers and the comparative absence of full-time ministers. The *Aelwyd*, being a non-sectarian body, has been able to bring the youth of these small groups together into a larger society. Thus, although the *cyfarfod bach* and *eisteddfodau* are still held from time to time at the chapels, there is an increasing tendency for the youth of all denominations to look towards the hamlet for their every-day social requirements.

The *Aelwyd* meets once, and sometimes twice, a week in winter and less frequently in summer. As yet its programmes have been very similar to those of the old chapel societies, with the addition of indoor games such as table-tennis and darts, short courses of lectures on Welsh literature and on the old art of *Penillion* singing[6] arranged in conjunction with the Extra-Mural Department of the University College of Wales, and the production of plays. Although Llanfihangel has an informal and spontaneous young men's society concerned with activities in which older people cannot share, the formal segregation of youth for indoor meetings is a product of urban culture which cuts across the customary unity of old and young in the home and the chapel. At the *Aelwyd* in Llanfihangel, as in many other rural centres in Montgomeryshire, the youth show more interest in the open meetings and in preparing programmes for such meetings than they do in playing with the games set at their disposal in the Old Schoolroom. Socially approved accomplishments bring the greatest satisfaction when they are acclaimed by acquaintances, of all ages. Hence the popularity of drama and *eisteddfodau*, as opposed to table-tennis and darts which never draw many spectators.

Today, with chapel life losing its vitality, the Llan has become once more the channel through which new forms of recreation, as well as new forms of merchandise, are being introduced, or re-introduced into the culture. For example, card-playing was long regarded with disapproval by the Nonconformists, and I came across at least one family that had left a chapel and returned to a church some two or three decades ago because of unpleasantness aroused by their participation in a whist-drive. During recent years, however, whist-drives, although still taboo in the chapels, have become a popular source of entertainment at the three hamlets, as well as a method of raising money for such causes as the Nursing Association, the Choir, the Women's Institute and the School. A whist-drive at the Llan now attracts from seventy to a hundred people, and while the organisation is still largely in the hands of Church people, Nonconformists contribute towards the prizes and often constitute the majority of the players.

Drama has reappeared again during recent years, and, unlike most new things, it has been accepted by the chapels as readily as by the Llan. The prejudice of the Nonconformists was overcome by its advocacy by ministers who came to the locality from other parts of Wales where the ban had already been raised. The rehearsal of plays has now replaced the Literary Meetings of the chapels, and their performance is a convenient way of augmenting chapel funds. The chapels, however, are structurally unsuitable for staging them, and the actual performances are given in the Old Schoolroom at the Llan where a stage is available.

Significantly, sports on a larger scale than those of the chapels are held at the Llan once or twice during the course of the summer. Competitors and spectators assemble from as far afield as Llanwddyn, Llanfyllin, Pontllogel, Dolanog, Pontrobert and Llangynyw, making a total of a few hundred. For a week or two before such an event the local youths practice racing and jumping and tug-of-war at the Inn Field, coached by one or two of the older inhabitants of the hamlet. There is nothing distinctive in the competitions, except that the tug-of-war between local teams and teams from neighbouring hamlets is the chief event of the evening, a contest which reveals much local patriotism. The sports continue until nightfall and supper is prepared at the Old Schoolroom.

Thus, three stages may be distinguished in the history of organised recreation in the parish. Like religion it was centred at first at the Llan, and its main occasion was a religious feast-day. Later, it was carried with religion into the neighbourhoods and revivified. Now, with the self-contained life of the neighbourhoods and the chapels waning, it is returning again to the hamlet where it is being supported largely by organisations the fountain-heads of which, like those of the Church, lie outside the parish.

Chapter XII

STATUS AND PRESTIGE

CLASS distinction is comparatively weak in Llanfihangel and it never interferes with free social intercourse between individuals and families. Almost every family until recently has held land direct from the landlord, and therefore the division between farmer and wage-earner has been less definite than in the neighbouring low-lands with their system of tied cottages. One class merges imperceptibly into the other. One man with twenty acres may be a full-time farmer, while another with the same acreage is a roadman or forestry-worker. A childless farmer will sometimes retire to a small-holding in his old age, and will not consider it beneath his dignity to earn a little money by helping a neighbour in busy seasons. The distinction between farmers, smallholders and cottagers is one of degree rather than of kind, and it is further weakened by the custom whereby farmers' sons become farm-labourers during their youth.

Another factor which has prevented the rise of separate classes is the greater opportunity for advancement in the uplands than in the lowlands. The amount of capital required to start farming on an upland farm is smaller, and it is by no means impossible for a thrifty and industrious farm-labourer to scrape together the necessary minimum, especially if he marries a girl who has economised in the same way. Nearly sixteen per cent of the farmers of over 20 acres were the sons of farm-workers or other wage-earners.[1] The same process has been going on from generation to generation so that a third of the present farming families may have belonged to the wage-earning class two generations ago. Owing to this elasticity of the social system, kinship groups, although they vary considerably in their collective wealth and prestige, tend to cut across class boundaries, and even the richest families have some poor relatives.

Still more important is the fact that every family has, broadly speaking, the same cultural and educational background, and that they are therefore at ease with one another. They all went to the same elementary schools, and that was all the formal education that the vast majority received. Only ten per cent of occupiers' children (of all ages over twelve) have ever attended the secondary

school at Llanfyllin or at Llanfair, and little more than one per cent
have been to a residential school. Even among some of the largest
farmers it is more usual to send girls to the secondary school than
boys, and such boys as do go are usually brought back to work on
the farm as soon as they reach the age of fourteen. With this
common educational background, the farmer and his employee
work together at the same tasks, eat at the same table, sleep in the
same house and talk about the same things.

Again, the varied social activities already described reflect a
system of values which attaches some importance to non-economic
techniques and accomplishments. Criticism of a neighbour for
being improvident or lazy is often qualified by some such remark as
' but he is a good Sunday-school teacher ', ' a good poet ', or ' a
great man on his knees '. And these qualities add to a man's
prestige and provide a measure of compensation for his shortcomings
as a producer of wealth. In this sphere of non-material culture,
distinction depends upon native talent, and a man of humble
position can gain considerable repute as a bard, a singer or a leader
in public worship. As a competitor at local *eisteddfodau*, or a
candidate in denominational scriptural examinations, he may sur-
pass his employer.

Economic status carries considerable weight in the democratic
election of Nonconformist deacons. The chapels rely on voluntary
contributions and it is prudent to place men of means in responsible
positions. But faithfulness and an ability to ' take part ' often
outweigh such considerations, and there are farm-labourer and
smallholder deacons in Llanfihangel as in other districts. Thus, in
chapel the employee can be the leader who sits in the ' big pew '
and brings the communion bread and wine to his earthly master.
Again, hospitality and generosity, which are so pre-eminent among
the traditional virtues, continue to be determinants of status, while
niggardliness, in spite of its increasing prevalence, is a weakness
harmful to prestige. A few farmers and farmers' wives commanded
a respect which was out of proportion to their wealth through their
readiness to help the needy and their magnanimity in forgiving
debts that could not easily be paid.

All these qualities contribute to prestige, but those people held
in highest esteem possessed a fair measure of all of them. An
all-round competence and versatility commands greater confidence
than any form of specialisation. A weakness is sensed in the
character of an unsuccessful farmer however accomplished he
may be in other respects, and the same applies to a successful

farmer who has no wider interests. There is something ' odd ' about both of them. But a well-balanced man who combines rectitude, industry and sound farming with a range of other interests and accomplishments is a man to be taken seriously. He is known as a *dyn o bwysau* (a man of weight), or a *dyn o farn* (a man with judgement) whose opinion on any matter is valued and quoted.

I have been told by several people who have studied Welsh farming from a technical standpoint that the upland farmer tends to be conservative in his methods, unambitious and often even lazy. This view overlooks the fact that he has not yet completely succumbed to the materialistic values of the modern world which tends to measure everything in terms of production and profit. Such judgements which measure one society by the standards of another are, of course, quite unscientific. The countryman is content with a relatively low standard of living only to the extent to which prestige in his community is not determined by economic factors. It is not always easy for an observer, obsessed with the value which the modern world attaches to ' efficiency ', to appreciate that to many a Welsh farmer, even today, writing a poem or an essay for an *eisteddfod*, or attending a drama practice or a preaching festival may be more important than producing surplus wealth. There is hardly a farmer in Llanfihangel who would suffer the loss of face involved in carrying hay on Sunday, however tempting the weather. Loss of crops is preferable to the loss of status which would result from unfaithfulness, not only to one's God, but to the standards cherished by one's forebears. Again, the countryman is fond of conversation, and his status is affected by the number of friends he has outside the locality. Therefore, he may consider it well worthwhile to lose a day's ploughing in order to attend an auction, even though there is nothing he wants to buy or sell. There will be the exchange of news with friends from a wider area, and this will enrich the discussion on his own hearth and on the hearths of his neighbours during subsequent evenings. People who neglect the non-economic aspects of life are criticised by their neighbours on the ground that ' they think of nothing but the penny '.

This emphasis upon non-economic determinants of status is superficially contradicted by the high position which money occupies in the scale of values, and by the distinctive attitude towards it. Indeed, the casual observer, who has already decided that the upland farmer is lazy, might easily be led to the contradictory conclusion that he is both generous and miserly at the same time.

Plate XI. Interior of a Nonconformist Chapel.

Plate XIIa. Llwydiarth Hall today

Plate XIIb. Plas Dolanog and the Vyrnwy Valley

Money is valued more than the commodities it can buy, and a farmer, who will freely give away a sack of potatoes, a bushel of grain or a basketful of apples without thought of payment, will often be found haggling over a sixpence. It is often said by people who have dealings with Welsh farmers that ' they will give you anything except money '.

The possession of money affects status far more than does its display in the form of luxuries. *Arian sych* (' dry money ') which is not needed for current expenditure is a treasure to be stored away, and nothing is more disheartening to a countryman than to have to fall back on these savings to make ends meet in bad years. This is called *dwyn mêl o'r cwch* (stealing honey from the hive). It would be impossible to grade families into economic classes by the quality of their furniture, their clothes, their motor-cars or where they go for their holidays. These things are not prized so highly as in modern communities, except by a few families with close connections with lowland farmers, and these are criticised by their neighbours for trying to live above their station. Neighbours have a rough idea as to whether a person is rich or poor ; they and their parents before them have observed the extent to which he has made, spent and inherited money. But no one would think of divulging the extent of his own money-wealth, neither would he try to give the impression that he is wealthy—except indirectly by pretending to be poorer than he is.

These pre-industrial standards are, however, being rapidly replaced by modern ones, and the change has been accelerated by the prosperity brought by the two Great Wars. During these periods of scarcity money could be made so easily and quickly that it became worth seeking it to the exclusion of all other values. To sacrifice a day's work in the interests of religion or art may have been worth while when the financial loss was only a few shillings, but suddenly it became a few pounds, and Mammon triumphed. Urban conceptions of the use of money are also spreading. Well-grates and three-piece suites are beginning to appear in the unfrequented parlours of farmhouses, and more attention is being paid to dress and ornament.

II

Notwithstanding the free social contact between families, there remains a considerable distinction between the independent farmer of, let us say, a hundred acre farm and a wage-earner who supplements his earnings from a smallholding. This arises partly from a difference in wealth, but the prestige of being one's own master is also valued. Craftsmen and tradesmen occupy an intermediate position socially, though some of the latter are probably richer than many of the larger farmers. Class-distinction expresses itself above all in marriage preferences. A farmer's son is expected to marry the daughter of a farmer of comparable wealth, and, although this rule ,is inevitably broken from time to time in such a closely knit community, the independent farming class remains very largely endogamous. Thus, of the wives of 38 farmers with over fifty acres who were themselves farmers' sons, 32 were farmers' daughters, and only 5 were the daughters of wage-earners.[2]

When a farmer's son insists on marrying below his class considerable resentment is generally felt by his family and other relations, but it is not an unpardonable offence, and if the girl is a ' good worker ' the resentment does not last long. The marriage of a farmer's daughter[3] to a labourer is a more serious matter, sometimes leading to lasting estrangements. These attitudes were explained locally in economic terms. The parents of both partners are expected to contribute stock and money towards the establishment of the young couple in a new farm, and this is often beyond the means of wage-earners. The loss of dowry incurred through the marriage of a farmer's son to a labourer's daughter is, however, only a minor calamity since the major contribution comes from the bridegroom's parents. But when a farmer's daughter marries a wage-earner the farmer may be faced with the dilemma of either allowing his daughter to suffer a permanent loss of status or accepting responsibility for stocking a new farm. And the choice affects not only himself but also the unmarried sons whose futures will be prejudiced by an additional and unexpected drain upon the family resources.

Although there is an important element of truth in these economic explanations, they are really rationalisations of more complex social attitudes. If the additional cost of marriage to a partner of lower status were the only objection, it should worry rich farmers less than the poorer ones. As we should expect, the contrary is the case. The richer the parents, the greater is their concern lest their children should choose impecunious spouses. Again, the particular objection to a poor marriage in the case of a farmer's daughter can be only partly explained in economic terms. In Llanfihangel, as in most Western societies, a man tends to raise or lower his wife to his own status. It is much easier for a farmer's wife, whatever her origin, to gain recognition in her husbands' class than it is for the antecedents of a labourer, who has become a farmer at his father-in-law's expense, to be overlooked.

The average farmer is relatively satisfied with his occupational station, and desires no better future for his children than that they too should become farmers or farmers' wives. Children who show no aptitude or who are physically unsuited for farming are educated, if means allow, for other careers. But the farmer is less interested than are the urban middle classes in this kind of social climbing. Thus, 78 per cent of the sons of farmers become farmers themselves, while only 10 per cent enter occupations which have no direct connection with the life of the countryside,[4] and the figures showing the occupations of the husbands of farmers' daughters are very similar. The farmer's ambition for himself and his children is not so much that they should rise into a profession which carries greater prestige, but that they should acquire bigger or better farms and so become more substantial farmers.

For the large farmer economic advancement involves leaving the district. As we have seen, Llanfihangel looks towards the Severn lowlands and the Shropshire Plain, and in so far as the large farmers may be said to emulate their social betters it is the farmers of the lowlands that they take as their pattern. They will tell you that Shropshire people are very nice people, that Shrewsbury is a very nice town, and that 50 acres of good land is worth 200 in Llanfihangel. They themselves may not move, but if they amass enough capital their children may be able to go. That is why a few of them try to send a daughter, and occasionally a son, for a few terms to a boarding school. It is not with the view to their climbing out of the farming class, but in order that they may have the same social prerequisites as the more class-conscious lowland farmers. For the same reason, it is more fashionable to shop in Oswestry than in Llanfyllin. These aspirations are more discernible in some families than in others, and on the whole the non-economic factors which have been discussed in the preceding chapters prevent them from becoming pronounced.

It may be mentioned by way of comparison that the external relationships of the farmers of the Border counties differ from those of West Wales. The latter have fewer contacts with English farmers, and the coastlands of Cardigan Bay offer but limited scope for advancement. In West Wales a larger proportion of farmers' sons are educated for black-coated and professional work, and when they go to England they become London tradesmen rather than lowland farmers.

The small farmer in Llanfihangel can better himself by acquiring a better farm within his native district.[5] Such farms become available from time to time through the migration of the most prosperous and the retirement or death of unmarried or childless occupiers. On the whole, farms have changed hands fairly often. While a fifth of those over 50 acres have been occupied by the same family for over a century, half of them were acquired by new tenants between 1910 and 1940. A fifth changed hands between 1930 and 1940. Smallholdings changed tenants more frequently than larger farms, while only a sixth of the occupiers of houses without land were born in their present homes.

The lowlands are of economic importance to the sons and daughters of cottagers and smallholders as well as to the larger farmers. A fair proportion of the youths have always been able to find work on local farms, but as they grew older the demands for their services declined, and the cottages in which they might settle were very few. As often as not, by the time they reached the age of marriage, the sons of their employer were old enough to take their places, and migration to the lowlands solved both their domestic and their employment problem. During recent decades, increased pastoralism and mechanisation have severely reduced the numbers required in both the uplands and the lowlands alike, and at the same time the higher wages of the towns offered a means of betterment to those who left the land.

Thus, while 78 per cent of the farmers' sons born between 1870 and 1905 became farmers, only a little more than half the sons of smallholders and wage-earners remained in agricultural occupations. The others entered such occupations as mining, quarrying, dock and transport work, travelling and shopkeeping, while an appreciable number emigrated to the United States and the Dominions.[6] Therefore, whereas the larger farmer's conception of a better life is mainly derived from his relatives and friends in lowland farms, the wage-earner's standard of values is more influenced by letters and visits from relatives doing well, or not so well, as miners, factory-workers, insurance collectors, or what not, in industrial towns. The bonds of kinship and locality retain their hold upon those who have gone away, and several have returned home to retire.

While the people of Llanfihangel respect wealth and ability of all kinds, they are very quick to see the ridiculous side of social snobbery and humbug. Indeed, there is little scope for pretentiousness in a community where the past history of every individual and his relatives is known to everyone else. And the community has

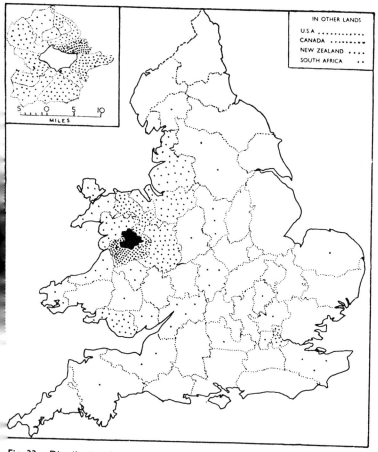

Fig. 33. Distribution, by counties, of children (over 16 years of age) and siblings of occupiers and of wives of occupiers in 1940—excluding children and siblings dwelling within the parish. One dot equals one person. Inset : the parishes around Llanfihangel.

very effective methods of keeping people in their places and helping them to cultivate a sense of proportion. For example, topical verses are recited or sung at social gatherings, alluding to the oddities of some of the people present, or to some amusing and embarrassing incidents in their lives.[7] It is done without malice, but it provides the victims with the wholesome experience of seeing themselves in a distorting mirror, and many things may be said in verse which would be offensive in prose. The more popular an individual may be, the more likely he is to be subjected to this form of verbal caricature. On the other hand, it is not usually indulged in publicly against those who are known to resent it, but because of their inability to accept it they do not ' belong ' in the fullest degree. Beyond these again, really unfriendly people may be subjected to more relentless treatment by the youth group.

To the classes which have their roots in the indigenous community must be added a small group of professional people, clergymen, ministers and teachers, and the visiting doctors and veterinary surgeons, who provide the community with specialised services. Few of these have kinship ties with the remainder of the people, and they are separated from them by their education and wider social contacts and interests. They are the only people usually addressed as ' Mr. ——— '. Their position depends not only upon the prestige of their offices as judged by the local community but also upon their relation to the world outside the parish and upon their function as a link between the community and that wider world. Still, their relation with the local community is much closer than is usual in an English village. The majority of them were brought up in simple homes like those of the people among whom they now live. Their original social background was the farm, the smallholding or the miner's cottage, and they are entirely at home with the people they serve. Their children attend the same elementary school as other children, and, while the children naturally tend to follow their fathers into the professions and thus leave the parish, their up-bringing does not make them a class apart. The son of a late rector of Llanfihangel married the daughter of a local farmer, and the marriage registers show that several clergymen and ministers have found wives among the daughters of farmers and smallholders of Llanfihangel.

This relatively classless society has now very little contact with people whose prestige stands higher than that of farmers and professional workers. There are no resident members of the old landed aristocracy, and an industrialist who has a residence called ' The

Cottage (not ' The Hall ') near Dolanog is their only contact with the newer aristocracy of the modern world. The latter takes a friendly interest in the people and is generous to the church and the school at Dolanog. He visits the area for short periods as often as his other activities permit, and derives great pleasure from the land which he farms with the aid of a bailiff. But his main business in life, the source of his wealth and position, lies outside the experience of the country-folk. His affairs depend upon factors other than the vicissitudes of the weather and agricultural prices, and he naturally cannot play a role comparable to that of the gentry of a former generation.

Mention has already been made of the Vaughans of Llwydiarth Hall who were the great landowners in the district until some two centuries ago. This family held a prominent position among the gentry of Montgomeryshire, and its two last male representatives sat as Members of Parliament during a large part of the seventeenth century.[8] Early in the eighteenth century the Vaughans became extinct through the lack of male heirs and the Llwydiarth Estate passed through marriage into the hands of Watkin Williams, grandson of Sir William Williams, a Welsh lawyer and speaker of the House of Commons. Watkin Williams succeeded his father to the baronetcy, and through his mother he inherited the great estates of John Wynn of Wynnstay and Gwydir. He changed his name to Watkin Williams Wynn—a name that has been handed down from father to heir ever since.[9] When the Vaughans died out, their

Fig. 34. Llwydiarth in 1684.

ancestral hall was occupied intermittently by relatives of the great landlord of Wynnstay, but it was subsequently allowed to fall into decay and later converted into a large farmhouse which still bears the name of Llwydiarth Hall. Thus, Llanfihangel ceased to have a resident squire. Local tradition knows nothing of the Vaughans except that they lived at Llwydiarth ' in the old days ', and since a book called ' The Story of Montgomeryshire ' is used in the schools it is doubtful whether even this is genuine ' folk-memory '.

Until the close of the nineteenth century, successive Williams Wynns played a much larger part in the life of the tenants than in later decades. They used the land for hunting and shooting, they were benefactors of the schools and churches, and the church and vicarage at Pontllogel were built at their sole expense. Rent-dinners were given which Sir Watkin would sometimes attend in person, and great feasts were held periodically at Wynnstay (Sir Watkin's residence near Ruabon) to celebrate such events as the coming-of-age of an heir, a wedding, a recovery from an illness or a return from a sojourn abroad. Details of some of these feasts are available.[10]   At a coming-of-age in 1770 it was said that 15,000 people all dined at the same time at Wynnstay Park, three coachfuls of cooks having been brought specially from London for the occasion. The enormous bill of fare on a similar occasion in 1841 included such items as 21 oxen, 146 sheep, 135 pickled tongues, 10 flitches of bacon, 5 Westphalia hams, 4 Strassburg hams, 6 Cumberland hams, 25 York hams, 3608 eggs, 28 turkeys, 40 ducks, 701 fowls, 204 grouse, 400 partridges, 267 lbs. of turtle, 280 lbs. of salmon, 2 stags, 17 bucks, 207 quarts of cream, 464 lbs. of butter, 51 hogsheads of ale, 829 bottles of sherry, 558 bottles of port, and so through the wines and spirits, 2136 peaches and nectarines, 1200 apricots, 12 bushels of apples for tarts, ... a spread which it took a week to consume.

A feast held in 1875 appears to have been a more modest affair, the Welsh guests at least being limited to a little over 700 tenants who paid rents of £10 a year or more. At these celebrations the tenants had an opportunity of renewing their allegiance. Toasts were drunk to the King, to the Prince of Wales, to Bishops and Archbishops, and to Sir Watkin's aristocratic guests. There were many speeches in appreciation of the benevolence of Sir Watkin, " The Uncrowned Prince in Wales ', and his praises were sung in Welsh and in English verse by rustic bards.

Again, Sir Watkin played an active part in the formation of the Yeomanry, and this brought a number of his tenants or their sons into closer contact with him. Incidentally, this contact with aris - tocracy was not without its repercussions upon the class conscious-ness of the tenants. The discrimination between those who paid rents above, and below, ten pounds per annum, and the fact that the Yeomanry could be joined only by men able to provide their own horses, helped to foster the mild class-distinction which we have observed between farmers and smallholders.

The festivities we have described belong to the past, and during the present century the landlord has made little effort to keep in touch with his tenants. ' Old Sir Watkin ' (d. 1944) hardly ever visited Llanfihangel during the last two decades of his long life, and many of his younger tenants had never seen him. To understand the reasons for this change it is necessary to consider the parts played by landlord and tenants in the politics of Wales in the past three-quarters of a century.

Chapter XIII

POLITICS

SIR Watkin's gradual withdrawal from the affairs of his tenants, culminating recently in a complete severance of the connection with the lands of Llwydiarth, is but one instance of the general decline of the land-owning class.[1] Until some sixty years ago the great landlords and the gentry were a real power in the Welsh countryside. They, mainly, were responsible for local administration, they interpreted the law and they commanded the militia and the yeomanry. They represented their constituencies in Parliament, and elections were usually contests between two or three rival county families. Thus, a Sir Watkin represented Denbighshire almost continuously for nearly two centuries, while the Montgomeryshire seat was held by one of his relatives, intermittently in the eighteenth century and continuously in the nineteenth century until 1880. The family also played a leading part in the formation of a Jacobite society among the gentry of north-eastern Wales.

With the last quarter of the nineteenth century the power of this ruling class dwindled rapidly. The new popularly elected County Councils and Parish Councils took over local administration, and as time went on the gentry were outnumbered on local Benches by people from a different social stratum. Legislation was passed giving the tenant some measure of protection, and at the same time far-reaching economic changes, the taxation of land and death-duties all combined to undermine the landlord's economic foundations. Generally speaking, the lesser gentry succumbed to these adverse conditions after the first World War, and now the great landlords are going. Many country-seats have become unoccupied while others serve as guest-houses, schools or temporary residences for industrialists and businessmen who play the squire in their spare time.

Although much of the prestige and power of the landlord survived at least to the end of the nineteenth century, his links with the peasantry were far more tenuous than in England. Anglicisation had separated the aristocracy from the Welsh people. They had become strangers in their own land, and their ignorance of Welsh life made it difficult for them to play an active part in it.

However well-disposed they may have been, they could be little more than patrons of a culture which existed apart from them and which was moved by forces from outside their world. Sir Watkin could give his tenants an occasional introduction into his own social milieu, but he could not enter fully into theirs. Wynnstay has had many a distinguished guest. Handel is said to have played its organ, and the second Sir Watkin has been described as a cultured country squire, a grand seigneur influential among his own people and a patron of the arts.[2] He counted Sir Joshua Reynolds and David Garrick among his friends and entertained them in his home. During that century Welsh literature was being enriched by the *cywyddau* of Goronwy Owen, the dramatic interludes of Twm o'r Nant, and the hymns which immortalised William Williams and Ann Griffiths in the hearts of the Welsh people. But it may be safely assumed that none of these was ever an honoured guest at Wynnstay. At the great feast of 1875 Sir Watkin's praises were sung in Welsh verse by the poet Mynyddog, but the former's attitude to the vernacular was fully revealed by his opening remarks : ' You will hear most of the toasts given you in *your* native tongue ', and the only words that he himself seems to have uttered in that tongue were ' *Iechyd da i chwi* ' (Good health to you.)[3]

With the great religious revivals of the eighteenth and nineteenth centuries, and the development of Nonconformity among the people, the separation between the world of the landlord and that of the tenant became well-nigh complete. The religious awakening gradually stimulated political and national consciousness and the landlord became increasingly identified with the *ancien regime*. The aristocracy as a class upheld the Church and resented the Nonconformity of their tenants. Howell Harris, the eighteenth century revivalist, maintained that ' the gentlemen hunt us like partridges ', and the first Sir Watkin was one of his greatest enemies. Indeed, Sir Watkin's death through falling from his horse on the way home from a hunt coincided with a Methodist prayer-meeting at which the following petition was made : ' *O Arglwydd cwympa Ddiawl Mawr y Wynnstay* ' (O Lord, cast down the Great Devil of Wynnstay).[4] Again, Sir Watkin was a Conservative who upheld the privileges of his class and a representative of English culture in Wales. His tenants were predominantly Nonconformist, radical and Welsh. The political history of Wales from the early decades of the nineteenth century until a generation ago consisted primarily of the intensification of the struggle between these two groups of interests, a struggle which, after passing through the bitter days of political evictions following the elections of 1859 and 1868, and the tithe war of the 1880s and 1890s, culminated in a victory for Non-conformity and Liberalism.

The year 1880 marks the turning point in the struggle so far as Montgomeryshire is concerned. In that year the Wynn candidate was defeated in a lively Parliamentary election by Stuart Rendel, a Liberal industrialist, and the seat has been a Liberal stronghold ever since. In 1886 Sir Watkin himself lost his seat in Denbigh-shire. At this time the main bone of contention between Tories and Liberals was the question of principle involved in the payment of tithe by Nonconformists to an Established Church in which they no longer believed. The sense of injustice aroused by the privileges of the Church was further aggravated by economic depression, and when a resolution to disestablish the Church in Wales was defeated in Parliament in 1886 a tithe-war broke out throughout North Wales. Riots occurred in Denbighshire, and attempts to sell the goods of farmers in order to recover the tithe proved abortive, until the Bishop of St. Asaph introduced a Bill by which the tithes were made payable directly by the landowner. This became law in 1891, although all the Welsh members voted against it.[5] The tithe was thus added to the rent, a stratagem which increased the unpopularity of the landlord, and corroborated the Nonconformist view that the landlord and the parson were political allies. At least two farmers in Llanfihangel refused to pay tithe during this controversy, with the result that sales of their farm-properties were held, and one of them was further penalised by an increase in rent. Ultimately, the tithe problem was settled by the Welsh Disestablishment Act of 1914. But the Churchmen in Llanfihangel maintain that the Nonconformists were cheated of their victory, because the tithe must still be paid to public bodies whereas they had expected that it would be abolished.

The conflict extended to matters other than tithe. About 1908 the parish churchyard had become full, and the rector and his followers planned to extend it. The Nonconformists insisted on an undenominational cemetery where they could bury without having to submit to the ministrations of the incumbent. The landlord acceded to the extension of the churchyard, but refused repeated requests for land for the cemetery. The controversy became heated, some Nonconformists insisting that the ground acquired by the Church was quite unfit for burial, that it was so rocky that people were being buried with their heads down ! A Parish Council election was fought in which the Nonconformists gained a substantial majority. The landlord gave way and about four acres of land near the Llan were purchased by the Parish Council which has since functioned as the Burial Ground Committee. In the adjoining parish of Meifod the squirearchy and the Church were more powerful, and the churchyard remains the only burial ground to this day. After the Nonconformists had won the day in Llanfihangel, the Churchmen on the Parish Council brought forward a motion demanding that a part of the cemetery be consecrated for their use. Some Nonconformists admitted the fairness of this claim since Churchmen also paid rates, but it was opposed by the majority. The motion remained on the agenda for a whole year before it was passed by a majority of one at a meeting from which some of the extremists were absent.

The politico-religious cleavage bears some relation to economic status. In 1940, the Nonconformist group comprised four-fifths of the farmers of holdings over 20 acres, and half the smallholders and cottagers, leaving the Church with half the smallholders and only a fifth of the farmers. It is difficult to generalise as to whether this is true of rural Wales as a whole, but it is my impression that the traditional poor, together with the richer members of the community, predominate in the Church, while people of intermediate status form the majority of chapel congregations.

Throughout the inter-War period the alignment of Church-Tory versus Nonconformist-Radical persisted in local politics, and County Council and District Council elections consisted of contests between them in which the Tory was always worsted. In one such election a Nonconformist farmer defeated the rector of the parish, and the present County Councillor is the son of one of the farmers penalised for non-payment of tithe. On one occasion a chapel-goer came forward as a Tory candidate, but the Nonconformists interpreted this as a bait set by the Churchmen and he also was defeated. Nevertheless, the fact that a Nonconformist should openly declare himself a Tory was indicative of a weakening of the unity of religion and politics.

During the last decade the old dichotomy has broken down with remarkable rapidity. It is not that Nonconformists have become Tories or Churchmen Liberals, but, its purpose achieved, the Liberal-Nonconformist movement has lost its *raison d'être*, while any desire on the part of the opposition to restore the old order has been rendered hopelessly impractical by its complete and general collapse. At the County Council election of 1945 the retiring County Councillor was returned unopposed, and the chairman at the public meeting which re-nominated him was a Churchman whose brother was once a candidate for the Church party. Old allegiances were completely glossed over in the same way throughout the County. In a total of 43 electoral divisions, only nine retiring councillors refused re-nomination, and only nine divisions were contested in the whole county. None of the candidates, including those returned unopposed, commended himself to the electors as either a Tory or as a Liberal.[6] The only candidates who wore party labels were seven Labour ones, two of whom were returned unopposed at Newtown and one at Llanidloes, but none in the rural areas.

Not so long ago the old schism permeated every sphere of social life, and in some extreme cases it served as a barrier to business transactions and marriage alliances, but it no longer interferes with any social relationships. Nonconformist leaders who once championed the Liberal cause now serve as managers of the Church School, the daughter of a Nonconformist teaches at the school, the rector is asked to adjudicate at chapel *eisteddfodau*, and, as we have seen, nonsectarian societies are gaining in popularity.

The general attitude towards Sir Watkin also shows that the old animosities have been almost entirely forgotten When the news came that the estate was to be sold to pay death-duties, the general reaction was one of apprehension and regret. From generation to generation, ' Sir Watkin ', as a landlord, had been taken for granted, and his fundamental right to his economic position was never really questioned even when his political power was most bitterly opposed. He was a personage who existed before his tenants were born and it was assumed that he would continue to exist when they had passed away. As an institution ' Sir Watkin ' did not die. He had a number of traditional attributes. He was generally praised for his paternal consideration for his tenants (in matters which did not involve a great deal of expense). When a farm became vacant ' Sir Watkin ' usually gave first preference to the sons of present and past tenants, and he was generous when misfortune caused tenants to fall behind with the rent. In discussing land-nationalisation the farmers were inclined to doubt whether the Government would show the same consideration.

Although the last ' Old Sir Watkin ' hardly ever visted the parish, his name was a household word and his photograph, or that of his heir taken on his twenty-first birthday, hung on the walls of Church and Nonconformist homes alike. Occasionally, one heard adverse criticism as in the following summing up on the passing of the landlords as a class :

On the whole you must say that the gentry were a poor lot, living luxuriously on the hard labour of their impoverished tenants. You could never get anything out of them ; they just collected the rent and lived as parasites on the country. They were no good to the nation, and Sir Watkin was as bad as any of them.

But, on the whole, such views were exceptional, the general attitude being one of kindliness and respect. When long-promised repairs were interminably delayed, there was a marked tendency to blame the agent rather than his master, and such criticisms as were voiced against Sir Watkin himself were usually couched in the friendliest terms. Of the fourteen inhabitants of the parish who attended the funeral of ' Old Sir Watkin ' at Llangedwyn in 1944, the majority were Nonconformists. Thus, the average view of the disruption of the old order falls in between that of a Nonconformist whom I have just quoted and that of a Churchman which follows :

There will be no history as one might say in a few years' time. Everybody will be the same and all the mansions will have been turned into boarding-schools and youth centres. There will be no gentry ; everybody will be ' scraping ' for all they are worth. It will be a bad thing for the countryside. It will be a great loss for this area when Sir Watkin goes. In the old days the gentry were generous, and they brought wealth into the country. Their sports gave pleasure to the tenants as well as to themselves—the beaters were as excited as those who were shooting. Now, it will be officials, and a lot you will get from them. They go away on their holidays and enjoy them on their own. I don't like living in a society where there is no one you can look up to and to whom you can raise your cap. It will be strange for our children in the new age to read of the way we used to live in the old days. They may think we were fools, but I should not be surprised that they will say that we were much happier than they.

To compensate for the conscious acceptance of Sir Watkin as the somewhat distant father of the community, an element of unconscious antagonism was sometimes revealed, even among Church people, in the evident satisfaction given by stories of contests of wit between an ' Old Sir Watkin ' and his fool Twm Siambr Wen. Here are two examples. Sir Watkin and his fool are out shooting hares, but Twm misses every shot. He sees a donkey and shoots it. Sir Watkin asks why he has shot the donkey, and Twm replies : ' I saw you shooting long-eared things and I did the same '. Sir Watkin, on horseback, is about to jump a fence, and he asks Twm whether there is a firm bottom on the other side. Twm replies in the affirmative, and Sir Watkin jumps and lands in a bog. Sir Watkin : ' I thought you said there was a firm bottom here '. Twm : ' Yes,

but you have not reached the bottom yet '. Pleasure was derived
from the knowledge that at least one commoner could make a fool of
Sir Watkin and get away with it.

In its widest context in Britain the conflict between Liberal
and Tory was primarily a conflict between industrial and landed
interests, while the opposition of tenants to landlords and of chapels
to churches were only subsidiary issues. But it was the latter that
the Welsh countryman understood, and it was through the eleva-
tion of these above the major economic issue that he was able to
make the Liberal Party his own. As yet he has found little in the
more recent struggle between capital and labour that corresponds
to the circumstances of his life and expresses his aspirations. And
the conflict in its urban form can have no meaning in a society
where a clear-cut division between employer and employee is lacking.
The only socialists that I came across in the parish were one or two
men who had spent many years as miners in South Wales.

In Parliamentary elections the majority continue to vote as
their fathers did, the Nonconformists for the Liberal candidate and
the Church people for the Conservative, but there is little enthusiasm.
The loyalty of many an old Radical with whom I discussed the
matter was severely shaken in the 1945 election by the mild Socialism
of the Liberal candidate's speeches. They were apprehensive of his
advocacy of land nationalisation, and were not very impressed by
his enthusiasm for conferring upon the countryside urban domestic
and social amenities, ranging from bathrooms to cinemas and
luxurious community centres. His concern about the depopulation
of the rural areas and his plea for more houses were better understood, though many of his fellow-Liberals would probably disagree
with him as to where they should be built.

While Socialism has aroused no direct response, class conscious-
ness is nevertheless emerging in a different form. Some years ago
a branch of the Farmers' Union was formed in the locality. Farmers
irrespective of sect became nominal members, and a Churchman
was elected secretary. Subsequently their adherence has become
gradually more positive. When a rumour reached the parish in
1945 that the Llwydiarth estate would be sold *en bloc* to a syndicate
which would then offer the farms at exorbitant prices to the
tenants, the Branch met as a body under the leadership of the Nonconformist District Councillor to protest against the injustice.
Again, it was as farmers with a common interest that they re-
elected their County Councillor and afterwards their District

Councillor in the recent elections. Both were farmers who no longer emphasised their old party allegiances, and both were returned unopposed. It was as though the inhabitants realised in some intuitive way that no party now represents their particular interests.

In several neighbouring constituencies farmer candidates in their election addresses stressed that they were supported by the Farmers' Union as well as by the public meeting at which they were nominated, and there were examples of well-known Liberal families giving the use of their cars to equally well-known Tory candidates who were supported by the Farmers' Union against Independent candidates with no interest in the land. The same state of mind is expressed, though not yet in Llanfihangel, in the preference in many districts for Young Farmers' Clubs rather than the Welsh League of Youth or the more anglicised County Youth Movement, both of which are concerned with wider, but non-occupational, aspects of culture. Similarly, ministers and school-masters tell me that it is becoming increasingly difficult to bring people together to a lecture or discussion on religious or educational subjects which were once of general interest, but if the subject has to do with farming there is a great response.

Thus, class solidarity in a form which first appeared among English farmers is spreading in the Welsh hills. Based upon a unity of economic interest and concerned solely with occupational matters, it is a rural counterpart of urban trade unionism. As such it re-mains unintegrated with the wider complex of traditional culture. It lacks the vitality and idealism of Welsh Radicalism which appealed to people's sense of justice as well as to their self-interest, and invoked principles which could be expounded from the pulpit as well as in the market-place.

Chapter XIV

EPILOGUE

I

EVERY ethnographic description is more or less selective, and in this study prominence has been given to those elements which distinguish the rural culture of Wales from that of rural England and still more from that of modern urban communities. Much of what is most distinctive is an inheritance from the pastoral and tribal past. Greatly modified, it persists in the high evaluation of family and kindred, in the hospitality extended to strangers and in the maintenance of a pattern of community life which is specially adapted to a scattered habitat. From the same past comes specialisation in arts and recreations which demand the minimum material equipment, and the fact that so many social institutions have no permanent habitation.

The contrast with the village traditions of the greater part of England is striking. There the inheritance of land was impartible and kinship weakly developed. To quote a modern social historian:[1]

'. . . upon the whole there is little evidence that the inhabitants of an English village in the thirteenth century thought of themselves as a body of kinsmen. When marriage of the heir customarily coincided with his taking over the management of the holding, the history of the blood which held the tenement became the history of a single sequence of small families, each pulsing in its time, each dying away. Since in every generation the sons who were not to inherit either left the holding or did not marry, the number of actual kinsmen could not increase rapidly '.

The Englishman's attitude towards kinship is well symbolised by the modern designation of distant relatives as ' Welsh cousins '.

Again, community life and economic co-operation in England are traditionally bound up with close settlement. The community centre was the village green, the church, the inn, rather than the home. This social system was thoroughly undermined by the scattering of farms as a consequence of the Agrarian Revolution. Seen upon a map the distribution of rural population in England and Wales became more alike, but their social inheritance remained different. In Wales, the social pattern as well as the settlement was diffuse, whereas the English farmer, in spite of dispersal, continued to regard the village or the town as the centre of community life. This consideration strengthens Mr. G. C. Homans' comment on the implications of the weak blood ties in village communities :[2]

'Better than many another society could have prepared them, this society prepared western Europeans and their descendants for the social isolation in which so many families live in the great urban agglomerations of today'

The Welsh people, on the other hand, had no such preparation for an age in which urban standards are supreme and human beings tend to be regarded as so many interchangeable individual units rather than as families and neighbours, an age in which the popular panacea for social disintegration is the ' community *centre.*'

Furthermore, the class configuration of upland Wales stands in marked contrast to the tripartite division of the rural society of lowland England into squire landlords, capitalist farmers and landless labourers. The ratio of labourers to independent farmers is much lower in Wales than in England, and over two-thirds of the land-holdings are under fifty acres.[3] The labourer is often a smallholder himself, his cottage is seldom ' tied ', and the freedom to choose his employer without losing his home, together with the proceeds of his holding, gives him a measure of independence.

This distinction between rural England and rural Wales again has a long history which cannot be recapitulated here, but it may be recalled that it started with the contrast between the English manorial system and medieval Welsh society which was essentially a society of freemen, the ' nobility ' being tribal chieftains bound to their followers by ties of blood, and the serfs forming a small minority of the population. The ' detribalisation ' of Welsh society saw the rise of a land-owning class, and landlordism became the order of the day in Wales as in England. But the anglicisation of this class ultimately prevented them from performing the normal functions of a local aristocracy, and they became thoroughly discredited.

The repudiation of the aristocracy and the ' Church of England ' and the retardation of acculturation during the past two centuries was the negative side of a renaissance of the native culture which began with the religious awakening and then spread to the realms of learning, literature, music and politics. Viewed externally, this transformation emerged from the ultimate acceptance of Puritanism. But this acceptance was no ordinary case of cultural diffusion by which an overt element is borrowed and gradually integrated with the pre-existing elements through being endowed with function and meaning. Nonconformity and chapel-building were the unforeseen *consequences* of a spiritual experience and a regrouping of emotional attachments at the core of the culture. The external forms of Nonconformist organisation were for the most part copied, but the meaning and emotive energy emerged from within.

Imbued with this new spirit an appreciable proportion of the ordinary men and women of Wales attained some of the ideal attributes of an aristocracy and a clergy, and it was these that set the standard and acted as spiritual guides for the remainder. Their *buchedd* (way of living) became the pattern for others to emulate, they were the *blaenoriaid* (leaders), and to them fell the task of *hyfforddi* (instructing) and *disgyblu* (disciplining). The traditional functions of a clergy and an aristocracy were assumed by a spiritualised laity, by an ennobled commonalty. It was the common people that maintained the academies and contributed funds for the foundation of the University, and it was from them that the ministers, educators and politicians of modern Wales emerged. For wellnigh a century, members of the landed aristocracy have seldom reached positions of real prominence in any sphere of Welsh life. The real leaders of modern Wales were reared in farmsteads and cottages, and there are few outstanding figures in Welsh affairs to-day of whom one has not heard it said by some workman or other : ' He is a cousin of mine ', or ' His uncle lives next-door to me '.

II

This society of modern Wales, exceptional as it has been in many ways, has not stood the test of time. There are at least three reasons for this. The first is inherent in its very nature, the second arises partly from the geographical position and political condition of Wales, and the third is the impact of modern industrial and urban civilisation. They can only be touched upon here.

First, although the new synthesis in Wales was a religious one, it was of a kind that could not be crystallised in institutions that would ensure the maximum continuity. It was a religion of the prophet rather than the priest, emergent rather than traditional. The unifying factor was not so much a body of doctrine as a direct religious experience gained in a revival, and its perpetuation depends not only upon the transmission of a teaching and a moral code, but upon a recurrence of the actual experience—and revivals cannot be repeated at will. Without vision a society of this kind becomes moribund much more rapidly than one in which tradition and authority play a larger part.

Secondly, Wales is geographically and politically united to England, and for the more talented Welshman the road to success is also to a large extent the road to England. As the outlook becomes more secular, the *mores* of the native society become increasingly irrelevant to the educated, and the acquisition of English culture seems more profitable than the cultivation of the national inheritance. As they achieve success anglicisation sets to work on the sons of the cottage as it did on the former gentry, and this precludes the development of a hereditary Welsh aristocracy. Modern Wales has continually exported its aristocracy and replaced it in each generation with a new élite promoted from among the people themselves.

Under such circumstances, the standards of the leaders have been essentially those cherished by the community generally, and, while that community retained its cohesion and nobility, discontinuity in personnel could be afforded. The new leaders were similar to the old, and replacement strengthened the unity of leaders and followers. But today, as the soil from which they grow becomes more sterile, replacement hastens degeneration, whereas continuity in the composition of the elite might have retarded it.

A lack of continuity of residence also weakens the social influence of professional people and administrators who remain in Wales— a condition which is universal in Western societies. The further one proceeds from manual work, the more migratory do people become. In any normal society ' the natural place of an exceptional man is to be leading his own people and helping them to bear their burdens. Your exceptional brain is serving the nation best if it remains racy of its own particular soil.'⁴ The modern system uproots the ablest members of the community, educates them and scatters them indiscriminately into official positions up and down the country. They are birds of passage and their interest in their adopted localities is not, generally speaking, as great as it might have been in their native localities among their own kith and kin. It is noteworthy that the *alltud* (exile) in medieval Wales, far from being an official, ranked next to the serf. In these days when conditions are so changeable, and when so many are 'on the move and on the make ', one wonders whether Llanfihangel, failing an Ann Griffiths or a John Hughes, could not do with an Edward or John Vaughan, or even a Sir Watkin—if only to save its trees, the heritage of generations, from being hastily cut down in order to secure quick returns in a seller's market.

Thirdly, the eighteenth century saw the birth, not only of Methodism, but of the Industrial Revolution, the effects of which eventually transformed the material life of the Welsh countryside and proved highly disruptive to the social fabric generally. Technical advancements are more easily communicable and more obviously advantageous than any other element of culture, and there is no doubt that their importation into Wales from and through England has gone on throughout history, and for that matter throughout pre-history. The material culture of Wales is far less ' Welsh ' than its non-material culture. But the results of the Industrial Revolution were fundamentally different from the older kind of diffusion. Wherever the pre-industrial techniques and styles came from, the actual products were for the most part made locally. Industrial civilisation, on the other hand, offered the products ready-made, thus depriving the local society of its craftsmen. The workshop was replaced as a social centre by the retailer's shop. The home crafts have also died out and with them has gone one of the reasons for congregating around the fire on winter evenings. It might be argued that people could continue to meet simply for companionship, but in practice this tends to confine social contact to groups of friends with strong common interests. Generally speaking, when men come together they come together to do things, and when the things they do together become fewer, social intercourse also declines. The social significance of a meeting or a visit often outweighs its practical purpose, but without such a purpose it would rarely occur at all.

With the adoption of modern inventions, commercial relationships are spreading at the expense of the traditional local reciprocities. In the old days horses and waggons were readily lent to take the Sunday School or the choir for an outing without thought of payment. Today buses are used and paid for. A horse eats and grows old whether it works or not, and to lend it to a neighbour involves no obvious material loss. A tractor or a motor-car, on the other hand, eats only when it works, and wears out with use. Inasmuch as it is not freely interchangeable for the older kind of services, it makes for social isolation. Experiments might, however, be made in inducing the spontaneous mutual-aid groups of the countryside to purchase some of the more expensive machines between them, thus developing a form of co-operation that is already there.

Furthermore, the quickened tempo of life has turned many an old custom into an anachronism. A countryman who has walked a few miles to a farm, or even travelled on horseback or in a trap appreciates a meal and there is a point in offering it to him. But, travelling by car, he can be home before the kettle boils, passing on his way many a friend with whom he would have stopped for a chat were it not for the car. In the same way, every official who has to do with the countryside arrives by car, performs his mission and departs. He seldom needs a meal, to say nothing of a night's hospitality, as did the visiting craftsmen and preachers of a former generation. In these days it is only the unprosperous that appreciate hospitality, a circumstance which is not without its repercussions upon the inhabitants' evaluation of their own inherited liberality.

At the same time as the farmers were enthusiastically winning their independence from landlord and church, and extending their control over politics and religion, they were rapidly losing their control over their economic life and becoming increasingly dependent upon the caprice of an international market and the policies of governments dominated by industrial interests. The replacement of subsistence agriculture by the specialised production of pastoral products for cash involved the introduction of capitalist standards and the conversion of a way of life into a means of production. The partial acceptance of these standards robbed Llanfihangel of half its inhabitants and seriously impoverished its social life and institutions. The ruins of habitations, the large but little-used farmhouse living-rooms, the spare rooms in the school at the Llan and the more than half-empty chapels are all symptoms of a social shrinkage. The community life of this type of society never depended upon large numbers, but it cannot function well without fair-sized household groups. The decline in the size of families, the fall in the number of men-servants, and particularly of maids, have all detracted from the richness of life at the homestead and weakened its attraction as a social centre.

Not only has the farmer's life become more lonely, the demands of his occupation have become more exacting. Labour-saving as machines may be, tasks cannot be *delegated* to them as they can to workmen and maids. The greater 'time-off' granted to the remaining servants has brought them new opportunities to seek fellowship away from the homestead, and the bicycle and motor-cycle have increased their mobility. Meanwhile, leisure has become scarcer for the farmer and his wife, and much of the time formerly spent in entertaining and visiting is now spent on routine jobs about the farm. Thus does the intrusion of industrial standards, with their sharp distinction between the place of work and the place of recreation,

undermine the old way of life in which work and play were inter-
mingled or were complementary aspects of the same activity.

III

Viewed from without, the old social life displays a remarkable
tenacity, and, in spite of the spread of machine-made goods, recreation and entertainment are still almost entirely home-produced.
But the picture appears quite different to those who live within
the culture.   Their invariable answer to the question whether any
of the traditional features survive today is: ' No, nothing like what
it used to be '.   And they will explain that in these days people
are too preoccupied with their own affairs to be neighbourly, too
busy to visit and entertain, in too much of a hurry to tarry and talk.
It is *mynd* (going, movement) that appeals to the young, and the
rest are too busy ' scratching ' for money to live the leisurely life
of the old days.   Again, they will point to the emptiness of the
chapels and churches, and the older ones will insist that the standards
of concerts, *eisteddfodau* and Sunday Schools are much lower and
the preparation for them much more perfunctory than in former
times.   And the evidence they adduce proves that they are not just
romanticising their own youth.   Judged by urban standards the
culture retains many of its old characteristics ; judged by its own
past it is in full decline.

The word decline is used advisedly, for little that is new has
come in to replace the old.   The traditional extra-occupational
activities have not been ousted to any appreciable extent by the
mass amusements of the modern age.   It is significant that recent
attempts to make a paying concern of a travelling cinema visiting
the hamlets of Montgomeryshire have ended in failure. It is just that
everyone is more engrossed in his own little concern than he used to be,
and has less time for other people and other things.   The farmer
tends to become a specialist in his own line, leaving the preaching
to the preacher and the educating to the schoolmaster.   In more
general terms, the little community in Llanfihangel, through accepting current values and becoming part of the contemporary economic
system, is already in the initial stages of the social atomisation which
is general in Western Civilisation.

This weakening of social ties is still more marked in modern
urban society.   The further one proceeds from the countryside the
more narrowly concerned do people become in their own specialised
little worlds, the more lacking in social wholeness.   It is therefore
inevitable that their most well-meaning efforts to reform rural

society, by making it more like their own, should only hasten the process of disruption. It is difficult for the planners of housing schemes, in their eagerness to confer urban amenities upon country people, to appreciate that the whole pattern of social relationships in a diffused society becomes meaningless when settlement is concentrated. There is no need to offer hospitality to the man who lives next door.

The traditional way of life seems, however, to have had some influence upon the work of local government bodies. A few years ago a new Central School was built in the countryside of the parish of Llangadfan and to it the older children went daily from the surrounding localities, including Pontllogel. But on the whole, educational reforms, designed as they are for a predominantly urban world, may well result in a further impoverishment of the life of the Welsh countryside. In Llanfihangel, the number of children attending the schools at Dolanog and Pontllogel became too small to conform with modern standards and both were closed while this book was being written. The children are now brought in cars to the Primary School at the Llan until they are eleven years of age, and then, apart from the few who go to Llangadfan, they proceed to the Secondary School at Llanfyllin. Judged by contemporary standards this is all to the good. The new Education Act is giving the country child an equal chance to compete with the urban child in the general struggle for social advancement—and, in that struggle, to have stayed at home reflects to no one's credit. But the countryside is thus being deprived of schoolmasters and schoolmistresses who used to be local leaders, and the children are being taught by implication to regard the town as the source of learning and culture. At the same time ministers are becoming fewer in the rural areas, and there are schemes afoot to group country parishes together into larger units to be served by centrally-placed clergymen.

The absence of real society in advanced circles is also manifested in the diversity of organisers, maintained by official and unofficial bodies, who visit the parish in turn, each offering his own particular brand of social activity: an adult class—to study any subject under the sun, with local option, a Youth Club, a Young Wales Club, a Young Farmers' Club, a Women's Institute, a Branch of the Farmers' Union. It is profoundly significant that none of these activities is designed for the community as a whole. They appeal, respectively, to the intellectually-minded, the young, the young farmers in particular, the women, and the farmers—the Old Age Pensioners' Club has not yet arrived. Each local group established in this way is linked organisationally with others of the same type in other localities and with a central office. The officials of the various organisations may meet occasionally at some county or national ' co-ordinating committee ', but there is nothing to tie the local units together on the spot, or to justify the one to the other. Indeed, one often finds them in competition, and there are several hamlets in Montgomeryshire where a succession of them has been established, each on the ruins of its predecessor. Thus does modern society try to instil new life into the countryside by commending to it its own specialisms. It is true that the pre-industrial rural society also had its itinerant specialists in the arts and crafts, but these, far from founding new social groups, were content to enrich the native life as they found it on the hearth and at other meeting-places.

Any social activity aroused in the countryside by remote control is bound to be superficial and short-lived, but modern society can do little else. Least of all can it prescribe a cure for the loosening of social ties until it achieves a new cohesion within itself. The failure of the urban world to give its inhabitants status and significance in a functioning society, and their consequent disintegration into formless masses of rootless nonentities, should make us humble in planning a new life for the countryside. The completeness of the traditional rural society—involving the cohesion of family, kindred and neighbours—and its capacity to give the individual a sense of belonging, are phenomena that might well be pondered by all who seek a better social order.

NOTES.

CHAPTER 1.   INTRODUCTION.

[1]The adjoining parishes are Llanfyllin (including the borough), Llan-rhaeadr, Llanwddyn, Llangadfan, Llanerfyl, Llanfair Caereinion, Llangynyw and Meifod.

[2] PLACES OF BIRTH OF OCCUPIERS, THEIR WIVES AND THEIR PARENTS.

Parish	Occupier	Occupier's		Wife	Wife's	
		Father	Mother		Father	Mother
	%	%	%	%	%	%
Llanfihangel	54.0	47.9	26.2	36.5	30.7	26.1
Adjoining Parishes	27.4	30.8	45.8	47.9	45.5	46.7
Neighbouring Parishes (not adjoining) ..	10.6	12.1	15.9	4.2	10.2	5.4
Other Districts	8.0	9.2	12.1	11.4	13.6	21.8

[3] DEMOGRAPHIC TABLES.

(a) *Census Figures for Llanfihangel Parish.*

Year.	Total.	Males.	Females.
1801	814	409	405
1811	818	407	411
1821	938	496	440
1831	906	594	412
1841	1041	545	496
1851	1029	542	487
1861	950	494	456
1871	883	477	406
1881	818	457	361
1891	767	410	357
1901	643	331	312
1911	661	364	297
1921	639	345	294
1931	590	320	270
1940*	498	270	228

* The figures for 1940 do not include the staff and pupils of a small private school which was temporarily evacuated to Dolanog, nor the small number of other evacuees who still remained in the parish.   According to the National Registration Census, the population in September, 1939, was 544 (including many evacuees).   In mid–summer 1948 it was estimated to be 520.

(b)   *Age and Marital Condition*, 1940.

Age Group	Total Pop.	Males. Single.	Married.	Widow-ed.	Total.	Females. Single.	Married.	Widow-ed.	Total.
0-9	62	28	—	—	28	34	—	—	34
10-19	87	50	—	—	50	37	—	—	37
20-29	68	35	5	—	40	13	14	1	28
30-39	81	17	26	—	43	10	27	1	38
40-49	63	7	25	—	32	5	24	2	31
50-59	66	11	21	2	34	3	25	4	32
60-69	39	4	15	5	24	1	9	5	15
70-79	29	—	9	8	17	1	6	5	12
80-	3	—	1	1	2	1	—	—	1
Totals	498	152	102	16	270	105	105	18	228

(c)   *Percentage of Population in Different Age-Groups.*

Age Group	Total Population Llanfihangel	England and Wales	Males Llanfihangel	England and Wales	Females Llanfihangel	England and Wales
0-9	12.4	13.9	10.4	14.7	14.9	13.2
10-19	17.5	16.0	18.5	16.8	16.2	15.2
20-29	13.7	15.8	14.8	16.2	12.3	15.4
30-39	16.3	16.0	15.9	16.2	16.7	15.8
40-49	12.7	13.3	11.9	12.7	13.6	13.9
50-59	13.3	11.4	12.6	11.0	14.0	12.2
60-69	7.9	8.4	8.9	8.1	6.6	8.8
70-79	5.8	4.0	6.3	3.6	5.3	4.4
80-	.6	1.0	.7	7.7	.4	1.2
Totals ..	100.0	100.0	100.0	100.0	100.0	100.0

(d)   *Percentage of Males and Females in Different Age-Groups.*

Age Group	Llanfihangel Males	Females	England and Wales Males	Females
All Ages	54.5	45.5	47.8	52.8
0.9	45.2	54.8	50.7	49.3
10-19	57.5	42.5	50.5	49.5
20-29	58.8	41.2	49.3	50.7
30-39	53.1	49.9	48.6	51.4
40-49	50.8	49.2	45.7	54.3
50-59	51.5	48.5	45.8	54.2
60-69	61.5	38.5	46.0	54.0
70-79	58.6	41.4	42.6	57.4
80-	66.7	33.3	35.6	64.4

[4] The Church of ' Lannyhagel ' was included in Pope Nicholas's Taxation, circa 1291, *Montgomeryshire Collections*, II (1869), p. 89.

[5] See R. Williams, ' History of the Parish of Llanfyllin ', *Montgomeryshire Collections*, III (1870), pp. 51 ff.

[6] See J. E. Lloyd, *A History of Wales* (London, 1911), I, pp. 247-8 ; J. E. Roberts and R. Owen, *The Story of Montgomeryshire* (London, 1916), pp. 169-72, 140.

[7] See *Montgomeryshire Collections*, V. (1872), pp. 399 ff., XIV. (1881), pp. 355 ff.

CHAPTER II. THE ECONOMY.

[1] SIZE OF HOLDINGS INCLUDING ROUGH GRAZING.

Acreage of Holding	1840		1940	
	Number	Percentage	Number	Percentage
House and Garden ..	19	11.6	16	12.3
1-5 acres	19	11.6	4	3.1
5-10 acres	14	8.5	15	11.5
10-15 acres	10	6.1	10	7.7
15-20 acres	6	3.7	3	2.3
20-30 acres	10	6.1	9	6.9
30-40 acres	10	6.1	5	3.8
40-50 acres	11	6.7	7	5.4
50-100 acres	23	14.0	18	13.8
100-150 acres	27	16.5	29	22.3
150-200 acres	10	6.1	5	3.8
200-300 acres	4	2.4	5	3.8
300-400 acres	—	—	3	2.3
Over 600 acres ..	1	.6	1	.8
Totals ..	164	100.0	130	100.0

[2] I have been unable to trace the papers of the Vaughans of Llwydiarth which might have thrown light on the early history of the holdings. A Latin document of 1309 gives a list of land holders, without naming the holdings (*Mont. Coll.* I. (1868), p. 157), and there are passing references in early fifteenth century papers to three settlements whose sites are still occupied and also to a *gafael* of free land called ' gavell Lloidiarth ' of which Sir Griffith Vaughan held a twentieth part. (*Mont. Coll.* IV. (1871), pp. 342-4 ; V. (1872), pp. 400-1.

[3] For a recent study of the dispersal of plots in the *gafael* see T. Jones Pierce, ' The Gafael in Bangor MS ' 1939,' *Trans. Hon. Soc. Cymmrodorion*, 1942, pp. 158-89.

It is also noteworthy that joint occupation of poor unenclosed land survived in northern Montgomeryshire until recent times. Dr. I. C. Peate quotes the following evidence from the nearby Parish of Garthbeibio. ' The Waun . . was divided between a number of farmers, each piece being known as a ' parcel ' . . . No such term as acre . . . was used, the land being measured in another way : the term used was ' the work of a scytheman ' (' gwaith gŵr a phladur '). The parcels varied from the ' work of two ' to ' the work of ten men with scythes ' . . . The boundary between each parcel was formed by a narrow piece of unpared land.' The former existence of such a practice in Llanfihangel is shown by such field-names as *Rhos dengwr*

(the *rhos* of ten men) and *Gweirglodd pedair pladur* (the meadow of four scythes). In the case cited by Dr. Peate (*Welsh House*, p. 119) the parcels did not necessarily belong to the farms adjoining them, and such an arrangement would explain some of the unattached fields of Llanfihangel in 1842. This method of parcelling open land without fencing is analogous to the way in which mountain pasture is still divided into sheep-runs. Although there are no fences each farmer knows his boundaries, and so do the old wethers and ewes kept to prevent the younger sheep from trespassing. The old sheep are always bought by an incoming tenant so that a knowledge of the boundaries may be preserved in the flock.

⁴ Powis Court Rolls, N.L.W. MSS.

⁵ A copy of the Award under this Act is in the custody of the Rector of Llanfihangel.

⁶ In order to compare the intensity of stocking at different dates and to measure the relative importance of cattle and sheep, the various classes of animals have been measured in Fig. 8 by a common denominator, the equivalent of one cow, known to agricultural economists as a ' stock unit '. Dairy cattle, 'other cattle over 2 years old,' and horses are represented as full units, while 1 cow equals 2 ' other cattle under 2 years old ' : 9 sheep : 15 lambs : 9 pigs : 100 poultry.

⁷ The following statistics have been extracted from the files of the Ministry of Agriculture.

LAND UTILISATION

Crop.	1870. Acres.	1890. Acres.	1914. Acres.	1918. Acres.	1939 Acres.
Wheat	426	293	106	369	12
Barley	245	226	196	269	28
Oats	707	757	639	1028	477
Mixed Corn	x	x	x	39	58
Rye	—	8	4	—	—
Beans and Peas	3	2	—	2	—
Potatoes	82	60	46	57	27
Turnips and Swedes	160	172	133	112	31
Mangolds	—	—	5	6	10
Rape (or Cole)	—	—	—	—	55
Vetches and Tares	1	1	2	—	7
Other tillage crops	—	1	1	1	—
Total acreage of tillage	1624	1520	1132	1883	705
Bare fallow	130	18	8	—	3
Clover, sainfoin and Temporary Grasses : (a) For mowing	556	453	520	458	566
(b) Not for mowing	298	269	300	195	329
Total Acreage of Arable Land	2608	2260	1960	2536	1603
Permanent Grass : (a) For mowing this season	919	1187	1034	981	1156
(b) Not for mowing this season	2474	4457	5160	4403	4779
Total Cultivated Area	6001	7904	8149	7918	7536
Rough Grazing	x	x	1500	2019	2351

Stock	1870.	1890.	1914.	1918.	1939.
Horses for Agricultural purposes (including mares for breeding)	178	246	213	226	170
All other horses	150	210	264	262	157
Total Horses	328	456	477	488	327
Cows and heifers in milk			478	429	430
Cows in calf, not in milk	573	611	51	58	48
Heifers in calf with first calf			40	33	91
Bulls used for service	x	x	x	x	14
Bulls and bull-calves reared for service	x	x	x	x	2
Other cattle : 2 years and above	365	279	156	154	133
1 year and under 2	596	785	501	594	628
Under 1 year			588	557	562
Total Cattle	1534	1675	1814	1825	1908
Ewes kept for breeding	3267	3233	4199	4586	6374
Other sheep over 1 year old			672	538	940
Ewe lambs for breeding in current year	1850	2450	4168	4191	590
Other sheep and lambs under 1 year					5406
Total Sheep and Lambs	5117	5683	9039	9315	13310
Total Pigs	546	604	542	391	559
Total Poultry	x	x	x	x	8793

x – no information available.

8 See A. W. Ashby and I. L. Evans, *The Agriculture of Wales* (Cardiff. 1944), pp. 100 ff.

9 The rents varied from 4/9 to 14/9 per acre for holdings over 50 acres, according to altitude, aspect, accessibility and condition of buildings, while the most representative figure was about 10/6 per acre. On holdings of 20-50 acres the rent ranged from 8/- to 20/- per acre, but the average did not exceed 11/6. The rents of holdings under 20 acres varied from 8/- to 30/- per acre, but this is a misleading measure since the rent of the house formed an appreciable part of the total for holdings of this size. Houses without land on the estate were usually small and primitive and their average rental did not exceed £4 per annum.

10 OCCUPATION OF SMALLHOLDERS.

	Holdings under 20 acres.	Holdings of 20 - 50 acres.
Full-time farming	9	15
Estate, forestry and road workers	13	2
Farm-workers	4	—
Craftsmen	3	1
Shopkeepers and postmen	3	2
Totals	32	20

[11] Cf. Elwyn Davies, 'Sheep Farming in Upland Wales', *Geography*, XX. (1935) pp. 97-111.

[12] Data : 366 marriages recorded in the Registers, 1885-1940.

[13] A. W. Ashby and I. L. Evans, *op. cit.*, Ch. X.

CHAPTER III. HOUSE AND HEARTH.

[1] I. C. Peate, *The Welsh House* (London, 1940), Ch. IV.

[2] For hall plan see N. Lloyd, *A History of the English House* (London, 1931) ; J. A. Gotch, *The Growth of the English House* (London, 1928), Chs. II and III.   For houses in Northern England analogous to the oblong house of Llanfihangel, see S. O. Addy, *The Evolution of the English House* (1933 ed.), pp. 68, 71, 73.

[3] *Ancient Laws and Institutes of Wales* Ed. Aneurin Owen, (London, 1842), I, pp. 78-9, 192-3, 486-7.

[4] *ibid* II, pp. 584-7.

[5] I. C. Peate, *op cit.*, p. 126.

[6] The *cegin* is called *y neuadd* in parts of Carmarthenshire, see W. Ll. Williams, *Gwilym a Benni Bach* (1945), *passim* ; Mr. T. J. Hughes who is making a social survey of Aberdaron in the Llŷn Peninsula informs me that the same term is used there.

[7] N. Lloyd, *op. cit.*, pp. 292-3.

[8] Both Aneurin Owen (*op. cit.*, I., pp. 292-3) and Dr. Peate (*op. cit.*, p. 131), translate *cell* as 'chamber'. Mr. S. J. Williams and Mr. J. E. Powell interpret it as 'store', and draw attention to the current use of *cell* for 'pantry' in parts of South Wales (*Cyfreithiau Hywel Dda yn ôl Llyfr Blegywryd*, Caerdydd, 1942, Geirfa).

[9] S. O. Addy, *op. cit.*, pp. 81, 82.

[10] N. Lloyd, *op. cit.*, p. 14.

[11] A barn at Tŷ Brith, located between Llanfihangel and Llanfyllin, contains three pairs of crucks arranged as shown in Fig. 35a, and a fourth pair (Fig. 35b) helps to support the roof of a cowhouse.   The ruins of a farmhouse in Llanfihangel called Halfen Uchaf contain the rotting remains of crucks and in 1940 those indicated in Fig. 35c were still standing.   On cruck construction generally, see C. F. Innocent, *The Development of English Building Construction* (London, 1916) ; S. O. Addy, *op. cit* ; H. H. Hughes and H. L. North, *The Old Cottages of Snowdonia* (Bangor, 1908) ; I. C. Peate, *op. cit.*, Ch. VIII.

[12] See, for example, A. Bertram, *The House, A Machine to Live In* (London) 1935), p. 17 ; N. Lloyd, *op. cit.* pp. 18 ff. ; A. H. Thompson, *The English House* (London, 1936), *passim*.

[13] *Pentan*, which means 'hob' in modern Welsh, is translated in the Latin texts of the Welsh Laws sometimes in the restricted sense of *pentanfaen* (*lapis focarius*), while in other places it is given the more general meaning of *focarius*.   It is derived from *pen-tân* (fire-end) and this adds to the significance of such medieval terms as *gwyl bentan* (fire-end festival), *chwedlau pentan* (fire-end stories) and *tuddedyn pentan* (a garment of homespun,—i.e. a garment made on the hearth).   For these terms see *Ancient Laws*, I., 308, II, 744, ix. ; *Myvyrian Archaiology*[2] (1870), p. 825a. 18.   The fireplace of a smithy is still called *y pentan* in modern Welsh.   The wider meaning is also suggested by the proverb : *Angel pen ffordd a diawl pentân* (an angel on the highway and a devil on the hearth), as well as by the triad which lists the three essentials of a serf,—his vat, his lance and his *pentan*.   *Ancient Laws*, I., 76-7.   A small cottage near Pontardulais, in Carmarthenshire, is known as Pentan Iago, which suggests a meaning analogous to " fire-house", one of the oldest English terms for 'living-room '.

[14] This description is limited to observations made in Llanfihangel ; for further details as to household furnishings in general, see I. C. Peate, *Guide to the Collection of Welsh Bygones* (in the National Museum of Wales,

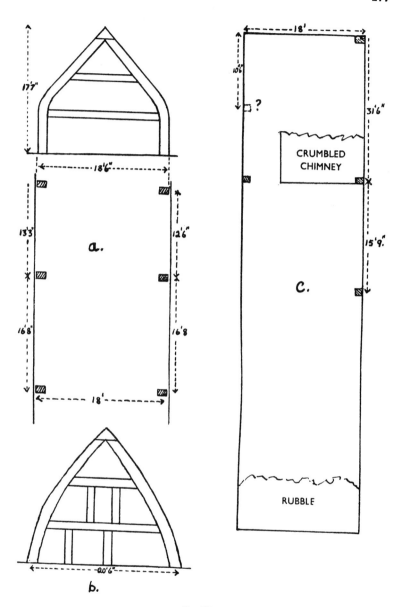

Fig. 35.

Cardiff 1929) ; *Guide to the Collection Illustrating Welsh Folk Crafts and Industries* (in the National Museum of Wales, Cardiff 1935).

[15] See S. O. Addy, *op. cit.*, pp. 68-9 ; E. E. Evans, *Irish Heritage* (Dundalk, 1942), p. 68.

[16] S. O. Addy, *op. cit.*, p. 79.

[17] E. E. Evans, *op cit.* pp. 72-3.

CHAPTER IV. FARMSTEADS.

[1] E. E. Evans, *Irish Heritage*, p. 79.

[2] Literally *y penllawr* means ' the floor-end,' and Dr. Peate, influenced perhaps by the fact that the living-room is called *y llawr* (the floor) in parts of North Wales, interprets it as ' the end, or head of the floor ' of the dwelling-part of the ' long-house ' (*The Welsh House*, p. 65).   But whereas *pen-y-llawr* might give us *penllawr* it does not easily become *y penllawr*. Cf. *Pen-y-bont* may become *Penbont*, but it is not called *Y Penbont*. It seems to me more likely that *penllawr* connotes ' the end (or place ?) where the (threshing)-floor is, c.f. *pentan* (fire-end), the end where the fire is) and *pen-tŷ* (house-end)— the end where the house is, not the extremity of the house—a word which is now used in Llanfihangel for a dwelling-house as opposed to a smallholding). In South Cardiganshire long houses the *penllawr* is often a step lower than the house-floor and is called *y llawr isaf* (the lower floor), which shows that it is a floor in itself and not the ' head ' of another one.   Whereas Dr. Peate equates *penllawr* with *bing* or ' feeding-walk,' the majority of the examples which he depicts are between 5½ and 6½ feet wide.   This extravagant use of space has to be accounted for.   It is true that *barn*-floors are generally wider than this, but I have seen the use of the flail demonstrated on a floor-space which was at least as narrow as the average *penllawr*. Addy's descriptions of English ' long-houses ' similar to the Welsh type prove the origin of the feature beyond all reasonable doubt.   In these ' the main entrance to the building was a passage which divided the ' fire-house ' from the ox-house or barn, and which was the threshing floor. This passage was known by various names. Anciently it was called the ' floor ' or ' threshold,' a word which means threshing floor, because in ancient times the floor at the entrance was for threshing.' (*The Evolution of the English House* (London, 1933 ed.), pp. 81-3, 97-8.)

[3] *Ancient Laws*, I., p. 321.

[4] For numbers of horses see Note 7 to Chapter I.

[5] C.f. W. Llewelyn Williams, '*Slawer Dydd* (1918), p. 12.

CHAPTER V. THE FAMILY

[1] A. W. Ashby and I. L. Evans, *The Agriculture of Wales*, p. 7.

[2] MALE LABOUR ON FARMS OVER TWENTY ACRES.

Age Group	Occupier	Sons		Other Relatives	Non-relatives	
		Single	Married		Single	Married
14-19	—	9	—	3	13	—
20-29	5	10	2	2	11	—
30-39	21	6	3	1	2	—
40-49	13	3	1	—	1	1
50-59	14	1	—	3	—	1
60-69	12	—	—	3	1	1
70 and over	7	—	—	2	—	—
Totals	72	29	6	14	28	3

FEMALE LABOUR ON FARMS OVER TWENTY ACRES.

Age Group	Female Occupier	Occupier's Wife	Daughters Single	Daughters Married	Other Relatives	Non-relatives Single	Non-relatives Married
14-19	—	—	8	—	1	3	—
29-29	—	10	8	3	3	4	—
30-39	—	15	3	1	4	2	1
40-49	—	13	1	1	1	1	—
50-59	1	12	—	—	2	1	—
60-69	5	5	—	—	1	—	—
70 and over	3	2	—	—	1	—	—
Totals	9	57	20	5	13	11	1

³ *Ancient Laws*, I, pp. 516-7.

⁴ The graphs were constructed from the following data : *England and Wales* : Table G in *Registrar General's Statistical Review* (1938). *Llanfihangel* : First marriages entered in the Registers of Llanfihangel and District, 1886-1940, in which one or both parties resided in Llanfihangel Parish. Numbers : Males, 307, Females, 320. Between 1890 and 1940:—111 farmers' sons, 163 farmers' daughters ; 132 sons of labourers and craftsmen, 113 daughters of labourers and craftsmen. The occupations of the fathers of bride and bridegroom are entered in the Registers, but it is possible that some labourers occupying smallholdings have been described as farmers. There may therefore be a margin of error in these calculations.

⁵ *Disparity in Ages of Spouses* (Sample : 322 first marriages).

	Per cent.
Wife older than husband	16.7
Husband and wife approximately the same age	12.5
Husband older than wife by one to three years	22.7
Husband older than wife by four to seven years	26.1
Husband older than wife by eight years or more	22.0

⁶ See C. M. Arensberg, *The Irish Countryman* (London, 1937), pp. 85 sq, *et passim*. H. Miner, *St. Denis : A French Canadian Parish* (Chicago, 1939), p. 63 sq. *et passim* ; G. C. Homans, *English Villagers of the Thirteenth Century* (Harvard, 1942), pp. 135 sq.

⁷ See for example A. Myrdal, *Nation and Family* (London, 1945), p. 51; E. M. Hubback, *The Population of Britain* (London, 1947), p. 106.

⁸ See T. P. Ellis, *Welsh Tribal Law and Custom in the Middle Ages*, 2 vols., (Oxford, 1926) ; F. Seebohm, *Tribal System in Wales* (London, 1904) ; J. E. Lloyd, *History of Wales*, I., pp. 283 ff.

⁹ *Ancient Laws*, I, p. 761, II., p. 64.

¹⁰ G. C. Homans, *op cit.*, pp. 170 sq ; T. P. Ellis, *op cit.*, I., p. 390.

CHAPTER VI. KINDRED.

¹ T. P. Ellis, *op cit.* I., pp. 432-3.

² On Alternate Generations see A. M. Hocart, *Man.*, 1931 §214 ; 1938, §31 ; A. D. Rees, *Man*, 1938 §168, J. L. Myres, *ibid.* §169.

³ Of 74 eldest sons 32 inherited their paternal grandfather's name, combined with that of the maternal grandfather in 16 cases, while the latter occurred without the former in 8 cases. The father's name occurred in 14 cases, either alone or combined with others. The names of other relatives or the mother's maiden name were present in 11 cases, again either singly or joined to others. There were only 16 of these 74 full names which, as far as I could judge from the incomplete genealogies at my disposal, had no family significance.

CHAPTER VII. YOUTH.

[1] For ' Consociation ' see A. R. Radcliffe Brown, *Africa*, XIII. (1940, pp. 195-210 ; R. E. Moreau, *ibid*, XIV. (1944), pp. 386 sq. ; F. Eggan (Ed.) *Social Anthropology of North American Tribes* (Chicago, 1937), pp. 75-81.

[2] A. Myrdal, *Nation and Family* (London, 1945), pp. 42–4.

[3] A. M. Hocart, *Kings and Councillors* (Cairo, 1936), p. 132.

[4] *Black Venus* (London, 1944).

[5] For a comprenhensive study, see K.R.V. Wickman, ' Die Einleitung der Ehe : Eine vergleichend ethnosoziologische Untersuchung über die Vorstufe der Ehe in den Sitten des schwedischen Volkstums.' *Acta Academiae Aboensis*, XI. (Abo. 1937), pp. 1–384.

[6] C. R. Baskervill, English Songs of the Night Visit. *Publ. Mod. Lang. Ass. Amer.*, XXXVI. (1921), pp. 565-614.

[7] T. Gwynn Jones, *Welsh Folklore and Folk Custom* (London, 1930), p. 186.

[8] Of another sample of 95 families from the district, 16 had no issue, while in 36 cases (45.6 per cent) the first child was born within 8 months of marriage.

[9] *Registrar General's Statistical Review* (1939), Pt. II., pp. 107–109.

[10] The illegitimacy rate per thousand live-births is, of course, a misleading abstraction since the factors affecting the number of legitimate and illegitimate births are not the same. It has to be used here owing to the absence of statistics giving age and sex distribution per parish, but it should be realised that the incidence of illegitimacy in rural areas is actually higher than is indicated by this method, because the proportion of unmarried to married women is relatively small. Thus, during the Census year of 1931, the illegitimacy rate per thousand unmarried women aged 15–45 was as follows : England and Wales, 5.7 ; Montgomeryshire, 10.6 ; Montgomeryshire Rural Districts, 13.4 ; Llanfyllin Rural District, 15.9.

[11] For distribution maps and analysis see A. Leffingwell, *Illegitimacy and the Influence of the Seasons upon Conduct* (1892). On Wales, see *Royal Commission on Land in Wales* (1893), *Report*, pp. 632 ff.

[12] C. M. Arensberg, *The Irish Countryman*, pp. 94 sq.

[13] T. P. Ellis, *Welsh Tribal Law and Custom*, I., pp. 450 sq.

[14] *Itinerary through Wales*, Ed. W. Ll. Williams, p. 195. (London, 1908.)

[15] T. P. Ellis, *op. cit.* I., p. 392.

[16] G. C. Homans, *op. cit.*, p. 166.

CHAPTER VIII. NEIGHBOURS.

[1] See G. C. Homans, *op. cit.* pp. 216-7.

[2] Lord Raglan writes of lowland Monmouthshire : ' Another thing that I noticed is how very rarely country people go into one another's houses, unless they are relatives or have some business there. It is not unusual to find a farmer's wife who has never set foot inside the next farmhouse '. (*Folk-Lore* (1946), p. 101.

[3] See for example M. J. Herskovits, *The Economic Life of Primitive Peoples* (New York, 1940), pp. 82 sq. ; A. M. Hocart, *Kings and Councillors* (Cairo, 1936), pp. 215, 218 ; J. F. Embree, *A. Japanese Village* (London, 1946), pp. 75, 95.

[4] C.f. T. Hughes Jones, *Scweier Hafila* (Llandebie, 1941), pp. 40 ff.

[5] Giraldus Cambrensis, *op. cit.* p. 184.

[6] *ibid.*, p. 169.

CHAPTER IX. NEIGHBOURHOODS AND HAMLETS.

[1] The Parish contains a Melin-wnfa and a Melin Cadwnfa, and there is a township of Cadwnfa. But *Gwynfa* seems to have been the original form. An early fourteenth century manuscript mentions *Guinna* and also *molendino de Guinna* (*Mont. Coll.* I. (1868), p. 157), and an early fifteenth century document mentions *Melyn Gwynva* (*Mont. Coll.* IV (1871), pp. 342-4 ; V. (1872), pp. 400-1). Cadwnfa is spelt *Cadwynfa* in seventeenth and eighteenth century Powjs Court Rolls (N.L.W. MSS).

[2] M. C. Jones, The Territorial Divisions of Montgomeryshire, *Mont. Coll.* II. (1869), p. 108 sq.

[3] See R. Williams, History of the Parish of Llanfyllin, *Mont. Coll.* III (1870), pp. 51 sq. ; E. A. Lewis, *Mediaeval Boroughs of Snowdonia*, (London, 1912), pp. 11, 14 ; *English Historical Review*, XV. (1900), p. 318.

[4] Compare the lists of Commotes, Manors and Hundreds in *Royal Commission on Land in Wales, Report*, p. 16, *Appendices*, p. 451, pp. 371-2.

[5] Two of the townships of Llanfihangel are mentioned in a Latin document written in 1309—Garth g[   ] and Finnoun Arthur. *Mont. Coll.* I., p. 157).

Mr. Glanville Jones, M.A., who has made a special study of the political and economic geography of medieval Wales, has given me the following statement regarding the antiquity of townships in general.

' The *tref* envisaged in the Welsh Laws and subsequently described as *vill* by the Anglo-Norman surveyors was essentially a rural administrative district, similar to the modern parish, but usually less extensive. For instance, there were within the parishes of Brithdir and Dolgelley no less than seven vills in 1293(a). Today there are within these two parishes a corresponding number of sub-units with well-defined physical boundaries described as townships. Five of them bear the same names as the vills of the thirteenth century. As far as can be ascertained from data included in an Elizabethan survey of the commote(b), the boundaries of the present townships appear to coincide with those of the medieval vills. A similar survival of medieval administrative structures is apparent even on the Welsh border. For instance every medieval vill in the Chirkland commote of Nanheudwy as recorded in 1293(c), and 1391-93(d) was represented in recent years by a township bearing the same name. Wherever reasonably detailed evidence is available the administrative *tref* or vill of medieval Wales appears to have been co-extensive with the township of the present day '.

(a) P.R.O. Lay Subsidy, 242/53 ; (b) P.R.O. Misc. Land Revenue, 2/236 folios 1-49 ; (c) P.R.O. Lay Subsidy, 242/55 ; Jones, G. P., ' The Extent of Chirkland ', 1391/1393 (1833), pp. 1/62.

The boundaries of the Townships in Fig. 30 have been taken from the maps contained in the Award under the Enclosure Act of 1811 to which reference has already been made.

[6] T. Rees and J. Thomas, *Hanes Eglwysi Annibynnol Cymru* (Liverpool, 1871), I, pp. 862-4.

[7] See T. Jones Pierce, A Caernarvonshire Manorial Borough, *Caern. Hist. Soc. Trans.*, 1941, pp. 9 ff.

[8] The Welsh elements in the culture of the industrial towns of Wales, such as the strong home life, extreme hospitality and perpetual visiting characteristic of mining communities, are also transplantations from the countryside. Even some of their less reputable traits, such as the nepotism of which their local government committees are often accused, appear to be cases of what was social in a familistic society becoming anti-social under urban conditions. A consideration ot the ancestry of candidates may not be very relevant to the selection of a schoolmaster, but it can at least be understood in terms of the rural society with its loyalty to kinsmen and its

assessment of a person's qualities by reference to the rock from which he was hewn. Again, the well-known practice whereby councillors appoint one another's friends and relatives in turn, on the principle that one good turn deserves another, may have little to commend it, but, to whatever extent it is more prevalent in Wales than elsewhere, it can be explained as an unworthy relative of *talu'r pwyth* (repaying the stitch) which is rooted in the reciprocities of the countryside.

CHAPTER X.   RELIGION.

[1] Ralph Linton, *The Study of Man* (New York, 1936), pp. 302-3.

[2] *ibid.* p. 463

[3] R. T. Jenkins, *Hanes Cymru yn y Ddeunawfed Ganrif* (Caerdydd, 1931), pp. 74-5, 102-3.

[4] See Owen M. Edwards, *Gwaith Ann Griffiths* (Conwy, 1905) ; Evan Isaac, *Prif Emynwyr Cymru* (Lerpwl, 1925) ; *Cymru* (1906).

In 1904 an Ann Griffiths Memorial Chapel was erected at Dolanog and paid for by a nation-wide collection. The nineteenth century farmhouse which now stands on the site of Ann Griffiths' birthplace, the Memorial Chapel, and her grave in Llanfihangel Churchyard attract dozens of summer visitors. The parlour at Dolwar Fach has been set aside as ' Ann Griffiths' Room ' for the reception of the pilgrims. Her picture, reproduced from an effigy in the Chapel, hangs on the wall, and there is a chair alleged to be Ann Griffiths' chair and a visitors' book. At Llanfihangel Rectory the visitor may call to see her signature in the Marriage Register and the relevant entries in the Register of Baptisms and Burials.

The visitors seldom stay more than an hour or two, and its historical associations have little effect upon the daily life of the parish. Strangers in the hamlet of Llanfihangel arouse a momentary interest, but if they are making their way towards the church they are soon dismissed as " *rhai o blant Ann* "(some of Ann's children). A few families claim to be of the same stock as Ann Griffiths or her husband, and most of the inhabitants are familiar with her more well-known hymns. On the other hand, nothing seems to be known of her life apart from what the more interested may have culled from literary sources. She is sometimes referred to as " *Yr Hen Ann* " (the old Ann) in Llanfihangel as elsewhere, and one legend may be cited here as an example of the unreliability of ' folk-memory.' There is a narrow path along the side of a deeply embedded stream between Dolanog and the neighbouring hamlet of Pontrobert where Ann Griffiths used to attend a place of worship. It is said that while walking along this dangerous path she composed the well-known hymn :

> *Cul yw'r llwybyr i mi gerdded,*
> *Is fy llaw mae dyfnder mawr,*
> *Ac 'rwy'n ofni yn fy nghalon*
> *Rhag i'm traed i lithro i lawr.*

(Narrow is the path I tread, below me is a great depth, and I fear in my heart lest my feet should slip). The metaphor fits the setting well, but the hymn was written by William Williams of Pant–y–celyn, around whose home in the hills of north-eastern Carmarthenshire one would doubtless find many a precipitous path.

[5] See Robert Gittins, Dolanog, *Cymru* (1906), pp. 93 ff., p. 98.

[6] See for example, E. G. Bowen, *Wales, A Study in Geography and History* (Cardiff, 1941), pp. 85 ff.

[7] J. Morgan Jones, Eglwys Maldwyn, in *Hen Gapel Llanbrynmair.* (Llandysul, 1939), ed. I. C. Peate, pp. 24-5.

ᴰDATES OF ERECTION OF PLACES OF WORHSIP.

Episcopal Church.	*Independents.*	*Baptists.*
Parish Church, rebuilt 1862.	Dolanog, 1810 (now closed).	Pontllogel, 1823 (now closed).
Dolanog, 1855.	Pen–llys, 1822.	
Pontllogel, 1864.	Sardis, 1827.	
	Braich-y-waun, 1842.	

Methodists (Calvinistic).	*Methodists (Wesleyan).*
Siloh, 1832.	Braich-y-waun, 1842-3.
Dolanog, 1830.	Dolwar, 1843.
Gad, 1858.	

T. Rees and J. Thomas, *Hanes Eglwysi Annibynnol Cymru* (1871), Vol. I., pp. 370-1, 862-4 ; J. Spinther James, *Hanes y Bedyddwyr yng Nghymru* (1893-8), Vol. IV., pp. 224-5 ; H. Jones, *Hanes Wesleyaeth yng Nghymru* (1911-13) ; Vol. II., p. 734 ; E. Griffiths, *Hanes Methodistiaeth Trefaldwyn Uchaf* (1914), pp. 113 sq., 143 sq ; D. R. Thomas, *History of the Diocese of St. Asaph* (1874), pp. 758-61.

The Calvinistic Methodists are now officially called The Presbyterian Church of Wales, and the Wesleyan Methodists have become The Methodist Church of Wales. The new names are, however, hardly ever used. To the average Welshman, the former are ' the Methodists ' and the latter ' the Wesleyans.'

[9] G. D. Owen, *Ysgolion a Cholegau yr Annibynwyr* (Abertawe, 1939) pp. 112-5.

[10] H. Jones, *op. cit.* II, p. 734.

[11] See *Cymru* (1906), pp. 98-9.
> *Nid a Harri Parri per—i wrando*
> *Ar Rowndiaid na Chwacer,*
> *Dynion sydd o dan y ser*
> *Yn peidio dweyd eu pader.*

[12] Bernard Manning, *The Making of Modern English Religion,* (London, 1929), p. 104., c.f. E. A. Payne, *The Free Church Tradition in the Life of England* (London, 1944), p. 143.

[13] See R. T. Jenkins, Hywel Dda : Some Afterthoughts, *Welsh Outlook,* XV., (1928), pp. 146 ff.

[14] References to play-acting and dancing in medieval Welsh literature are extremely rare, and throughout subsequent centuries the role of these arts in Welsh culture bears no comparison with that of poetry. The poor development of drama in modern Wales has often been attributed to religious prejudice, but it is noteworthy that its history before the Methodist Revival—when it flourished in England—was extremely unpromising.

There seem to be no Welsh words of native origin for ' dance '. Both *carol* and the current *dawns* are borrowed terms. References to dancing in sixteenth and seventeenth century literature are vague, satirical or condemnatory, or couched in English terms. The ' folk-dances ' recorded in recent times—generally in areas open to English influence—have English names in most cases, and little can be said with any certainty about the history of the art in Wales. For what is known and surmised see W. S. Gwynn Williams, *Welsh National Music and Dance* (London, 1932) ; H. Mellor, *Welsh Folk Dances* (London, 1935) ; and Lois Blake, *Welsh Folk Dance* (Llangollen, 1948). It is significant that in Ireland " The professional poet did not care for songs. There could be nothing like a ballad, in the old sense of a song to accompany a dance, for dancing was unknown in Ireland until modern times. In the old Gaelic world the chief delight of the cultivated classes was to listen to a poem, often as unrhythmical as the Welsh *cywydd*, recited or

chanted to harp music. . . . Choirs and community singing were also un-
known. Until recently all songs in Irish were solos." (O. J. Bergin, On the
Origin of Modern Irish Rhythmical Verse, in *Mélanges Linguistiques offerts à
M. Holger Pedersen*–Copenhagen, 1937), p. 284.

[15] T. Gwynn Jones, *op cit.*, p. 218.

[16] Giraldus Cambrensis, *op. cit.*, p. 174.

CHAPTER XI. RECREATION AND ENTERTAINMENT.

[1] Walter Map, *De Nugis Curialium*, Ed. E. S. Hartland (London, 1923),
p. 99.

[2] Giraldus Cambrensis, *op. cit.*, p. 175.

[3] T. Gwynn Jones, *op. cit.*, pp. 161-2.

[4] The name is reminiscent of the medieval ' Festival of Fools ', but this
was usually' held during the Christmas season and not in May. See E. K.
Chambers, *The Mediaeval Stage* (Oxford, 1903), I., pp. 274 ff.

[5] John Jones (Ioan Lenydd), *Llef yn Erbyn Ofergoeledd ac Ysbrydegaeth*
(1901). I am indebted to the Reverend J. H. Richards of Llanfyllin for draw-
ing my attention to this tract.

[6] In *Canu Penillion* (lit. singing of stanzas) the singer does not sing the
notes of the tune : the melody is played by the accompanist, traditionally a
harpist, while the singer chants his stanzas in a simple counterpoint to the air,
starting each verse a bar or more after the instrument.

CHAPTER XII. STATUS AND PRESTIGE.

[1] Sample : 70 farmers of holdings over twenty acres. An investigation
of the social origin of a sample of 834 farmers from eleven Welsh counties
undertaken in 1925 produced comparable results to those obtained from Llanfihangel. Of this sample, 75 per cent were sons of farmers, 11 per cent were
sons of farm-workers, and 7.5 per cent were sons of other manual workers.
See A. W. Ashby and J. Morgan Jones, The Social Origin of Welsh Farmers,
Welsh Journ. Agri., II., p. 12.

[2] Of the wives of 7 farmers of over 50 acres who were themselves sons of
farm-workers, 5 were farmers' daughters and 2 the daughters of farm-workers.

[3] The occupation of the husbands of 114 farmers' daughters over 40 years
of age were as follows :

Farmers	76.3 per cent.
Labourers and smallholders	8.0 per cent.
Craftsmen	7.0 per cent.
Others	8.7 per cent.

[4] *Occupations of Farmers' Sons.*
Sample : 218 sons and brothers (over 35 years of age) of occupiers of
over 20 acres who were themselves the sons of farmers. Farmers, 78 per cent;
smallholders, bailiffs, farm-workers, 9 per cent ; craftsmen, miners, shopkeepers, railwaymen and professional workers, 13 per cent.

[5] The exact date at which the families of present occupiers or their wives
acquired their holdings could not be ascertained in many cases, but the following table, based on local memory and upon lists of tenants dating from 1842
and 1875, may be taken as a rough summary for the 61 farms over 50 acres.

Date	Percentage.
Before 1840	20.0
1840 - 1879	8.3
1880 - 1899	15.0
1900 - 1909	5.0
1910 - 1919	15.0
1920 - 1929	13.3
1930 - 1940	21.7

The evidence is more scanty for holdings of less than 50 acres. Only 7.8 per cent can be shown with any certainty to have remained in the same family since 1840, and this suggests that the smaller farmers have been more inclined to move in search of better holdings. On the other hand, the proportion of occupiers and their wives born on their present holdings was roughly the same as for larger holdings.

The testimony given by Sir Watkin's Agent before the Royal Commission on Land in Wales included the following figures : Out of 111 holdings on the Llwydiarth estate, one had been held by the same family for 300 to 400 years, 11 for about 200 years, 12 for about 150 to 200 years and 5 for about 100 to 150 years. This implies that 82/111 had changed hands at least once between 1783 and 1883. The figures varied for different estates but they all showed considerable changes. See ' Length of Tenancies ' in *Royal Commission on Land in Wales, Report* (1883), pp. 290 ff.

The length of occupation of holdings in Wales is nevertheless considerably greater than in England. See the Ministry of Agriculture's *National Farm Survey of England and Wales, A Summary Report* (1946), pp. 31-4.

[6] *Occupations of Sons of Smallholders (under 20 acres), Farm labourers and other Wage-earners.*

Sample : 154 sons born between 1870 and 1908.

	Per cent.
Smallholders, farm workers and other rural workers	44.8
Farmers	10.7
Miners, quarrymen and other industrial workers	17.5
Dock and transport workers	8.4
Clerks, travellers, shopkeepers, postal workers, etc.	9.0
Other occupations	1.8
Emigrated to Dominions and to the U.S.A.	7.8

[7] For satire as a traditional method of punishment see D. Lleufer Thomas, *The Welsh Land Commission, Digest of its Report* (London 1896), p. 48 ; c.f. *The Academy* for 21st Dec. 1895.

[8] See W. R. Williams, *History of Parliamentary Representation of Wales* (Brecknock, 1895), pp. 143 sq.

[9] See Askew Roberts, *Wynnstay and the Wynns* (Oswestry, 1876).

[10] *ibid.* pp. 96 sq.

CHAPTER XIII. POLITICS.

[1] See H. M. Vaughan, *The South Wales Squires* (London, 1926), pp. 2-4 *et passim.*

[2] See Gwyneth Evans, Charles Watkin Williams Wynn, (Unpublished Thesis, N.L.W.), pp. 8-9 ; Cecil Price, *The English Theatre in Wales* (Cardiff, 1948), pp. 61 ff.

[3] Askew Roberts, *op. cit.*, p. 82.

[4] *ibid*, p. 12.

[5] In this paragraph I have followed Professor D. Williams' summary of the general succession of events, *History of Wales*, 1485-1931 (London, 1934), pp. 94-6.

[6] *Merioneth County Times* (Welshpool), February, 16, 23, 1946.

CHAPTER XV. EPILOGUE.

[1] G. C. Homans, *op. cit.*, p. 216.

[2] *ibid.*, p. 217.

[3] A. W. Ashby and I. L. Evans, *op. cit.*, p. 95.

[4] H. J. Mackinder, *Democratic Ideals and Reality*[4], (London, 1943), p. 141

INDEX

alternate generations, 79.
Ann Griffiths, 17, 110 f., 126, 155, 165.
aristocracy, 150 f. ; decline of, 154 f. ;
   164 ; anglicisation of, 154 f., 163 ;
   adherence to Church of England,
   155 f; Conservative, 155 : absence of
   in modern Welsh Society, 163-4.

bachelors, 66, 69-70.
bargaining, 96-7.
Blygain Fawr, Y, 126.

Calvinism, 111, 113-4.
cattle, 22-3, 55 ; sale of, 25.
cefn gwlad (rural neighbourhood), 100,
   101, 108, 129, *et passim.*
cegin (living room), 32, 39, 40 f.
cemetery, controversy over, 156-7.
choirs, 133, 138.
class configuration, 142 f., 163-4.
commerce, 25, 27 f.
common land, 20-1.
competition, 133-4, 136.
Conservatives, 155 f.
consociation, 84.
conversation, 97, 131 f., 144.
co-operation between farms, 92 f.
Co-operative Society, 28, 107.
courtship, hostility to suitor from
   outside locality, 83-4 ; secretive-
   ness, 85 ; girl's home as meeting-
   place, 85-6 ; *cnocio,* 86 ; night
   visit, 85-7 ; pre-marital pregnancies, 87.
crafts, decline of, 27, 166 ; social aspect of, 133, 166 ; domestic, 139.
craftsmen, scattered dwellings of, 103.
crops, 21, 22, 24.
crucks, 40, 176-7.
cyfarfod bach, 136.
cymanfa bregethu, 100, 118.
cymanfa ganu, 100, 117-8, 124.

dairy products, 23-4 ; marketing of,
   28.
dancing, absence of, 127, 129, 183.
deacons, 115, 124-5, 143.
Disestablishment of Church, 156.

Dissent, see Nonconformity.
division of labour between sexes, 62-3
Dolobran, 17, 113.
Dolwar Fach, 17, 110, 182.
dresser, 44.
drovers, 27.

economic changes, 21-2, 27 f., 166-7.
economic depressions, 29 f.
education, see schools.
eisteddfod, 100, 132, 133, 136-8, 143,
   158.
elections, 156-8, 160-1.
electricity, 48.
emigration, 148, 149.
enclosure, 20.

fairs, 26, 63, 133-5.
family farming, 60 f.
family names, 79.
farm-buildings, 51 f.; cowhouses, 55,
   57 ; barns, 55-9 ; granaries, 57 ;
   stables, 57 f.
farmers' sons, at home and as farm-
   workers, 61 ; dependence on
   parents, 63-4 ; marriage of, 64 f. ;
   inheritance, 68.
Farmers' Union, 160-1.
farmers' wives, 14, 62-3, 146.
farmsteads, location, aspect, shelter,
   47 ; water supply, 48 ; layout,
   50 f. See also farm-buildings.
farm-workers, as smallholders, 21 24 ;
   hired in May, 25 ; include farmers'
   sons, 61 ; unmarried men, 61 ; conditions of service, 62 ; status and
   opportunity for advancement, 142
   f. ; decline in numbers, 21, 43, 167.
feats at Wynnstay, 152-3.
feeding-stuffs, 24, 28.
' folk-memory,' 152, 182.
food, 29.
funerals, 81, 92-3, 98-9, 125.
furniture, 43 f., 145.

games, 82, 135, 139-40.
Giraldus Cambrensis, on incest, 79 ;
   on cohabitation, 89; on hospitality,
   100, on settlements, 100.
gwylmabsant, 133-4.

' halves,' 30.
hamlets, description of, 11-13 ; meet-ing-places for youths, 82 ; social life, 99 f. ; as social centres, 104, 106, 140.
Harvest Thanksgiving, 118.
hearth, 43-4, 107. See *pentan*.
holdings, 18-21.
Homans, G. C., 163.
homes as social centre, 43, 100, 105, 107, 129, 131 f.
horses, social significance of, 57 f.
hospitality, 97, 100, 129, 131, 143, 167.
houses, building materials, 32 ; ob-long farmhouse, 32-5, 38, 39, 47 ; cottages, 35 f., 39 ; antiquity of, 39-40 ; crucks, 40 ; square farm-house, 40 f. ; living-room, 39, 40-1; back-kitchen, 41 f. ; 45 ; fireplace, 33, 43-4 ; parlour, 46.
households, composition of, 70 ; de-cline in size of, 71.
Howell Harris, 155.
humour, 132, 137.
hymns, 110 f. ; hymn-tunes, 129.
illegitimacy, 87 f.
income, 30.
Industrial Revolution, effects of, 166-7.

Jenkins, Professor R. T., 109-10.

kindred, classification, 72-4 ; physical consanguinity, 74-7 ; social signifi-cance of, 77 f. ; kinship groups, their physical and cultural traits, 78 f. ; solidarity of, 79-80 ; med-ieval society, 81 ; dispersal of kindred, 149 ; weakness of blood-ties in English village, 162-3.

Labour Party, 158. See socialism.
labour per hundred acres, 24.
Lake Vyrnwy, influx of English workers, 16.
land-owning class, See aristocracy.
land tenure, conditions of, 25-6, dura-tion of tenancies, 148.
lectures, 136, 139.
Liberals, 156 f.
lighting, 48.
Linton, Professor Ralph, 109, 112.
Llanfihangel yng Ngwynfa, meaning of name, 101.
Llanfyllin, 13 ; church, 16 ; market-town, 27-9 ; social centre, 107 ; Nonconformity, 113 ; borough of,

16, 101 ; manor of, 101 ; hundred of, 103 ; Rural District, 103; Fairs, 134.
Llwydiarth Estate, 17, 18, 20, 160.
Llwydiarth Hall, 16-17, 106, 151-2.
Lord Powis, 17.
luck-money, 96-7.

marriage, seasonal distribution, 26 ; establishment of couple in a farm of their own, 64-5; age of marriage, 65 f. ; disparity in ages of spouses, 66 ; consanguine marriages, 79, 84 ; choice of spouse, 84-5, 146-7 ; wedding customs, 90.

Mathrafal, 16, 108.
meals, 45, 95.
Mechain, Cantref of, 16.
Meifod, 16, 157.
Methodist Revival, 104, 109 f., 120, 126, 155, 163-4.
migration to lowlands and to towns, 14, 148, 149.
money, attitude towards, 127, 144-5.
moral code, 126 f.
mutual aid, 91 f., 99.
Mynyddog, 155.

neighbourhoods, 104 f.
neuadd, 38-9.
Nonconformity, 119-20, 124, 126-7, 129-31, 155 f. See also religious denominations, and religious ob-servance.
Nonconformist chapels, see places of worship.

Old Schoolroom, 82, 89, 106, 126, 138, *et passim*.
Oswestry, 13, 28, 29, 107.

Parish Church, 16, 101, 104, 113.
pastoral tradition, 20-23.
Peate, Dr. Iorwerth C., 34, 57, 178.
penllawr, 34, 57, 178.
pentan, 43, 176.
physical features, 11-12.
places of worship, distribution, 102, 104-5 ; dates of erection, 113-14, 183 ; Nonconformist chapels, 124-5; grouping of chapels, 116 f.
plays, 129, 135, 139, 140.
poets, 132-3, 143.
population, 13 ; origin of, 14 ; de-cline of, 14-15 ; decline in size of families, 71 ; excess of males, 71 ; statistical tables, 171-2.

Powys, 103.
practical jokes, 83-4.
pre-industrial standards, 29 f., 144-5.
professional class, 150.
proverbs, 136.
purchase of farms, 30.
puritanism, 113, 126.

Quakers, 17, 113, 124.

religious denominations, relative numerical strength, 112 ; history, 112-4 ; social significance, 114 f. ; grouping of chapels of same denomination, 115-18 ; organisation, 119.
religious observance, 118 ; Nonconformist services, 120 f. ; sermons, 121-3, 129 ; prayer-meetings, 120, 123-4 ; *seiat, cyfeillach*, 113, 123 ; communion, 125 ; scriptural knowledge, 125 ; Episcopal Church, 126; relation to prestige, 143. See also Sunday School.
rent, 23, 25.
ridicule, 83-4, 149-50, 137.

satire, 133, 150.
schools, 106, 129, 142-3, 150, 158.
sectarianism, 114 f.
sermons, see religious observance.
settlements, 12-13.
sheep, 21-3 ; sheep sales, 27 ; sheep shearing, 94, 95-6.
shops in hamlets, 28 ; shop as social centre, 82, 99 ; shop-car, 28.
singing, by youths, 82 ; in church, 126 ; in harmony, 129 ; tonic-solfa, 129, 136 ; choirs, 138 ; *penillion*, 139.
Sir Watkin Williams-Wynn, 45, 105, 151 f., 154 f., 158 f.
smallholders, 18, 20, 21 ; occupations of, 24, 175 ; characteristic of Wales, 163.
smith, 27.
social advancement, 142, 147 f.
socialism, 160.
sports, 135, 140.

squatting, 20, 106.
standard of living, 29-31.
stories and story-telling, 43, 97, 129, 131 f., 136, 159 f.
succession to paternal holding, 68-70.
Sunday observance, 128, 144.
Sunday schools, 116, 120, 130, 143.

tai unnos, 20.
temperance, 127-8.
theology, 111, 113-14.
threshing, 55-7, 94, 95.
Tithe Survey and map, 18-21, 39.
Tithe War, 156.
townships, 102 f.

urban culture, relative absence of in Wales, 108, 181-2.
Urban and industrial influence, 31, 62, 71, 145, 148.
Urdd Gobaith Cymru (Welsh League of Youth), 82-3, 85, 139-40.

values, 29 f. 143 f.
Vaughans of Llwydiarth, 16-17, 106, 151-2.
visiting, 26, 91 f. 97, 131 f.

water-power, 48.
water-supply, 47-8.
wealth, 30, 127, 145.
wedding customs, see marriage.
Welsh language, 14-16, 129-30.
Welsh Laws, on houses, 38-9 ; re. horses, 58 ; on rights of wife, 63 ; on family and kindred, 71-2, 80-1 ; on marriage, 89.
whist-drives, 140.
Women's Institute, 138-9, 140.
Wynnstay, 17, 59, 151, 152, 155.

Yearly round of agricultural work, 24-5 ; relation to social life, 25-6.
Yeomanry, 69, 152-3.
Young Farmers' Clubs, 161.
Young men's society, 82 f., 139.
Young People's Society, 138.
youngest son, 68-70, 71.